LGBTQ Life in America

Recent Titles in Contemporary Debates

Climate Change: Examining the Facts
Daniel Bedford and John Cook

Immigration: Examining the Facts
Cari Lee Skogberg Eastman

Marijuana: Examining the Facts
Karen T. Van Gundy and Michael S. Staunton

Muslims in America: Examining the Facts
Craig Considine

Prisons and Punishment in America: Examining the Facts
Michael O'Hear

American Journalism and "Fake News": Examining the Facts
Seth Ashley, Jessica Roberts, and Adam Maksl

Free Speech and Censorship: Examining the Facts
H. L. Pohlman

Poverty and Welfare in America: Examining the Facts
David Wagner

Voting in America: Examining the Facts
H. L. Pohlman

Race Relations in America: Examining the Facts
Nikki Khanna and Noriko Matsumoto

Guns in America: Examining the Facts
Donald J. Campbell

Public and Private Education in America: Examining the Facts
Casey D. Cobb and Gene V Glass

LGBTQ LIFE
IN AMERICA

Examining the Facts

Melissa R. Michelson and Brian F. Harrison

East Baton Rouge Parish Library
Baton Rouge, Louisiana

Contemporary Debates

An Imprint of ABC-CLIO, LLC
Santa Barbara, California • Denver, Colorado

Library of Congress Cataloging-in-Publication Data

Names: Michelson, Melissa R., 1969– author. | Harrison, Brian F., author.
Title: LGBTQ life in America : examining the facts / Melissa R. Michelson and Brian F. Harrison.
Description: 1st Edition. | Santa Barbara : ABC-CLIO, 2022. | Series: Contemporary debates | Includes bibliographical references and index.
Identifiers: LCCN 2021012406 (print) | LCCN 2021012407 (ebook) | ISBN 9781440875052 (cloth) | ISBN 9781440875069 (ebook)
Subjects: LCSH: Sexual minorities—United States—Social conditions. | Sexual minorities—Identity. | Transgender people—Civil rights—United States. | Sexual minorities—United States—Social life and customs.
Classification: LCC HQ73.3.U6 M53 2022 (print) | LCC HQ73.3.U6 (ebook) | DDC 306.760973—dc23
LC record available at https://lccn.loc.gov/2021012406
LC ebook record available at https://lccn.loc.gov/2021012407

ISBN: 978-1-4408-7505-2 (print)
 978-1-4408-7506-9 (ebook)

26 25 24 23 22   1 2 3 4 5

This book is also available as an eBook.

ABC-CLIO
An Imprint of ABC-CLIO, LLC

ABC-CLIO, LLC
147 Castilian Drive
Santa Barbara, California 93117
www.abc-clio.com

This book is printed on acid-free paper ∞

Manufactured in the United States of America

Contents

How to Use This Book   ix

Introduction   xi

1   The Origins of LGBTQ Identity   1
   Q1. How are sexual behavior, sexual orientation,
      and gender identity related to each other?   2
   Q2. Is it true that there are LGBTQ animals in the wild?   5
   Q3. Is being LGBTQ a choice?   12
   Q4. Does LGBTQ identity exist outside of Western
      societies such as those in North America and
      developed European countries?   15
   Q5. Have there always been LGBTQ people?   19
   Q6. Has the idea that LGBTQ orientations stem from
      childhood sexual trauma been debunked by
      researchers?   25
   Q7. Is the word "queer" a slur against the LGBTQ
      community?   29

2   LGBTQ Political and Legal Treatment Over Time   33
   Q8. Did the gay rights movement begin at Stonewall
      in 1969?   34
   Q9. Is it true that some vocal opponents of LGBTQ
      rights are closeted gay people?   39

Q10. Do laws protecting LGBTQ people affect the
freedom of religious Americans who oppose LGBTQ
people on religious grounds?   43

Q11. Does giving rights to LGBTQ people lead to the
legalization of practices like pedophilia, bestiality,
and necrophilia?   49

Q12. Have hate crimes against LGBTQ people in the
United States increased over time?   53

Q13. Do LGBTQ people in the United States still suffer
from legal discrimination?   57

3 Public Visibility of LGBTQ People   61

Q14. Has the public become more supportive of same-sex
relationships and marriages?   62

Q15. Has the public become more supportive of same-sex
people being parents?   66

Q16. Are major religions in the United States more
supportive of LGBTQ people than they used to be?   70

Q17. Are more people coming out as LGBTQ?   75

Q18. Are there more openly LGBTQ elected officials
than there used to be?   79

Q19. Are there more LGBTQ people on TV and in
movies than there used to be?   84

4 Gender Identity, Performance, and Dynamics   91

Q20. Do LGBTQ relationships have the same dynamics
that straight relationships do?   92

Q21. Do lesbians and straight women harbor different
views and attitudes toward men?   95

Q22. Do gay men hate women, especially lesbians?   98

Q23. Are bisexual people just confused gay (or straight)
people who can't make up their mind?   101

Q24. Are gay men less masculine than straight men?   104

Q25. Are lesbians less feminine than straight women?   109

Q26. Why are LGB people (people with nonheterosexual
sexual orientations) grouped together with T people
(non-cisgender gender identities) into one LGBTQ
community?   112

Q27. Are men who enjoy cross-dressing or drag
transgender?   115

5   **Transgender and Nonbinary Identity**   **119**
    Q28. Is it true that gender is not binary?   120
    Q29. Do medical and psychological authorities regard
         transgender or nonbinary gender identity as a
         mental illness?   125
    Q30. Can children really know that they are transgender
         from an early age?   128
    Q31. Do all transgender and nonbinary people feel the
         need to change the way their body looks through
         surgery?   132
    Q32. Are more Americans using nonbinary pronouns?   135
    Q33. Is transgender identity related to sexual
         orientation, in that transgender men are former
         lesbians and transgender women are former gay men?   138
    Q34. Is there tension between the feminist movement
         and people who identify as transgender and/or
         nonbinary?   140

6   **Behaviors and Outcomes Associated with LGBTQ People**   **145**
    Q35. Do LGBTQ people contract HIV/AIDS at different
         rates than straight people?   146
    Q36. Are LGBTQ people more prone to mental illness
         than straight people?   150
    Q37. Can conversion therapy change someone's sexual
         orientation or gender identity?   154
    Q38. Do LGBTQ people abuse drugs and alcohol at
         different rates than straight people?   159
    Q39. Do straight people and LGBTQ people have
         different life expectancies?   163
    Q40. Are LGBTQ youth more likely to be homeless?   166
    Q41. Is bullying of LGBTQ kids for their sexual
         orientation becoming less common?   169
    Q42. Are children of LGBTQ parents worse off than
         children of straight parents?   172

7   **Diversity within the LGBTQ Community**   **177**
    Q43. Do LGBTQ people tend to be of a certain race,
         gender, or age?   178
    Q44. Do LGBTQ people tend to live in particular
         geographic regions?   181

Q45. Do LGBTQ people tend to be from a particular
    socioeconomic background?   183
Q46. Are LGBTQ people more sexually active than
    straight people?   186
Q47. Is there such a thing as a "gay lifestyle"?   189
Q48. Do LGBTQ and straight people display distinct
    differences in their physical appearance, behavior,
    or speech?   192
Q49. Have LGBTQ people made positive impacts on
    American life and culture?   195

Index   201

How to Use This Book

LGBTQ Life in America: Examining the Facts is part of ABC-CLIO's Contemporary Debates reference series. Each title in this series, which is intended for use by high school and undergraduate students as well as members of the general public, examines the veracity of controversial claims or beliefs surrounding a major political/cultural issue in the United States. The purpose of this series is to give readers a clear and unbiased understanding of current issues by informing them about falsehoods, half-truths, and misconceptions—and confirming the factual validity of other assertions—that have gained traction in America's political and cultural discourse. Ultimately, this series has been crafted to give readers the tools for a fuller understanding of controversial issues, policies, and laws that occupy center stage in American life and politics.

Each volume in this series identifies 30 to 40 questions swirling about the larger topic under discussion. These questions are examined in individualized entries, which are in turn arranged in broad subject chapters that cover certain aspects of the issue being examined, for example, history of concern about the issue, potential economic or social impact, or findings of latest scholarly research.

Each chapter features 4 to 10 individual entries. Each entry begins by stating an important and/or well-known **Question** about the issue being studied—for example, "Has the public become more supportive of same-sex relationships and marriages?"; "Can conversion therapy change someone's sexual orientation or gender identity?"; and "Are LGBTQ youth more likely to be homeless?"

The entry then provides a concise and objective one- or two-paragraph **Answer** to the featured question, followed by a more comprehensive, detailed explanation of **The Facts**. This latter portion of each entry uses quantifiable, evidence-based information from respected sources to fully address each question and provide readers with the information they need to be informed citizens. Importantly, entries will also acknowledge instances in which conflicting data exists or data is incomplete. Finally, each entry concludes with a **Further Reading** section, providing users with information on other important and/or influential resources.

The ultimate purpose of every book in the Contemporary Debates series is to reject "false equivalence," in which demonstrably false beliefs or statements are given the same exposure and credence as the facts; to puncture myths that diminish our understanding of important policies and positions; to provide needed context for misleading statements and claims; and to confirm the factual accuracy of other assertions. In other words, volumes in this series are being crafted to clear the air surrounding some of the most contentious and misunderstood issues or our time—not just add another layer of obfuscation and uncertainty to the debate.

Introduction

Figuring out how we are different and how we are the same has been one of the most fundamental struggles of culture and civilization for centuries, if not millennia. In some ways, it is human nature to make sense of who we are by negotiating the boundaries of who we are not: finding *our* people and distinguishing them from *others*. While that kind of boundary-making can generate benefits, it often creates obstacles to establishing common ground, understanding, and mutual respect across different groups. We need not be exactly the same as the person standing next to us to seek a common purpose or to treat other people with respect and dignity. It can be challenging, however, to live up to the foundational idea of the United States that all people are created equal.

Black poet, activist, and lesbian Audre Lorde exemplified that idea in a speech to Medgar Evers College in 1980 when she said, in part, "We sometimes find it difficult to deal constructively with the genuine differences between us and to recognize that unity does not require we be identical to each other" (Lorde 1980).

Part of the way forward in dealing constructively with our differences is to confront myths, misconceptions, and misinformation where they arise. For the LGBTQ community, that has been a particularly important and arduous task in recent decades. In 1967, CBS News released a documentary called *The Homosexuals*, an hour-long broadcast anchored by Mike Wallace. The original intent of the piece was to offer a research-based look into the lives of gay men in America: producers read books, consulted with experts in related fields, and conducted 30 hours of interviews. Despite the original intent, the documentary perpetuated misconceptions and false-hoods that had long plagued the LGBTQ community: gay men were described in the documentary as lecherous sexual predators, imminent threats to children, and deviants from what was considered ideal American values. Wallace described the average gay man this way:

> The average homosexual, if there be such, is promiscuous. He is not interested in nor capable of a lasting relationship like that of a heterosexual marriage. His sex life, his love life, consists of a series of one-chance encounters at the clubs and bars he inhabits. And even on the streets of the city—the pick-up, the one-night stand, these are characteristics of the homosexual relationship. (Tropiano 2002, 11)

Wallace also cited a CBS News poll from the previous year that found that Americans considered homosexuality more harmful to the United States than adultery, abortion, or prostitution. The poll also found that two-thirds of Americans reacted to homosexuality with "disgust, discomfort, or fear," with 1 in 10 people describing their reaction as "hatred" (Kaiser 1997). LGBTQ identity didn't start to exist in the 1960s, of course, but the CBS documentary is a prime example of how even a well-intentioned effort missed the mark in describing gay men in the not-so-distant past.

The task of more accurately describing the LGBTQ community—its diversity, expectations, challenges, and needs—has changed over time as the community itself changed. This book sets out to explain and to describe what it means to be LGBTQ and how that identity occurs in nature and in history; how what the public thinks and feels about the LGBTQ community has changed over time; what different segments of the LGBTQ community have in common and how they differ; how societal and cultural expectations can place an undue burden on LGBTQ people; and how the movement for equal rights for LGBTQ people remains ongoing.

Chapter 1 delves into the fundamentals of LGBTQ identity, tackling questions about whether being LGBTQ is a choice; whether it exists in nature; how it exists outside of Western societies; the origins of LGBTQ identity; how the meaning and use of the word "queer" has changed over time; and key differences between sexual orientation and gender identity. **Chapter 2** discusses the legal and political treatment of LGBTQ people, identifying misconceptions about how LGBTQ rights infringe on other rights in American life; how the LGBTQ movement began; the nature of opposition to LGBTQ rights; and how LGBTQ people have experienced discrimination and hardship, both past and present. **Chapter 3** focuses on public visibility of LGBTQ people, including how attitudes have changed over time in response to political, media, and interpersonal trends and developments. It also addresses questions about how public opinion toward LGBTQ people has changed over time as well as how LGBTQ people are perceived in the prominent areas of politics and religion. **Chapter 4** focuses on gender identity and performance, including ways that cultural norms and expectations surrounding masculinity and femininity can sometimes complicate interpersonal relationships. In particular, this chapter tackles misconceptions around gender dynamics in LGBTQ people; perceptions of animosity within the LGBTQ community; myths about bisexual and pansexual people; and how complicated norms and expectations of masculinity and femininity can be. **Chapter 5** addresses transgender and nonbinary identity, including discussions of whether gender is binary; differences between transgender identity and sexual orientation; and particular challenges that transgender and nonbinary people face in the United States. **Chapter 6** looks at the relationships between LGBTQ identity and different behaviors and outcomes from the standpoints of health and safety including substance abuse, mental illness, and homelessness. In particular, this chapter discusses myths and misconceptions about conversion therapy, HIV/AIDS, and questions about quality of life for LGBTQ people. Finally, **Chapter 7** underscores the idea that while the LGBTQ community is indeed one community, there is not a *correct* way for an LGBTQ person to look, to love, or to live. This chapter identifies diversity within the LGBTQ community, including race, geographic region, education, and socioeconomic status; whether LGBTQ people are more or less sexually active than heterosexual people; and what people mean when they discuss a "gay lifestyle."

Returning to Audre Lorde's idea of unity among difference, the spirit of this book is to provide factual information about LGBTQ people to demonstrate that it is, in fact, the appreciation of our differences that unlocks our collective potential. Unity does not require assimilation or the erasure of human diversity: true unity calls for us to take a moment to embrace the facts about those who are different than we are, to honor the ways we are the same, and to commit to the equal treatment of everyone under the law, all with the common desire to form a more perfect union.

ACKNOWLEDGMENTS

Helpful feedback on draft chapters of this book was provided by Finley Archer, Joshua Michelson, Francheska Privalova, Jessie Satovsky, Avyay Sriperumbudur, Layla Wallerstein, and, in a starring role, Indigo White.

We are also grateful for the comments and suggestions from our editor, Kevin Hillstrom.

FURTHER READING

Kaiser, Charles. 1997. *The Gay Metropolis: 1940–1996.* New York: Houghton Mifflin.

Lorde, Audre. 1980. "I Am Your Sister: Black Women Organizing across Sexualities." In Mark Blasius and Shane Phelan, eds., *We Are Everywhere: A Historical Sourcebook of Gay and Lesbian Politics,* 1997. New York: Routledge Press, p. 472.

Tropiano, Stephen. 2002. *The Prime Time Closet: A History of Gays and Lesbians on TV.* New York: Applause Theatre & Cinema.

1

The Origins of LGBTQ Identity

What it means to be LGBTQ has changed over time but one thing is clear: it is not a new concept or identity. This chapter starts with definitions of our contemporary understandings of gender identity, sexual orientation, and sexual behavior before turning to how these concepts exist in nature, throughout the world, and throughout history. Emphasizing that being LGBTQ is not a choice a person makes but rather is a part of their identity, chapter 1 tackles the broad concept of the origins of LGBTQ identity.

Q1 introduces definitions like sexual orientation and gender identity and describes why these definitions are important in understanding LGBTQ identity and life. Q2 documents same-sex behavior among animals in the wild and explains why that finding is important in understanding human behavior. Q3 addresses the common misconception that being LGBTQ is a choice, making the point that most identities tend to be immutable and static. Q4 explores how LGBTQ identity is expressed and appreciated in areas outside of Western culture while Q5 summarizes historical evidence that LGBTQ people have been around for millennia. Q6 debunks the myth that there is a connection between LGBTQ identity and sexual trauma during childhood. Finally, Q7 addresses the word "queer" and explains that despite its history as a hateful slur, many have embraced the term and have reclaimed it as a term of inclusion within the LGBTQ community.

Q1: HOW ARE SEXUAL BEHAVIOR, SEXUAL ORIENTATION, AND GENDER IDENTITY RELATED TO EACH OTHER?

Answer: Behavior, sexual identity, and gender identity are all different but interrelated concepts. Sexual *orientation* is about more than just sexual *behavior.* Having a clear understanding of sexual orientation and gender identity requires attention to many different concepts, including the definitions of gender identity and sexual orientation as well as the concepts of sex, gender, masculinity, femininity, attraction, and identity.

The Facts: To best understand the answer to the question, there are three main concepts to consider: the differences between sex and gender, between sexual orientation and gender identity, and between sexual behavior and sexual orientation.

First, sex refers to physical characteristics and attributes that differentiate men, women, and other people. These differences may be genetic or anatomical in nature and primarily relate to biology or physiology. *Gender,* on the other hand, refers to roles, behaviors, and activities that are socially constructed in a way that is deemed culturally appropriate for men and women (World Health Organization 2019). According to the *Publication Manual* of the American Psychological Association, "Gender is cultural and is the term to use when referring to women and men as social groups. Sex is biological; use it when the biological distinction is predominant."

In a 2010 TEDx Talk, historian Alice Dreger discussed how blurred the lines between sex and gender can be: "We now know that sex is complicated enough that we have to admit nature doesn't draw the line for us between male and female. . . . we actually draw that line on nature. . . . What we have is a sort of situation where the farther our science goes, the more we have to admit to ourselves that these categories that we thought of as stable anatomical categories that mapped very simply to stable identity categories are a lot more fuzzy than we thought" (Dreger 2010).

Because it is related to culture and societal norms, gender varies from society to society and can change over time. How a person sees themselves and their gender is called their *gender identity;* that is, one's internal and personal sense of being a man, woman, nonbinary, or something else. Most people have a gender identity as male (man, boy) or female (woman, girl) that is closely related to *gender expression*: external manifestations of gender expressed through someone's name, pronouns, clothing, haircut, behavior, voice, or body characteristics. Society identifies these cues as masculine, feminine, or androgynous, and the cues change over time (GLAAD 2019).

Most of the time, a person's sex assigned to them at birth lines up with their gender. However, it isn't always quite so simple. There are multiple identities where they don't line up; these identities are included in the umbrella term *transgender*, which includes *nonbinary* identities as well as transgender women (women assigned male at birth) and transgender men (men assigned female at birth). Individuals may refer to themselves as *intersex* (born with reproductive or sexual anatomy and/or a chromosome pattern that can't be classified as male or female); *androgynous or nonbinary* (not identifying or presenting as a man or as a woman); *gender nonconforming* (not following other people's ideas or stereotypes about how they should look or act based on the female or male sex they were assigned at birth); *genderqueer* (when gender identity and/or gender expression falls outside of the masculine/feminine gender binary); *two-spirit* (certain Native American and Canadian First Nation people who identify with a third gender, implying a masculine and a feminine spirit in one body); or *genderfluid* (shifting gender identity and/or gender expression over time) (Sylvia Rivera Law Project n.d.). For more on this topic, see Q28.

In short, sex, gender, gender identity, and gender expression have to do with a person's sense of who they are in terms of their gender and whether that sense is the same as or different from the anatomy with which they were born. It is all about a person's idea of who they are. By contrast, *sexual orientation* refers to "an individual's enduring physical, romantic and/or emotional attraction to others" (GLAAD 2019). *Straight* (heterosexual) refers to when a male person is emotionally, romantically, sexually, affectionately, or relationally attracted only to women or when a female person is only attracted to men. People need not have had specific sexual experiences to know their own sexual orientation; in fact, they need not have had any sexual experience at all.

LGBTQ is a commonly used acronym for lesbian, gay, bisexual, transgender, and either queer or questioning. There are, however, additional identity terms like intersex, asexual, agender, and pansexual (among others) that are sometimes included; the use of "LGBTQ" is expected to include all sexual and gender identities whether they are included in the acronym or not. The full acronym is LGBTQQ2SIAA (GLAAD 2019).

- *Gay* (or homosexual) is an adjective describing people who are sexually attracted to people of the same sex.
- *Lesbian* is the preferred term for gay women, though some lesbians may prefer to identify as gay.

- *Bisexual* refers to people who have the capacity to be sexually attracted to both men and women.
- *Transgender*, as opposed to *cisgender*, is an umbrella term for instances in which someone's gender identity does not line up with their sex that was assigned to them at birth. It is not a sexual orientation but is included in the LGBTQ acronym to acknowledge the shared experiences and challenges faced by all members of the LGBTQ community (Tannehill 2013).
- *Cisgender* refers to people whose gender identity matches the sex they were assigned at birth.
- Finally, *queer* is an adjective used by some people for whom sexual orientation is not exclusively heterosexual or straight or whose gender identity is not exclusively cisgender, or both. Some people who identify as queer find other terms (gay, lesbian, bisexual) too limiting or fraught with cultural connotations they feel do not apply to them. Once considered a derogatory term, queer has been reclaimed by some LGBTQ people as a way to describe themselves (for more information, see Q7). It is not a universally accepted term, however, even within the LGBTQ community. Additionally, the Q at the end of LGBTQ can also sometimes mean questioning—an acknowledgment of those who are questioning their sexual orientation or gender identity.

There are a variety of ways these identities can manifest themselves. One aspect is attraction: physiological, unconscious arousal toward others. *Romantic orientation* is a way of talking about attraction to others in terms of love and romance rather than just sexual contact. People use a variety of labels to describe their romantic orientation, including *aromantic* (not expressing romantic attraction in relationships), *homoromantic* (attraction to the same gender romantically but not sexually), and *heteroromantic* (attraction to a different gender romantically but not sexually). A person can experience attraction without necessarily acting on that attraction. For example, a man may find himself aroused by another man but that arousal does not necessarily dictate his sexual orientation or drive his sexual behavior. Some African Americans prefer to use the term "same-gender" or "same-sex loving" to describe their sexual orientation, seeing "gay" and "lesbian" as primarily white terms (Human Rights Campaign n.d.).

Another aspect is *sexual behavior*, the physical act of engaging in sexual conduct. Behavior does not always correspond to sexual orientation or identity. A woman may have sex with another woman but may still identify her sexual orientation as heterosexual; the behavior may simply constitute attraction. MSM and WSW are abbreviations for men who have sex with men and women who have sex with women, respectively, emphasizing the behavior rather than the identities of the individuals involved.

In short, there are many layers to take into account when characterizing and explaining the relationship among sex, gender, gender identity, and sexual orientation. A person may see themselves as fitting within the constructs of a gender binary (male/female) or they may not. A person may see congruence between the sex they were assigned at birth and their current gender identity or they may not. A person may identify with a sexual orientation that reflects the gender of the person with whom they have sex or they may not. In many ways, human sexuality and gender are very personal, individual-level endeavors; definitions, identities, and categories (or the lack thereof) are constantly shifting and changing based on prevailing conceptualizations of sex, gender, sexual orientation, gender expression, and gender identity. Norms and expectations are constantly shifting to meet the latest ideas of what it means to live and to exist in the social world.

FURTHER READING

Dreger, Alice. 2010. "Is Anatomy Destiny?" TEDxNorthwesternU, December. https://www.ted.com/talks/alice_dreger_is_anatomy_destiny

GLAAD. 2019. "GLAAD Media Reference Guide: Lesbian/Gay/Bisexual Glossary of Terms." https://www.glaad.org/reference/lgbtq

Human Rights Campaign. n.d. "Communities of Color." https://www.hrc .org/resources/communities-of-color

Sylvia Rivera Law Project. n.d. "Fact Sheet: Transgender & Gender Nonconforming Youth in School." https://srlp.org/resources/fact-sheet -transgender-gender-nonconforming-youth-school/

Tannehill, Brynn. 2013. "Why 'LGB' and 'T' Belong Together." *Huffington Post*, February 25. https://www.huffpost.com/entry/why-lgb-and-t-belong -together_b_2746616

World Health Organization (WHO). 2019. "Gender and Health." https:// www.who.int/health-topics/gender

Q2: IS IT TRUE THAT THERE ARE LGBTQ ANIMALS IN THE WILD?

Answer: Yes. Scientists in several different fields have documented same-sex attraction, behavior, and relationships among animals for several decades. While this behavior was originally seen as aberrant or as an

anomaly, more recently, biologists have studied same-sex mating and relationships more systematically to understand the implications of such
behavior in sociological, biological, and evolutionary terms. Same-sex
behavior and even lifelong same-sex partnerships do exist in the wild but
biologists are reluctant to classify same-sex behavior and sexual orientation
in animals the same way as they do humans. In other words, they distinguish between same-sex intimacy and LGBTQ identity.

The Facts: Animals have been observed engaging in same-sex sexual
activity for decades. However, many of these cases were dismissed as animal boredom, curiosity, or simply as anomalies. It wasn't until Canadian
biologist Bruce Bagemihl published his book *Biological Exuberance* in 2000
that these behaviors were seen as something worthy of study themselves;
scientists were encouraged to look at these cases not as something to ignore
but as something to study systematically.

Studying these cases was not as simple as it may seem. At the very core
of evolutionary biology—since the time of Charles Darwin, the pioneering
biologist who developed the theory of evolution in the late nineteenth
century—lies the concept that genetic traits and behavior that advantage
an animal will remain and will help it create a lot of offspring (and conversely, those without such advantages will vanish). In short, evolution
slowly optimizes an animal toward one singular goal: passing along its
genes. Yale ornithologist Richard Prum said, "Our field is a lot like economics: we have a core of theory, like free-market theory, where we have
the invisible hand of the market creating order—all commodities attain
exactly the price they're worth. Homosexuality is a tough case, because it
appears to violate that central tenet, that all of sexual behavior is about
reproduction. The question is, why would anyone invest in sexual behavior
that isn't reproductive?" (quoted in Mooallem 2010).

Scientists who study animal behavior address the complex question of
animal sexuality in different ways. One common element, however, is that
they encourage us to try not to compare humans and animals and to distinguish between identity and behavior. For example, Paul Vasey, professor
of psychology and director of the Laboratory of Comparative Sexuality at
the University of Lethbridge, suggests that humans are the only documented case of "true" homosexuality in animals, writing, "It is not the case
that you have lesbian bonobos or gay male bonobos." They do not identify
as homosexual. However, he adds, they do engage in homosexual *behavior*.
"What's been described is that many animals are happy to engage in sex
with partners of either sex" (quoted in Hogenboom 2015). While same-sex
behavior has been documented in hundreds of species on isolated

occasions, only a handful have made it a habitual part of their lives. In addition, we cannot ascribe a sexual orientation to a species with whom we cannot communicate; we can only observe and evaluate their behavior.

Since 2000, researchers have developed new hypotheses based on observations of different animals and how sexual behaviors might themselves fit within evolutionary boundaries. In other words, scientists have sought to discern ways that same-sex behavior has helped advance an evolutionary role of reproduction within individual species. For example, Bagemihl's research helped to spur interest and research into same-sex behavior in animals because he found that there is significant variety in nonreproductive sexual behavior, including same-sex courtship, pair-bonding, sex, co-parenting with same-sex animals, and instances of lifelong homosexual partnering in species that do not have lifelong heterosexual relationships. In fact, there are instances where couples have been beneficial to the survival of the species. In 2019, two male penguins cared for an egg that had been abandoned by a female of the species in the zoo. Zookeepers described the couple as "model parents, taking turns to keep the egg warm" and protecting it from jealous rivals (BBC 2019).

Scientists have known for some time that albatrosses—which can live to be 60 or 70 years old—usually mate with the same bird every year for life; their "divorce rate," as biologists term it, is among the lowest of any bird species. When they are together, birds copulate and incubate an egg together for 65 days, taking shifts protecting the nest while the other fishes and eats for weeks at a time. When together, these couples will preen each other's feathers and engage in elaborate mating behaviors and displays, according to Marlene Zuk, professor of ecology, evolution, and behavior at the University of Minnesota (quoted in Mooallem 2010). Lindsay C. Young, vice president and executive director of Pacific Rim Conservation, spent years studying the behavior of the Laysan albatross in Oahu, Hawaii, and observed the usual monogamous behavior. She and a colleague noticed that a third of the pairs at their study site consisted of two female birds, not one male and one female—a pairing easily missed because albatrosses are one of many species where the sexes look basically identical. The female–female pairs were behaving the same way as opposite-sex pairs, including incubating eggs and raising chicks and engaging in the same mating rituals. The chicks they parented were fathered by males from a different committed pair who mated with one or both of the female birds.

There are other examples as well. In certain species of penguins, males form long-term bonds with other males, sometimes engaging in sexual behavior with one another. Dolphins often touch genitals together and researchers have documented instances in which males go one step further by mounting another male and penetrating his blowhole (Jha 2009). Geese, particularly Canadian geese, are well-known for spending their lives with a single mate; they tend to search for another mate only if the first one dies. Bagemihl found that 30 percent of these mates for Canadian geese were the same sex (Bagemihl 2000).

Many animals do seem to create lifelong partnerships with others of the same sex but these animals typically are not labeled as "gay" or "lesbian." That's because scientists don't conceptualize animal behavior and identity in the way that we often do with humans. For example, Young does not use terms like "straight couples" or refer to female–female pairs as "lesbians" for a variety of reasons. She noted that the same-sex pairs do everything except have sex, which makes it unclear if that means they could be classified in the way humans are. "Lesbian is a human term. . . . The study is about albatross. The study is not about humans" (quoted in Jha 2009).

Other research finds that some species can adapt to their environment by changing their sex. Typically, the presence or absence of a Y chromosome determines whether an organism has a sex of male (XY) or female (XX). Studies of certain species of frogs, however, show that if the number of male and female frogs in the society are not proportional, a chemical trigger activates certain genes that disintegrate current sex organs and begins the development of the other sex organ (Main 2019). Flatworms are simultaneous hermaphrodites, meaning they have functioning male and female sex organs at the same time. When it is time for reproduction, the worms stab at each other in a duel known as "penis fencing," trying to be the first to inseminate the other and therefore function as the male (Tsang 2017). Crepidula, commonly known as slipper snails, are sequential hermaphrodites: they are born male but at a point in their life cycle, they become female. Researchers attempting to understand the reason and timing for this change point to several explanations. First, they have found that as females get larger, their chances at reproductive success increase so as males grow larger, becoming female may offer them an evolutionary advantage. They have also determined that these changes may be affected by environment, finding that if male Crepidula are in direct contact with female snails, they tend to delay a change in sex to increase the likelihood of reproduction (Tsang 2017).

Explanations for Same-Sex Behavior in the Animal Kingdom

There are generally three overarching explanations of why same-sex behavior can be found among animals: evolutionary, social, and sexual.

Scientists have identified several evolutionary reasons why animals engage in same-sex behavior. For example, male fruit flies will try to have sex with any other fly, male or female, within the first 30 minutes of life. Eventually, however, they learn to recognize the smell of virgin female flies and over time will focus solely on them. David Featherstone, biologist at the University of Illinois at Chicago, said that while it might be tempting to look at this trial-and-error approach as inefficient, it is a good strategy given different pheromone blends in different habitats. He said, "A male could be passing up an opportunity to have viable offspring if they are hardwired to only go for a certain smell" (quoted in Hogenboom 2015). Another example of an evolutionary advantage comes from male flour beetles: they frequently mount each other and even deposit sperm; if the male carrying this sperm mates with a female at a later point, that sperm may get transferred, meaning the male who produced it fertilized a female without the effort of having to court her (Jha 2009). In both cases, the males are engaging in same-sex sexual behavior to fertilize females indirectly, suggesting these behaviors may be favored by evolution. These examples also show how these insects are not at all homosexual in the way we conceptualize humans.

Sheep behavior provides even more evolutionary evidence. According to psychologist Paul Vasey, an expert in animal behavior, up to 8 percent of male sheep in flocks of sheep prefer other males despite fertile females being around. A 1994 study found these males have slightly different brain structures compared to the others: the part of their brain called the hypothalamus, known to control sex hormone, was slightly smaller in those preferring same-sex mates compared to those preferring opposite-sex ones. Neurobiologist Simon LeVay reports there is indeed an evolutionary component, suggesting that same-sex behavior could help fertility among female sheep and/or their desire to mate; the increased fertility and desire in mating can apply to other females nearby in an effort to spur procreation, likely due to an innate tendency to protect the species from an evolutionary perspective. Scientists believe that even female siblings of sheep who prefer same-sex mates could produce more offspring in a lifetime than average. In response to the sheep studies, LeVay said, "If these genes are having such a beneficial effect in females, they outweigh the effect in males and then the gene is going to persist" (quoted in Hogenboom 2015).

Similar to humans, animals use sex to gain all sorts of social advantages. For example, bottlenose dolphins engage in same-sex behavior to form strong social bonds but most will ultimately go on to have offspring with the opposite sex. Bonobos are sometimes described by biologists as our "oversexed" relatives because they engage in so much sexual behavior with both the same sex and the opposite sex. Researchers have found that sex among bonobos cements social bonds and is related to their concept of a social ladder. Junior bonobos may use sex to bond with dominant group members and to reduce tension. These cases suggest that sexual behavior is about more than reproduction, says Zuk, who also notes that female bonobos have sex when they are outside their reproductive period and can't get pregnant. "There's a whole range of behaviors that fit in well with how evolution happens that now include homosexual behavior" (quoted in Hogenboom 2015).

Scientists have also found a strong correlation between a species' mating system and same-sex behavior. In essence, the sex with fewer parental responsibilities is more likely to engage in same-sex behavior. The unburdened sex is free to take advantage of whatever mating opportunities come their way, according to Geoff MacFarlane, biologist at the University of Newcastle in Australia: "Homosexual behavior is more likely to be maintained and not be selected against than if you are a sex that cares a lot for offspring and only has one or few reproductive partners" (quoted in Kessler 2010).

Finally, some species have sex with same-sex mates because they are simply enjoying themselves, according to Vasey. "They're engaging in the behavior because it's gratifying sexually or it's sexually pleasurable," he says. "They just like it. It doesn't have any sort of adaptive payoff" (quoted in Owen 2004). Robin Dunbar, a professor of evolutionary psychology at the University of Liverpool, England, suggests that same-sex behavior doesn't need to have a specific function. "It could be a spin-off or by-product of something else and in itself carries no evolutionary weight. . . . An organism is designed to maximize its motivational systems" (quoted in Owen 2004). In other words, if the urge to have sex is strong enough, it may spill over into nonreproductive sex, as suggested by the actions of animals like bonobos.

In summary, animals in the wild may not identify as gay, bisexual, or straight in the way some humans do but there is a plethora of evidence to suggest that animals don't conform to traditional categories of sexual orientation: they engage in same-sex behavior to satisfy a variety of needs, whether they are evolutionary, social advancement, or simple pleasure and gratification.

FURTHER READING

Adkins-Regan, Elizabeth, and Alan Krakauer. 2000. "Removal of Adult Males from the Rearing Environment Increases Preferences for Same-Sex Partners in the Zebra Finch." *Animal Behavior* 60, 1: 47–53.
Bagemihl, Bruce. 2000. *Biological Exuberance: Animal Homosexuality and Natural Diversity*. New York: St. Martin's Press.

BBC. 2019. "Berlin Gay Penguins Adopt Abandoned Egg." *BBC News*, August 12. https://www.bbc.com/news/blogs-news-from-elsewhere -49318080

Brandlin, Anne-Sophie. 2017. "10 Animal Species That Show How Being Gay Is Natural." *Deutsche Welle*, August 2. https://www.dw.com/en /10-animal-species-that-show-how-being-gay-is-natural/g-39934832

Del Hoyo, Josep, Andrew Elliott, Jordi Sargatal, and José Cabot. 2005. *Handbook of the Birds of the World V1–V9*. Barcelona (Spain): Lynx Edicions.

Diamond, Jared M. 1989. "Goslings of Gay Geese." *Nature* 340, 6229: 101.

Hogenboom, Melissa. 2015. "Are There Any Homosexual Animals? Lots of Animals Engage in Homosexual Behaviour, but Whether They Are Truly Homosexual Is Another Matter Entirely." *BBC*, February 6. http:// www.bbc.com/earth/story/20150206-are-there-any-homosexual-animals

Jha, Alok. 2009. "Same-Sex Relationships May Play an Important Role in Evolution." *The Guardian*, June 17. https://www.theguardian.com/science /blog/2009/jun/17/same-sex-relationships-gay-animals

Kessler, Rebecca. 2010. "Why It's OK for Birds to Be Gay." *Live Science*, August 23. https://www.livescience.com/11125-birds-gay.html

Lombardo, Michael P., et al. 1994. "Homosexual Copulations by Male Tree Swallows." *The Wilson Bulletin* 106, 3: 555–557.

MacFarlane, Geoff R., Simon P. Blomberg, Gisela Kaplan, and Lesley J. Rogers. 2007. "Same-Sex Sexual Behavior in Birds: Expression Is Related to Social Mating System and State of Development at Hatching." *Behavioral Ecology* 18, 1: 21–33.

Main, Douglas. 2019. "Healthy Frogs Can Mysteriously Reverse Their Sex." *National Geographic*, March 21. https://www.nationalgeographic.com /animals/2019/03/frogs-reverse-sex-more-often-than-thought/

Mooallem, Jon. 2010. "Can Animals Be Gay?" *The New York Times Magazine*, March 31. https://www.nytimes.com/2010/04/04/magazine /04animals-t.html/

Owen, James. 2004. "Homosexual Activity among Animals Stirs Debate." *National Geographic*, July 22. https://www.nationalgeographic.com /science/2004/07/homosexual-animals-debate/

Schutz, Friedrich. 1965. "Homosexualität und prägung: Eine experimentelle untersuchung an enten [Homosexuality and Imprinting: An Experimental Study of Ducks]." *Psychologische Forschung* 28, 5: 439–465.

Tsang, Jennifer. 2017. "The Sex Life of Snails: Whitman Scientist Traces the Germline of a Hermaphrodite." *Marine Biological Laboratory*, July 3. http://social.mbl.edu/the-sex-life-of-snails

Tyler, Paul A. 1984. "Homosexual Behaviour in Animals." In Kevin Howells, ed., *The Psychology of Sexual Diversity*. Oxford: Blackwell, pp. 42–62.

Q3: IS BEING LGBTQ A CHOICE?

Answer: No. Sexual orientation is not a choice; it is a natural part of human diversity and scientists continue to study the combination of genetic markers, hormones, and social characteristics that play a role in sexual orientation.

The Facts: While there is no "gay gene," researchers have found that some genetic variations are correlated with same-sex sexual orientation. A team of geneticists led by Andrea Ganna examined genetic data from 2017 and 2018 from over 477,000 individual participants in the United States, the United Kingdom, and Sweden. Ganna's team found five genetic markers (loci) significantly associated with same-sex sexual behavior but the variants only accounted for 8–25 percent of variation in sexual behavior, only partially overlapped between male and female participants, and did not allow for prediction of an individual's sexual orientation (Ganna et al. 2019). In other words, genetics only account for explaining *some* of a person's sexual identity.

On their website designed to share the results of their academic study with the general public, the researchers caution that all human behavior is only partially genetic in nature and that sexual behavior and orientation "are also shaped in large part by a person's environment and life experiences." Sexual orientation is the result of a combination of genetic components, environment, and experiences. "Our genetic findings in no way preclude the additional influences of culture, society, family, or individual experiences, or of non-genetic biological influences, in the development of sexual behavior and orientation" (Genetics of Sexual Behavior 2020).

The myth of the *gay gene* stems from a 1993 study led by geneticist Dean Hamer that found families with two gay brothers were very likely to have certain genetic markers on a region of the X chromosome known as Xq28 (Hamer et al. 1993). The study found that "a locus (or loci) related to sexual orientation lies within approximately 4 million base pairs of DNA on the tip of the long arm of the X chromosome. Although this represents less than 0.2 percent of the human genome, it is large enough to contain several hundred genes. . . . Once a specific gene has been identified, we can find out where and when it is expressed and how it ultimately contributes to the development of both homosexual and heterosexual orientation" (Hamer et al. 1993, 326).

Other research also supports a biological basis to sexual orientation, including genetic studies and familial studies. According to clinical psychologist Khytam Dawood, familial studies find consistently that both male and female homosexuality run in families; homosexual women have more homosexual sisters than do heterosexual women and male homosexuals tend to have more homosexual brothers. Biological studies find the existence of certain genes on chromosome 8 and the X chromosome influence the development of male sexual orientation (see Dawood 2015). The fraternal birth order effect finds that homosexual men have a greater number of older brothers and that the estimated odds of being homosexual increase by approximately 33 percent with each older brother. Summarizing those studies, Dawood notes: "One in seven homosexual men owe their sexual orientation to the fraternal birth order effect" (Dawood 2015, 783).

Other studies have tried to find brain-based markers for sexual orientation. A 1992 study compared the brains of gay and straight men, looking specifically at the hypothalamus which controls the release of sex hormones from the pituitary gland. The third interstitial nucleus of the anterior hypothalamus (INAH3) was more than twice as large in heterosexual men; the findings of the study were later discredited, however, when it was discovered that all of the brains of the gay men were from individuals who had died from AIDS. A later study conducted by a group of doctors at New York's Mount Sinai School of Medicine found no differences in INAH3 volume or number of neurons between gay and straight men (Byne et al. 2001).

Neurobiology professor Dick Swaab has argued forcefully, based on his decades of research, that sexual orientation is determined in the womb. "All the research indicates that our sexual orientation is programmed in the brain before birth, determining it for the rest of our lives" (Swaab 2014, 64). One example Swaab provides is the impact of the treatment of pregnant mothers with the synthetic estrogen known as diethylstilbestrol (DES), meant to prevent miscarriages, between 1939 and 1960. While DES did not affect miscarriage rates, it did increase the rate of bisexuality and homosexuality in girls exposed to the drug while in the womb. This conclusion is supported by a review of the scientific literature by endocrinologist Louis Gooren (1990), who notes: "Studies assessing the effects of prenatal hormonal influences on later sexual orientation have in a number of cases established positive correlations between prenatal sex-steroid exposure and homosexuality" (p. 84). Swaab also cites research that finds hypothalamic structure differences between homosexual and heterosexual men.

Swaab is adamant that events after birth do not affect sexual orientation. Children brought up by lesbians are not more likely to be gay;

homosexuality should never be regarded as a "lifestyle choice"; and attempts by some religious groups to "cure" people of homosexuality are doomed. (Cookson 2014)

Alice Dreger, a historian of medicine and science, notes in a 2019 interview that "evolution would naturally favor heterosexuality because that's how you get babies" but that "scientists find evidence that there may actually be advantages to a family of having a certain percentage of the children be gay" (Dreger 2019). In other words, if an extended family has adults who produce resources that contribute to the standard of living of the household and its children but who do not use resources to raise their own children, resources are more abundant for children in the household. This phenomenon can take the form of the stereotypical gay uncle or lesbian aunt who showers their nieces and nephews with gifts and attention. Dreger notes that this theory is consistent with the fact that "if a mother has lots of pregnancies of males every successive male will be a little bit more likely to be gay."

Other scientists argue that biology shapes sexuality but is not determinative. Sociomedical scientist Rebecca Jordan-Young, author of *Brain Storm: The Flaws in the Science of Sex Differences*, asserts that "biology and culture interact to shape our sexuality." Similarly, Meg-John Barker, author of *Queer: A Graphic History*, notes that "most aspects of human experience are actually biopsychosocial: a long word which means that they involve our biology, our psychology, and the social world around us, with all of those things influencing each other in complex feedback loops, making it impossible to tease apart each element or the direction of any cause-effect relationships" (quoted in Dastagir 2018).

FURTHER READING

Byne, William, et al. 2001. "The Interstitial Nuclei of the Human Anterior Hypothalamus: An Investigation of Variation with Sex, Sexual Orientation, and HIV Status." *Hormones and Behavior* 40, 2: 86–92.

Cookson, Clive. 2014. "'We Are Our Brains,' by Dick Swaab." *Financial Times*, February 16. https://www.ft.com/content/b4d9a12c-901a-11e3-8029 -00144feab7de

Dastagir, Alia E. 2018. "'Born This Way'? It's Way More Complicated than That." *USA Today*, April 10. https://www.usatoday.com/story/news /2017/06/16/born-way-many-lgbt-community-its-way-more-complex /395035001/

Dawood, Khytam. 2015. "Sexual Orientation: Genetic Aspects." *International Encyclopedia of the Social & Behavioral Sciences, 2nd ed.*, 779–784.

Dreger, Alice. 2019. "What Makes Someone Gay? Science Is Trying to Get It Straight." *Big Think*, February 19. https://bigthink.com/videos/what -makes-someone-gay-science-is-trying-to-get-it-straight

Ganna, Andrea, et al. 2019. "Large-Scale GWAS Reveals Insights into the Genetic Architecture of Same-Sex Sexual Behavior." *Science* 365, 6456: eaat7693.

Genetics of Sexual Behavior. 2020. https://geneticsexbehavior.info/

Gooren, Louis. 1990. "Biomedical Theories of Sexual Orientation: A Critical Examination." In David P. McWhirter, Stephanie A. Sanders, and June Machover Reinisch, eds., *Homosexuality/Heterosexuality: Concepts of Sexual Orientation*. New York: Oxford University Press, pp. 71–87.

Hamer, Dean H., et al. 1993. "A Linkage between DNA Markers on the X Chromosome and Male Sexual Orientation." *Science* 261, 5119: 321–327.

LeVay, Simon. 2011. *Gay, Straight, and the Reason Why: The Science of Sexual Orientation*. New York: Oxford University Press.

Swaab, Dick Frans. 2014. *We Are Our Brains: A Neurobiography of the Brain, from the Womb to Alzheimer's*. New York: Spiegel & Grau.

Q4: DOES LGBTQ IDENTITY EXIST OUTSIDE OF WESTERN SOCIETIES SUCH AS THOSE IN NORTH AMERICA AND DEVELOPED EUROPEAN COUNTRIES?

Answer: Yes. Individuals have engaged in same-sex intimacy in countries outside of Western societies for centuries (see Q5). However, there is a difference between behavior and identity and the idea of a homosexual or queer identity is relatively modern (see Q1). That said, there are individuals who identify as LGBTQ in every country around the world. The degree to which those identities are accepted, tolerated, or recognized by law, however, varies widely.

The Facts: Countries around the world have generally opted for one of three basic methods of responding to LGBTQ individuals: to ignore them, to criminalize them, or to grant them legal rights. Many countries simply ignore the issue completely or consider it to be an issue of psychiatric illness, leading many individuals who wish to engage in same-sex intimacy to do so in secret. In other countries, often in the most conservative regions of the world such as predominantly Muslim countries in Asia and Africa, same-sex intimacy and partnerships have been and remain criminalized. Legal recognition for same-sex identity and couples is much more common in Western societies, although some countries provide for same-sex partnerships and other legal recognition but not full marriage equality.

Same-sex marriages are legal in North America (the United States, Canada, and most of Mexico); in much of Western Europe (except Italy and Switzerland); and in many Latin American countries (Argentina, Brazil, Columbia, Ecuador, and Uruguay). No countries in Central or Eastern Europe have legalized same-sex marriage. In Africa, same-sex marriage is only legal in South Africa; in the Asia-Pacific region, it is only legal in Australia, Taiwan, and New Zealand, although Israel and Armenia recognize same-sex marriages performed elsewhere. Additional countries allow for same-sex unions or registered partnerships but not for full marriage equality, including Italy and Switzerland as well as many countries in Central and Eastern Europe (Andorra, Croatia, Cyprus, Czech Republic, Estonia, Greece, Hungary, Liechtenstein, and Slovenia).

Nonetheless, same-sex relationships between consenting adults are illegal in many countries around the world, including throughout much of Africa and the Middle East. Many of these same countries also criminalize "posing as" or "imitating" a person of a different sex, which leads to arrest and punishment of people based on their gender expression. The range of punishments for offenses in these countries can include fines, jail time, lashings, life imprisonment, and even execution. Not surprisingly, then, openly LGBTQ people in these parts of the world are virtually nonexistent.

In April 2019, the kingdom of Brunei enacted laws that penalize same-sex relations with death by stoning. In Malaysia, individuals engaging in same-sex intimacy can face corporal punishment and up to 20 years in prison. In some countries, antigay laws are seldom enforced but are often used to harass and extort LGBTQ people. For example, while officials in Sri Lanka have not convicted anyone of violating LGBTQ laws since the country gained independence in 1948, statutes outlawing gay sexual activity are used by police to assault, harass, and sexually and monetarily extort individuals believed to be gay. In addition, transgender people continue to face arbitrary detention and mistreatment. At the same time, some countries have paused prosecutions despite leaving anti-LGBTQ laws on the books. For example, the Malawi government announced a moratorium on its antigay laws in July 2014 and police have been instructed to not arrest people for same-sex activity; no one has been arrested for breaking antigay laws in Malawi since 2012.

LGBTQ Activism Worldwide

Despite their lack of legal standing, individuals who identify as LGBTQ exist worldwide and continue to organize for equal rights. Since 1978, the International Lesbian, Gay, Bisexual, Trans and Intersex Association (ILGA), originally called the International Gay Association, has supported rights of the LGBTQ community around the world. As of June 2021, ILGA is a federation of 1,708 organizations from 167 countries and territories, including six regional chapters in Africa, Asia, Europe, Latin America and the Caribbean, Oceania, and North America (ILGA).

For example, in Africa, member organizations are united under the Pan Africa International Lesbian, Gay, Bisexual, Trans and Intersex Association (PAI). PAI is registered in South Africa, the African nation with the friendliest legal environment, but the group includes countries from across the continent. In 2018, representatives from 39 African countries attended their fourth regional conference in Gaborone, Botswana, hosted by LeGaBiBo (Lesbians, Gays and Bisexuals of Botswana). Conference organizers noted that the meeting was well attended despite some interested parties unable to attend because of "the ever-present homophobia in most governments in the continent." This homophobia resulted in the denial of visas sought by some delegates, particularly from Francophone West Africa (a group of French-speaking nations located in western Africa that were once colonial territories of France). Despite this challenge, the group voted to host a fifth gathering in 2020 in Accra, Ghana but the conference was canceled after protests from conservative religious groups in Ghana (Wakefield 2020).

There are also LGBTQ individuals and groups in countries around the world that continue to build community and visibility. In some countries such as Argentina and Brazil, this takes the form of visible activism such as Gay Pride parades and publications. In Argentina, the Argentine Homosexual Community (CHA), founded in 1984, supports members of the gay and lesbian community with legal and psychological counseling and HIV/AIDS prevention. Brazil has had an active LGBTQ movement since the late 1970s (Longaker 2019). In 2007, Buenos Aires hosted the Gay World Cup of soccer. The city of São Paulo hosts the largest annual Gay Pride parade in the world every year, and in June 2019, Brazil's Supreme Court criminalized both homophobia and transphobia. Nonetheless, Brazil remains one of the most dangerous countries in the world for LGBTQ people and violence against members of the community is reported daily. President Jair Bolsonaro, elected in 2019, declared in 2018 that he was a "proud homophobe."

Acceptance of LGBTQ individuals and identities is limited, both by the government and by the general public, in many other countries as well. In Japan and China, same-sex intimacy is not illegal but there is no recognition of same-sex partnerships. It wasn't until 2018 that India, home to more than 1.3 billion people, decriminalized homosexual behavior; however, homophobia remains a significant hurdle in the country. In Russia, homosexual sex was decriminalized in 1993 but discrimination is still widespread. Participants at a 2006 gay rights march in Moscow were assaulted by counterdemonstrators and not protected by police and two years later the mayor of Moscow banned gay events in the city. Support for LGBTQ people and rights has further decreased since 2012, during the administration of Russian president Vladimir Putin. In 2013, Putin signed a "gay propaganda" law banning the sharing of information about LGBTQ people and the country has since seen a dramatic increase in homophobic violence. In April 2021, Putin signed into law several constitutional amendments that, among other restrictions, formally and legally define marriage as between a woman and a man (Lavers 2021).

In Egypt, there are no specific laws outlawing same-sex intimacy and the government runs a confidential hotline that provides callers with information about HIV/AIDS. However, in 2001, 52 men nicknamed the Cairo 52 were arrested for their behavior while on a floating nightclub called the Queen Boat; 23 were found guilty of "debauchery and contempt of religion" and sentenced to hard labor. In Iran and Nigeria, gay men and lesbians are sometimes punished or even executed for their sexual orientation; Iran does allow sex reassignment surgery for individuals who want to "become heterosexual."

FURTHER READING

Avery, Daniel. 2019. "71 Countries Where Homosexuality Is Illegal." *Newsweek*, April 4. https://www.newsweek.com/73-countries-where-its-illegal-be-gay-1385974

Human Dignity Trust. n.d. https://www.humandignitytrust.org/

Human Rights Watch. 2019. "#Outlawed: 'The Love That Dare Not Speak Its Name.'" http://internap.hrw.org/features/features/lgbt_laws/

ILGA. 2021. "ILGA World—The International Lesbian, Gay, Bisexual, Trans, and Intersex Association." https://ilga.org

Jacobs, Sue-Ellen, Wesley Thomas, and Sabine Lang, eds. 1997. *Two-Spirit People: Native American Gender Identity, Sexuality, and Spirituality.* Springfield: University of Illinois.

Lavers, Michael K. 2021. "Putin Formally Bans Same-Sex Marriage in Russia." *Washington Blade,* April 6. https://www.washingtonblade .com/2021/04/06/putin-formally-bans-same-sex-marriages-in-russia/

Lipka, Michael, and David Masci. 2019. "Where Europe Stands on Gay Marriage and Civil Unions." *Pew Research Center,* October 28. https:// www.pewresearch.org/fact-tank/2019/10/28/where-europe-stands-on-gay -marriage-and-civil-unions/

Longaker, Jacob. 2019. "Brazil's LGBT Movement and Interest Groups." In Don Haider-Markel, ed., *The Oxford Encyclopedia of LGBT Politics and Policy,* November 22. New York: Oxford University Press. https://doi .org/10.1093/acrefore/9780190228637.013.1293

Masci, David, and Drew DeSilver. 2019. "A Global Snapshot of Same-Sex Marriage." *Pew Research Center,* October 29. https://www.pewresearch .org/fact-tank/2019/10/29/global-snapshot-same-sex-marriage/

Simon, Rita J., and Alison Brooks. 2009. *Gay and Lesbian Communities the World Over.* Lanham, MD: Lexington Books.

Wakefield, Lily. 2020. "A History-Making LGBT+ Rights Conference in Ghana Has Been Banned and No, It's Not Because of Coronavirus." *Pink News,* March 13. https://www.pinknews.co.uk/2020/03/13 /ghana-lgbt-rights-conference-coronavirus-pan-africa-ilga-nana-akufo -addo/

Q5: HAVE THERE ALWAYS BEEN LGBTQ PEOPLE?

Answer: Yes. While the word *homosexual* did not exist before 1869, evidence of same-sex attraction dates back as far as 1800 BCE in poems from ancient Egypt (Parkinson 2013). References to close friendships between men and between women that cross "a moving boundary between emotional and physical intimacy" exist "in Greek philosophy, Christian humanist treatises, medieval Arabic poetry, and tales of Chinese emperors and Japanese samurai" (Aldrich 2012, 12). Determining just how far back same-sex intimate relationships go, however, is tricky, because of the wide variation in how sex and sexuality have been understood over time. In addition, a distinction should be drawn between the modern phenomenon of identifying as gay, lesbian, bisexual, or transgender and the ancient tradition of same-sex desire.

The Facts: One possible ancient representation of same-sex sexual intimacy comes from 2400 BCE in ancient Egypt. Wall carvings in the Saqqara burial site of Niankhkhnum and Khnumhotep dating back to that era depict two men holding hands, looking into one another's eyes, and embracing. Some Egyptologists believe the men were twins, brothers, or just friends while others see the carvings as evidence of a more intimate, sexual relationship. Another representation in the Pyramid Texts, Egypt's oldest religious writings, suggests that Horus and Seth (both human males) engaged in reciprocal anal intercourse despite warnings against doing so from Horus's mother, the goddess Isis (Aldrich 2012, 16).

Evidence of early homosexual behavior between men is much more widespread in ancient Greece. Greek history and literature include abundant references to homosexual love, which according to scholar Louis Crompton "held an honored place in Greek culture for more than a thousand years, that is, from before 600 BCE to about 400 CE" (Crompton 2003, 2). The ancient Greeks did not use any words that would correspond to the modern word *homosexual*; instead, they spoke of *paiderastia*, which meant literally "boy love": "a relation between an older male and someone younger, usually a youth between the ages of fourteen and twenty" (Crompton 2003, 3). The term for such a relationship today is *pederasty*. (Modern law in many locations classifies sexual interaction with those younger than the age of consent, usually 16 years old, as statutory rape.)

There are more than 50 examples from ancient Greek art, history, and literature of young men loved by deities, including most of the principal male gods of the Olympian pantheon, famous poets, playwrights, political leaders, and artists. "This is an astounding record, including as it does most of the greatest names of ancient Greece during the greatest period of Greek culture," wrote Crompton. "For a man not to have had a male lover seems to have bespoken a lack of character or a deficiency in sensibility" (Crompton 2003, 2–3).

In the *Laws*, Plato praises the communities of Crete and Sparta for their approval of same-sex love. In *Politics*, Aristotle claims the Cretans encouraged "sexual relations among the males so that the women would not have children" (Crompton 2003, 7). Plato's *The Symposium* (c. 385–378 BCE) also describes love between men; wine cups from the era show erotic scenes between bearded men and younger, athletic youth. According to historian Robert Aldrich, ample evidence of gay male relationships from ancient Greece can be found in vase paintings, literature, history, and philosophy. Famous male couples from this period include Achilles and Patroclus, Harmodius and Aristogeiton, and Alexander and Hephaestion. "Those familiar with the Classics . . . knew that gods, as well as men, overflowed with homosexual passion" (Aldrich 2012, 24).

In Athenian society, emotional connections and sexual intercourse between men was accepted and celebrated but only under particular conditions. Specifically, older, adult men typically filled the role of the dominant sexual partner with younger men and adolescents. The older man was also expected to oversee the education and upbringing of the younger man while also marrying and fathering children. These same-sex relationships are often described as romantic and emotional, not simply about physical intimacy. In ancient Greece, wrote Crompton, "love between males was honored as a guarantee of military efficiency and civic freedom. It became a source of inspiration in poetry and art, was applauded in theaters and assemblies, and was enthusiastically commended by philosophers" (Crompton 2003, 536).

Homosexual relations were also common in the Roman Empire. The most famous example is the love story between a Roman emperor named Hadrian (76–138 BCE) and a handsome young man named Antinous (110–130 BCE). As Aldrich notes, "Antinous was apparently not the first of Hadrian's male partners . . . but the intensity and longevity of their relationship was remarkable" (2012, 30). The emperor renamed the city where Antinous died Antinoöpolis. In addition, he "proclaimed Antinous as a god, and promoted his worship with the building of temples. Yearly athletic contests were held in his memory. The emperor had coins minted and medals struck with the image of his friend, and statues of Antinous graced cities around the empire" (Aldrich 2012).

When Christianity took over in the fourth century, Roman law imposed a death penalty for homosexual behavior, citing scriptural condemnations of such acts in Leviticus. Men and women who escaped execution lived lives of intimidation, humiliation, and violence. "In the Middle Ages fierce laws were passed, at clerical prompting, that led to the burning, beheading, drowning, hanging, and castration of male 'sodomites' who, through the broadest possible interpretation of the Sodom story and other biblical texts, were blamed for such disasters as plagues, earthquakes, floods, famines, and even defeat in battle. Lesbian acts, too, were condemned, and women were executed" (Crompton 2003, xii).

Historic examples of homosexuality also come from imperial China, including famous verses from the seventeenth-century poet Chen Weisong (1625–1682) celebrating his relationship with Xu Ziyun (1644–1675), a young actor nicknamed Purple Clouds. The two men met when Chen was 35 and Purple Clouds was 15 and they lived together as a couple along with Chen's wife, two concubines, and several children. In an anthology of poetry written after Purple Clouds's death, fellow poets honored their relationship and one line from poet Wu Qing references the most famous stories in ancient Chinese homosexuality: the *shared peach* and the *cut sleeve*.

The story of the shared peach refers to Duke Ling of Wei (534–492 BCE), a provincial ruler who was in power from 543–493 BCE, and a young male court official named Mizi Xia, who, after eating half of a delicious peach, stopped and gave the other half to Duke Ling, who exclaimed, "How sincere is your love for me!" (Aldrich 2012, 33). The story of the cut sleeve refers to the relationship between Emperor Ai (28–1 BCE), a ruler during the Han dynasty from 6–1 BCE, and Dong Xian. As the story goes, Emperor Ai was napping with Dong Xian stretched out across his sleeve. In order to get up without disturbing his lover, he instead cut off his own sleeve. Aldrich notes: "The 'passion of the shared peach' and the 'passion of the cut sleeve' thus became bywords for the homosexual behavior that was commonplace in ancient China. At least ten emperors of the ancient Han dynasty openly engaged in same-sex affairs, male brothels operated for centuries in Beijing and other cities, and marriages between two men were occasionally celebrated in the province of Fujian" (2012, 34–35). In the late Wu and early Qing periods, homosexual behavior was considered praiseworthy and romantic. This acceptance of homosexuality persisted in China until the early twentieth century, when cultural changes brought in by the revolutions of Sun Yat-sen (1911) and Mao Zedong (1949) dramatically altered Chinese attitudes about same-sex sexual relationships.

Pre-Meiji Japan (800–1868) provides another example of same-sex intimacy. Because early Japan lacked a written language prior to 552, when Chinese characters (Kanji) were imported, we can't know how same-sex intimacy was treated before then. Kūkai (774–835 BCE), the founder of a major branch of Buddhism, is widely believed to have had multiple homosexual relationships with other men at his monastery. Stories of homosexual love and behavior also feature in many famous Japanese works, including the eleventh-century *Tales of the Genji*. Mirroring the mores of other ancient civilizations, most same-sex male Japanese relationships were between an older man and an adolescent, with the senior partner taking on the active sexual role and acting as a mentor to the younger partner. This practice was particularly widespread during the Tokugawa period (1600–1868).

When European explorers came to the eastern Pacific and Polynesia in the late eighteenth century, they often saw (and discouraged) homosexuality. Sometimes this resistance was restricted to sex between men when one of the two was a crossdresser (*mahu* in Tahiti or *fa'a fafine* in Samoa); in Hawaii, young masculine men called *aikane* had sex with the king. There is also evidence of same-sex relationships among Native Americans from before the arrival of Europeans. The Indian text the *Kama Sutra*, from the fourth century CE, includes a discussion of men who are sexually attracted to other men.

Homosexuality is also recorded in Africa, although sociologist and anthropologist Stephen O. Murray notes that since no written records were kept of social relations before the arrival of European colonists, little is known about the history there prior to the nineteenth century, corresponding with the time period when European colonial governments imposed laws to suppress nonheterosexual relationships (Murray 2015). One exception is the same-sex intimacy recorded for posterity in the rock paintings by San Bushmen. Historian Marc Epprecht notes that San art dating "from at least two thousand years ago"—at least 1,000 years before the arrival of colonists—depicts both group and partnered anal and intercrural (between the legs) sex. "Same-sex sexual practices not only existed in pre-modern milieux but were common enough to be socially acceptable" (Epprecht 2004, 26).

Historical evidence of same-sex relationships among both men and women comes from multiple areas of Africa, including reports of same-sex intimacy between men in Angola in 1625, the Congo in 1732, Nubia in 1882, French Senegal in 1893, Guinea in 1894, Zanzibar in 1899, Eritrea in 1900, and Ethiopia in 1909, to name just a few. Overall, numerous reports indicate that homosexual behavior and relationships were common in traditional African cultures for both men and women. The first Swahili-English dictionary, published in 1882, included terms for "man-woman" as well as other terms referencing alternative gender identities (Murray and Roscoe 1998, 30). "The colonists did not introduce homosexuality to Africa but rather intolerance of it—and systems of surveillance and regulation for suppressing it" (Murray and Roscoe 1998, xvi). Sometimes, natives resisted the negative labeling of homosexuality and cross-dressing; however, European efforts to suppress public homosexuality were eventually successful.

Homosexuality also has a long history in Russia. In the mid-1600s, the first commercial bathhouses appeared in Moscow and according to historian Dan Healey, these facilities were a site for sexual intimacy between men (Healey 2001). Russia's Military Articles of 1716 prohibited consensual sex between men in military service (Essig 1999), largely due to the influence of European ideas about sexual morality (Healey 2001). However, even after the prohibition was extended to civilian men in 1835 by

Nicholas I, same-sex desire and intimacy between men persisted (Healey 2001).

Same-sex intimacy between men was also common in medieval Islamic societies. Beautiful young men since early 'Abbāsid times (beginning in 761 CE) were assumed to be sexually receptive. They also were known to display "wit and flippancy, association with music and certain musical instruments, activity as go-betweens, and (sometimes) cross-dressing" (Murray and Roscoe 1997, 305). In the late eighth century, Persian households often kept a *ghulām*, a young male slave kept for sexual purposes. Generally, "the cultural expectation was for the boy to outgrow sexual receptivity" but there is also evidence from the Islamic world that some males continued to engage in same-sex intimacy deep into adulthood (Murray and Roscoe 1997, 305).

Same-Sex Intimacy Between Women in World History

In stark contrast to the abundant documentation of same-sex intimacy between men, women were almost invisible in most places. Same-sex contact between women was often not regulated; according to sociologist Laurie Essig, while men who broke these prohibitions were considered criminals, women were considered "less than full legal subjects, weaker and therefore more susceptible both to perverse desires and their necessary correctives" (Essig 1999, 4). The major exception is the ancient Greek poet Sappho (born in 612 BCE) from the Greek island Lesbos in the Aegean Sea. Her "avowals of love for women in her poems . . . made the word 'lesbian' a synonym for female homosexuality" (Crompton 2003, 18). Sappho also gives her name to what was called *sapphism* and is now called *lesbianism*, after the island of her birth. The fragments of her poetry that have survived speak of her love of the beauty of young women and the sexual consummation of her desires for those women. Other evidence from ancient Greece includes lasting relationships between women noted by Plutarch in *Lives* and a lesbian couple from one of Lucian's dialogues of the partnered women Demonassa and Megilla—the latter of whom hailed from Lesbos.

Another lesbian poet comes from the Islamic world. The eleventh-century princess Walladah bint al-Mustakfi (994–1091), sometimes called the Arab Sappho, uses her poetry to praise her female lover Muhjah, often with fairly explicit sexual language (Murray 1997). Writing in the twelfth century, Sharif al-Idrisi (1100–1166) noted that women "more intelligent than the others"—women who were "educated and elegant"—were choosing lesbian relationships (quoted in Murray 1997, 99).

FURTHER READING

Aldrich, Robert. 2012. *Gay Lives*. New York: Thames & Hudson.

Bullough, Vern L. 2019. *Homosexuality: A History (From Ancient Greece to Gay Liberation)*. New York: Routledge Press.

Crompton, Louis. 2003. *Homosexuality & Civilization*. Cambridge, MA: Harvard University Press.

Epprecht, Marc. 2004. *Hungochani: The History of a Dissident Sexuality in Southern Africa*. Montreal: McGill-Queen's University Press.

Essig, Laurie. 1999. *Queer in Russia: A Story of Sex, Self, and the Other*. Durham, NC: Duke University Press.

Healey, Dan. 2001. *Homosexual Desire in Revolutionary Russia: The Regulation of Sexual and Gender Dissent*. Chicago: University of Chicago Press.

Murray, Stephen O. 1997. "Woman-Woman Love in Islamic Societies." In Stephen O. Murray and Will Roscoe, eds., *Islamic Homosexualities: Culture, History, and Literature*. New York University Press, pp. 97–104.

Murray, Stephen O., and Will Roscoe. 1997. "Conclusion." In Stephen O. Murray and Will Roscoe, *Islamic Homosexualities: Culture, History, and Literature*. New York: New York University Press, pp. 302–319.

Murray, Stephen O., and Will Roscoe, eds. 1998. *Boy-Wives and Female Husbands: Studies in African Homosexualities*. New York: St. Martin's Press.

Murray, Stephen O. 2015. "Africa: Sub-Saharan, Pre-Independence." *GLBTQ, Inc.*, glbtq.com.

Parkinson, R. B. 2013. *A Little Gay History: Desire and Diversity across the World*. New York: Columbia University Press.

Q6: HAS THE IDEA THAT LGBTQ ORIENTATIONS STEM FROM CHILDHOOD SEXUAL TRAUMA BEEN DEBUNKED BY RESEARCHERS?

Answer: Yes. Researchers have found no evidence that childhood sexual trauma is linked to sexual identity or orientation.

The Facts: The myth that nonheterosexual sexual orientation is linked to childhood sexual trauma is related to a historical understanding of homosexuality as an illness and a belief that heterosexuality is the only normal and natural form of sexual expression. Heterosexism (discrimination against nonheterosexual people) and heteronormativity (that only heterosexuality is the norm) often lead to discrimination and prejudice against people who are outside of that norm (nonheterosexual people). These views encourage perceptions of LGBTQ people as inferior or mentally ill—possibly as a result of childhood sexual trauma. "Historically researchers and clinicians have been encouraged to describe or explain a *cause* for individuals who deviate from the culturally sanctioned norm of heterosexuality. For example, in the heteronormative society in which we live, one such myth has been that people begin to identify as nonheterosexual as a result of a traumatic sexual experience by someone of the opposite sex" (Walker, Hernandez, and Davey 2012, 386).

The misconception that physical and sexual abuse in childhood might lead to same-sex sexuality in adulthood stems from studies that have found these factors to be positively correlated. The heteronormativity of most societies encourages many individuals to seek a root cause of their sexual orientation. As Gartner notes:

Any boy growing up gay in our society is likely to endure painful psychological and social struggles as he comes to understand his orientation and deal with people's reactions to it. In reacting to these struggles, he will probably go through a period of wondering about how he came to be homosexual. At such a time, he will look everywhere for an answer to the question, "Why am I gay?" And, if he has been sexually abused by a man, it is easy for him to "blame" his sexual orientation on the abuse. (2000, 13)

It is true that multiple studies have reported that nonheterosexual individuals are more likely to report a history of child sexual abuse compared to heterosexual individuals. Experts note, however, that all of those studies suffer from "noteworthy methodological sampling limitations." As is often the case and as every statistician knows, correlation is not causation. These studies are not scientifically valid and no link has been proven (Walker et al. 2012, 387). In other words, just because people who are gay are more likely to have been victims of sexual trauma does not mean that the trauma caused or even influenced their sexuality. Same-sex attraction generally emerges prior to any physical or sexual experiences. Data show that predominant sexual orientation is established before latency (usually age 7–13); on average, same-sex sexual attraction among men emerges at age 10 and sexual experiences occur several years later (Rind 2013). In other words, same-sex intimacy often happens after—not before—a person has identified a same-sex attraction or a gay sexual orientation.

There are two major possible explanations for the persistent spurious correlation: 1) adolescents perceived by adults to be gay or lesbian are more likely to be targeted for abuse by adults; and 2) adults who are gay or lesbian are more likely to recall childhood trauma that is related to their sexuality.

The American Psychological Association (AGLP 2020) notes:

> No one knows what causes heterosexuality, homosexuality, or bisexuality. Homosexuality was once thought to be the result of troubled family dynamics or faulty psychological development. Those assumptions are now understood to have been based on misinformation and prejudice. . . . No specific psychosocial or family dynamic cause for homosexuality has been identified, including histories of childhood sexual abuse. Sexual abuse does not appear to be more prevalent in children who grow up to identify as gay, lesbian, or bisexual, than in children who identify as heterosexual.

Psychologists Richard Gartner and Bruce Rind note that the assumption that childhood sexual assault causes homosexual orientation requires that an assault happens first. However, no causal link exists between childhood sexual assault and subsequent predominant sexual orientation. Most sexual abuse of boys occurs after sexual identity has been established; many abused gay men have a clear sense of homosexual orientation before their abuse (Gartner 2000). Research scientist Andrea Roberts and her colleagues summarized the various explanations for the positive association between childhood maltreatment and adult same-sex sexual orientation.

1. Adolescents who reveal their same-sex sexual orientation are targeted for maltreatment.
2. Adolescents exploring same-sex attractions may put themselves in risky situations, increasing likelihood of maltreatment.
3. Sexual orientation minorities disproportionately exhibit gender-nonconforming behaviors in childhood and are targeted for maltreatment.
4. Differential recall of maltreatment by sexual orientation.
5. Maltreatment increases likelihood of same-sex sexuality. (Roberts et al. 2013)

Multiple scholars have responded negatively to the idea that childhood sexual abuse generates same-sex sexuality. Rind argues that the conflation of "positive/willing sexual relations between gay or bisexual boys and men" with unwanted sexual abuse is based on an assumption that all same-sex attraction and behavior is "a diversion from the natural state of exclusive heterosexual orientation" (2013, 1655). In turn, critics have accused Rind of downplaying the harm caused by childhood sexual abuse because children cannot legally consent to sexual intimacy and thus should not be considered willing participants.

As further evidence of his argument that childhood sexual abuse cannot be the cause of same-sex sexual orientation, Rind notes the inconsistent effects that such abuse is said to have on boys and girls: when men sexually abuse minor females, some assume that the victims lose sexual interest in men and thus become lesbians; however, when men sexually abuse minor boys, they are assumed to become more attracted to men and thus become gay (Rind 2013, 1657).

Another approach to explaining the correlation between childhood sexual abuse and same-sex sexual orientation incorporates measures of childhood gender nonconformity. Childhood gender nonconformity refers to behavior that is viewed as incompatible with societal expectations for boys to behave in masculine ways and girls to embrace feminine characteristics. Gay men and lesbians are more likely to be gender nonconforming compared to heterosexual men and women (Xu and Zheng 2017) and "gender nonconforming behaviors are often recognized by adults before a child is aware of a sexual identity" (Andersen and Blosnich 2013, 6). Thus, the correlation between childhood sexual abuse and adult sexual orientation may be a result of nonheterosexual children being more likely to be abused because they are exhibiting gender-nonconforming behaviors that are noticed (and acted on) by adults. In addition, teenagers exploring and questioning their sexual orientation may put themselves in situations where sexual abuse is more likely such as public sex environments (public areas where people go for consensual sexual contact) (Balsam, Rothblum, and Beauchaine 2005). Because they are putting themselves in riskier situations, they may run a greater risk of being abused by adults.

A final argument against a causal link between childhood sexual assault and same-sex sexuality is the simple empirical disconnect between the prevalence of sexual abuse of children and the prevalence of gay, lesbian, and bisexual adults in the general population. This stems from the very real (albeit unpleasant) fact that many children—about one out of five, according to researchers—are survivors of childhood sexual assault. If those assaults were affecting adult sexual orientation, there would be far higher rates of nonheterosexual orientation among adults (Andersen and Blosnich 2013).

The consistent conclusion reached in scientific research is that sexual orientation precedes childhood sexual assault and childhood sexual trauma does not cause individuals to become gay, lesbian, or bisexual.

FURTHER READING

AGLP. 2020. "LGBTQ Fact Sheets." The Association of LGBTQ+ Psychiatrists. http://www.aglp.org/Pages/factsheets.htm

Andersen, Judith P., and John Blosnich. 2013. "Disparities in Adverse Childhood Experiences among Sexual Minority and Heterosexual Adults: Results from a Multi-State Probability-Based Sample." *PLoS ONE* 8, 1: e54691.

Balsam, Kimberly F., Esther D. Rothblum, and Theodore P. Beauchaine. 2005. "Victimization over the Life Span: A Comparison of Lesbian, Gay, Bisexual, and Heterosexual Siblings." *Journal of Consulting and Clinical Psychology* 73, 3: 477–487.

Gartner, Richard B. 2000. "Sexual Victimization of Boys by Men: Meanings and Consequences." *Journal of Gay & Lesbian Psychotherapy* 3, 2: 1–33.

Rind, Bruce. 2013. "Homosexual Orientation—From Nature, Not Abuse: A Critique of Roberts, Glymour, and Koenen (2013)." *Archives of Sexual Behavior: The Official Publication of the International Academy of Sex Research* 42, 8: 1653–1664.

Walker, Monique D., Ana M. Hernandez, and Maureen Davey. 2012. "Childhood Sexual Abuse and Adult Sexual Identity Formation: Intersection of Gender, Race, and Sexual Orientation." *American Journal of Family Therapy* 40, 5: 385–398.

Xu, Yin, and Yong Zheng. 2017. "Does Sexual Orientation Precede Childhood Sexual Abuse? Childhood Gender Nonconformity as a Risk Factor and Instrumental Variable Analysis." *Sexual Abuse* 29, 8: 786–802.

Q7: IS THE WORD "QUEER" A SLUR AGAINST THE LGBTQ COMMUNITY?

Answer: *Queer* was once a pejorative slur but since the 1980s, it has been increasingly reclaimed as a term of inclusion within the LGBTQ community.

The Facts: A movement to reclaim queer as a badge of honor began with the gay rights movement of the 1970s and 1980s. In 1990, a group of gay rights activists formed the organization Queer Nation which used the term as a means of actively reclaiming it as a badge of pride rather than as a disparaging term. They used coming out as a political strategy in the 1990s, visiting heterosexual bars and suburban shopping malls while wearing T-shirts with LGBTQ pride slogans, staging kiss-ins, and chanting: "We're here! We're queer! Get used to it!" The intent in choosing the most popular epithet used against gay people was a way to confront and to fight homophobia (Brontsema 2004). Leaflets distributed by Queer Nation (2016) noted:

> When a lot of lesbians and gay men wake up in the morning, we feel angry and disgusted, not gay. So we've chosen to call ourselves queer. Using "queer" is a way of reminding us how we are perceived by the rest of the world. It is a way of telling ourselves we don't have to be witty and charming people who keep our lives discreet and marginalized in the straight world.

Despite this early attempt to reclaim the word, queer was considered a slur for many decades thereafter and is still considered pejorative when used by outsiders to refer in a derogatory way to members of the LGBTQ community. In the sixteenth century, the word "queer" originally meant strange or odd. By the late 1800s, it began to be used to refer to sexual deviance and to feminine or gay men in particular. The term "gay" rose to prominence in the 1920s as a code word that straight people would not understand. Within the subsequent two decades, queer became viewed as a derogatory label meant to imply that a gay person was deviant and abnormal and was used as a way to bully and harass those perceived to be violating gender norms while "gay" increasingly became the preferred term within the community (Brontsema 2004).

Some argue that hate speech terms can never be reclaimed and that attempting to reclaim "queer" is not only futile but self-defeating. They suggest that repeating the word can only reinforce a homophobic society's common stereotypes and fears. Some members of the LGBTQ community are still not comfortable with the word—particularly people who were on the receiving end of verbal harassment using the word when they were younger. Even today, when queer is used by people and organizations to identify themselves, it is not a slur, but it can still be offensive when used as an epithet. As with other historical slurs used to refer to members of the LGBTQ community, the word queer can still cause harm when used in a way meant to cause harm but reclaiming slurs can help to empower members of a marginalized group.

Many people believe that language is dynamic and ever-changing (Brontsema 2004). Jessica Stern, executive director of the LGBTQ advocacy group Outright International, explains that queer "has become a beautiful, inclusive term." While originally a term used scornfully, "since the 1980s, many LGBTQ people have reclaimed the word to remove the negative connotations that were used to dehumanize us" (Gander 2018). Similarly, National Public Radio's editor for standards and practices Mark Memmott notes, "for many people, it's still a difficult word to hear or read because of the past history. But language evolves. Words evolve" (Rocheleau 2019). Columnist Dan Savage explained the process of reclaiming antigay slurs this way (Wheeler 2020):

> For a person to use a word that once scared them and inhabit its power, what it really says is: "I'm not scared of you anymore *or* this word."

Many groups have added a Q for queer to the familiar LGBT acronym as a way of broadening the umbrella of inclusion to include people of fluid or intersecting sexual orientations and gender identities. (Others suggest the Q stands for "questioning" one's sexual identity.) LGBTQ Nation explains queer as including all lesbian, gay, bisexual, and transgender people because they fall "outside the heterosexual mainstream of the gender binary. . . . If you're gender-neutral, nonbinary, agender, genderfluid, pansexual, asexual, solosexual or something else not covered by LGBT, the Q has got you covered!" (Villarreal 2019). The word celebrates differences rather than putting people into boxes; queer allows and welcomes "a multiplicity of sexualities and genders" (Brontsema 2004).

Queer has gone mainstream in recent years. There are popular television shows that use the word in their titles, such as *Queer as Folk* (in 1999) and *Queer Eye for the Straight Guy* (2003). Academics have studied queer theory since 1991 and queer film and art festivals have been around since the early 1990s. While still harmful when used to marginalize and to demean people, the term queer is often used as a term of inclusion and diversity in contemporary language.

FURTHER READING

Brontsema, Robin. 2004. "A Queer Revolution: Reconceptualizing the Debate Over Linguistic Reclamation." *Colorado Research in Linguistics* 17, 1: 1–17.

Gander, Kashmira. 2018. "Is Queer an Offensive Slur?" *Newsweek*, March 30. https://www.newsweek.com/queer-offensive-slur-855703

Perlman, Merrill. 2019. "How the Word 'Queer' Was Adopted by the LGBTQ Community." *Columbia Journalism Review*, January 22. https://www.cjr.org/language_corner/queer.php

Queer Nation NY History. 2016. *Queer Nation NY*, August 25. https://
    queernationny.org/history
Rocheleau, Juliette. 2019. "A Former Slur Is Reclaimed, and Listeners Have
    Mixed Feelings." *NPR*, August 21. https://www.npr.org/sections/publiced
    itor/2019/08/21/752330316/a-former-slur-is-reclaimed-and-listeners-have
    -mixed-feelings
Villarreal, Daniel. 2019. "What Does Queer Mean? Well, There's No One
    Definition." *LGBTQ Nation*, September 21. https://www.lgbtqnation
    .com/2019/09/queer-mean-well-theres-no-one-definition/
Wheeler, André. 2020. "Why I'm Reclaiming the Homophobic Slur I
    Used to Fear." *The Guardian*, March 9. https://www.theguardian.com
    /commentisfree/2020/mar/09/lgbt-gay-men-slur-homophobia

2

❖

LGBTQ Political and Legal Treatment Over Time

When people think about the beginning of the fight for equal rights for the LGBTQ community, the first thought for many is the riots at the Stonewall Inn in New York City in 1969. While Stonewall was a pivotal and important part of LGBTQ history, Q8 notes that it did not mark the very beginning of the contemporary LGBTQ rights movement. There are other important aspects of LGBTQ political and legal treatment over time that have often gone unnoticed and this chapter provides key insights into the evolution of political and social debates regarding LGBTQ issues in our time.

Q9 delves into the claim that some of the strongest opponents of LGBTQ rights are, in fact, closeted LGBTQ people themselves. Several questions investigate the notion that equal rights for LGBTQ people will infringe on other important American rights. A perceived tension between religious freedom and LGBTQ rights, one that has lingered for decades, is addressed in Q10. The claim that granting LGBTQ rights will result in other consequences like legalized bestiality and necrophilia is addressed in Q11. Q12 investigates the rate of hate crimes against LGBTQ people over time. Finally, Q13 summarizes the ways that LGBTQ people continue to experience legal discrimination in the United States.

Q8: DID THE GAY RIGHTS MOVEMENT BEGIN
AT STONEWALL IN 1969?

Answer: No. The Stonewall Riots that occurred in New York City in 1969 are considered the symbolic launch of the modern gay rights movement but gay and lesbian organizations in the United States have been fighting for equality since at least 1924. In fact, important events prior to the Stonewall Riots give key context to how and why the riots took place.

The Facts: In our national memory, the Stonewall Riots of 1969 are remembered as the first time that LGBTQ people fought back against oppression. The Stonewall Inn, where the riots took place, was designated a National Historic Landmark by President Bill Clinton in 2000. In 2016, President Barack Obama elevated Stonewall to the designation of National Monument. However, although the Stonewall Uprising holds an important place in the history of the LGBTQ rights movement, it was not the first time that LGBTQ Americans took action on their own behalf.

The first documented gay rights group in the United States was the Chicago Society for Human Rights, established in December 1924. Founded by Henry Gerber and six other men, the organization aimed to bring homosexuals together and to educate legal authorities and legislators. The group published two newsletters before a police raid in 1925 led to the arrest of several members, including Gerber, and the confiscation of the group's property. A newspaper account of the raid caused Gerber to lose his job and the Society for Human Rights ceased to exist. In 2015, Gerber's home was designated a National Historic Landmark.

Post-WWII efforts by gays and lesbians to fight for their rights were more successful. These efforts include creation of the Veterans Benevolent Association (VBA) in 1945, the first gay and lesbian membership-based organization in the United States. It was followed by the founding of the Mattachine Society of Los Angeles in 1951 and the establishment of the Daughters of Bilitis in San Francisco in 1955.

The VBA was founded with the goal of fighting back against the military's use of not-honorable discharges (also known as blue discharges because they were handed down on blue forms) to dismiss homosexual men from the ranks. While dishonorable discharges were used in response to serious offenses such as not following orders or overt cowardice, blue discharges were used for character issues such as alcoholism, lying, and "sexual perversity" such as men having or suspected of having sex with other men. Those noted on their military records as being sexual psychopaths suffered consequences in civilian life, including challenges in finding employment. This problem was worsened with passage of the Servicemen's Readjustment Act (the GI Bill) in 1944, which made generous financial benefits available to most veterans but not to those with blue discharges. In 1945, four honorably discharged veterans formed the VBA to fight for the end of the use of blue discharges of gay men. In coalition with the NAACP, which was fighting against the excessive use of blue discharges of Black service members, the VBA conducted a media and lobbying effort against the discharges that lasted until 1954. Those efforts were largely unsuccessful in stopping blue discharges. Nonetheless, the VBA was valuable to members both for its legal advisory panel which helped members facing discrimination in employment or housing due to their sexual orientation and for its role as a social organization.

The Mattachine Foundation was formed in Los Angeles in 1950 by Harry Hay and Rudi Gernreich, soon joined by Bob Hull, Dale Jennings, and Chuck Rowland. It was renamed the Mattachine Society in 1953. In Europe in the Middle Ages, the Mattachines were societies of men who played the jester or fool in dance, performing veiled political satire. Harry Hay saw gay men in American society in a similar role: embodying the rejected but important elements of American culture. The Mattachine founders created and led discussion groups, developed research committees and speaker committees, and eventually, local chapters of the group opened in cities around the country. In 1951, the core group of founders crafted a statement of purpose and a membership pledge that reveal Hay's vision that gay people were a minority group, a status assigned at birth, living under heterosexual oppression. His overarching goal was to liberate gay men from this oppression. The three goals in the statement of purpose were to unify, to educate, and to lead. The Society believed it could serve as an example for homosexuals to follow so American society would begin to craft a different image of gay men: productive, beneficial, and dignified. When the original board was forced out in 1953 after rumblings of communist organizing, Ken Burns became the new chairman of the board of directors. Under his leadership, the focus of the organization changed to rely more on science and finding a cause for homosexuality. It also doubled down on focusing on gay people as sharing a core group identity as gay. This new philosophy helped to boost membership and increased the conversations about common problems among gay men. In 1955, the Society began publishing the *Mattachine Review*, a monthly magazine that published a diverse array of news, society, history, culture, and opinion pieces of interest to the gay community.

The Daughters of Bilitis (DOB), organized in San Francisco by Del Martin and Phyllis Lyon in 1955, was the first lesbian organization in the United States. Formed as a discussion and social group, DOB focused on the issues facing its members as lesbians. The organization took its name from a female character who was romantically associated with Sappho, the female Greek lyric poet, in a collection of poems written by Pierre Louÿs. In 1956, DOB began publishing *The Ladder*, a monthly (and later bimonthly) magazine that aimed to educate lesbians and the public as well as to advocate against homophobic laws. At first, DOB promoted a more passive, nonconfrontational, assimilationist stance to encourage conformity. In the 1960s, however, it became more politically active, focusing much of its energies on challenging laws that punished homosexuals for their sexual orientation.

These homophile groups (homophile meaning "loving the same") mostly engaged in closed-door activities meant to bring members of the gay and lesbian community together. But they also staged occasional protests against police harassment and began fighting for their rights in court, including the right to assemble and publish magazines. Publications were an important part of the homophile movement, as illustrated by the first issue of the *Mattachine Review*, published in January 1955, which professed a hope that readers would learn the truth about "the sex variant" as opposed to the falsehoods and misunderstandings that dominated many straight attitudes about homosexuality. Two years prior, in 1953, the Mattachine Society began publishing *One* magazine, but *One*, Inc. quickly became its own organization.

These groups operated against the backdrop of what has been dubbed the Lavender Scare, a fear in post-World War II America that homosexuals posed a threat to national security and needed to be systematically removed from the federal government. On April 27, 1953, Republican president Dwight Eisenhower issued Executive Order 10450, which made homosexuality grounds for dismissal from the federal government. In addition, the federal government encouraged local police departments to increase persecution and arrests of gay Americans and to share their arrest records. The reasoning for the purge was multifaceted: some politicians argued that gay people were moral deviants who were at increased risk of blackmail; others, including Senator Joseph McCarthy, a Republican from Wisconsin who emerged as the most powerful and unscrupulous of America's anticommunist politicians during this period, argued that gay people were of fragile mind and thus particularly susceptible to communism. In all, more gay men and lesbians were purged from the federal government than suspected communists, according to historian David Johnson, author of *The Lavender Scare*. It wasn't until 1995 that the federal government officially stopped using sexual orientation as grounds to deny employment; by then, more than 10,000 gay men and women had been driven from their jobs.

Gay and lesbian activism picked up during the 1960s, as did the number of organizations and publications, reflecting the era's culture of protest and demands for equality. While the 1950s were dominated by the postwar Red Scare and the Lavender Scare, the 1960s were a time when many groups, inspired by the Black civil rights movement, began to use street activism to achieve their goals. Local groups started to form larger coalitions, including the East Coast Homophile Organizations (ECHO) in 1963 and the North American Conference of Homophile Organizations (NACHO, pronounced Nay-Ko) in 1966. NACHO sponsored protests in cities around the country and created a national legal fund to challenge antigay policies. Its most influential work would come from its national conference in 1968.

In 1964, a handful of homophile activists staged the first public protest on behalf of gay people, in front of the Whitehall Induction Center in New York City in opposition to the military's exclusion of homosexuals. Multiple small protests were held in various cities in 1965, including one in front of the United Nations in April 1965 protesting discrimination, one in front of the White House in May 1965 by ECHO, one in July 1965 in front of the Pentagon to protest discrimination in the military, one in August 1965 in front of the State Department, and another one in front of the White House in October 1965, again by ECHO and this time including 35 picketers (an increase from the 10 participants recorded for the May demonstration).

On April 26, 1966, four members of the Mattachine Society—John Timmons, Dick Leitsch, Craig Rodwell and Randy Wicker—staged a "sip-in" at Julius', a bar in the West Village of New York City. Modeled after the sit-ins of the Black civil rights movement at segregated lunch counters, the sip-in was conducted to protest the common refusal by bars at the time to serve gay people. This policy was based on city regulations against serving people who were disorderly because at the time, being gay was by definition seen as disorderly. The protestors had invited the media and media coverage led the New York Commission on Human Rights to declare refusal to serve a homosexual as unlawful discrimination.

Less than three months later, on July 18, a group of radical young queers calling themselves Vanguard picketed outside of Compton's Cafeteria in San Francisco. At the time, Compton's was a well-known hangout for transgender women and drag queens located in the Tenderloin district, the city's gay neighborhood. San Francisco police officers, however, often arrested Compton's Cafeteria patrons for violating the city's anti-cross-dressing ordinance or for sex work. The demonstrations continued into August at which time one of the protesting women fought back against police seeking to arrest her. Her defiance, which took the form of throwing a steaming cup of coffee in a police officer's face, sparked a riot. The event is the first known instance of collective resistance to police harassment by the LGBTQ community.

Modeling of the gay rights movement after the Black civil rights movement is also evident in decisions made at the 1968 annual NACHO conference. Participants at that meeting adopted a slogan proposed by
Mattachine Society activist Frank Kameny, "Gay is Good," modeled after
the contemporary "Black is Beautiful" slogan of the Black Power movement. Also at that meeting, NACHO members adopted a five-point
Homosexual Bill of Rights:

1. Private consensual sex between persons over the age of consent shall
   not be an offense.
2. Solicitation for any sexual acts shall not be an offense except upon the
   filing of a complaint by the aggrieved party, not a police officer or agent.
3. A person's sexual orientation or practice shall not be a factor in
   the granting or renewing of federal security clearances or visas, or in the
   granting of citizenship.
4. Service in and discharge from the Armed Forces and eligibility for vet-
   eran's benefits shall be without reference to homosexuality.
5. A person's sexual orientation or practice shall not affect his eligibility
   for employment with federal, state, or local governments, or private
   employers.

All of this activism led to the event popularly remembered as the first of its
kind: the Stonewall Riots. The Stonewall Inn was a popular gay bar in
Greenwich Village that allowed dancing and welcomed drag queens and
homeless youths. As with all gay bars at the time, it was also frequently
raided by New York City police, with adverse consequences for the personal lives and livelihoods of those detained and named in the newspaper.
During one such raid, however, in the early hours of June 28, 1969, patrons
and neighborhood residents began throwing objects at police. The event
escalated into three nights of riots and five days of protests. Shortly after
the Stonewall Uprising, members of the Mattachine Society split off to
form the Gay Liberation Front, a radical group that launched public demonstrations, protests, and confrontations with political officials.
  On June 28, 1970, New York City community members marched
through local streets in commemoration of the one-year anniversary of the
Stonewall Riots. Named the Christopher Street Liberation Day, the march
is now considered the country's first gay pride parade. The event started
small, with just a few hundred people gathered outside of the Stonewall
Inn, but by the time the group arrived in Central Park, 50 blocks to the
north, the crowd numbered in the thousands, shouting "Say it loud, gay is
proud." Gay Liberation Front founder Michael Brown told the *New York
Times*: "We have to come out into the open and stop being ashamed, or

else people will go on treating us as freaks. This march is an affirmation and declaration of our new pride" (quoted in Fosburgh 1970).

FURTHER READING

Broverman, Neal. 2018. "Don't Let History Forget about Compton's Cafeteria Riot." *The Advocate*, August 2. https://www.advocate.com /transgender/2018/8/02/dont-let-history-forget-about-comptons-cafeteria-riot

Farber, Jim. 2016. "Before the Stonewall Uprising, There Was the 'Sip-In.'" *New York Times*, April 20. https://www.nytimes.com/2016/04/21 /nyregion/before-the-stonewall-riots-there-was-the-sip-in.html

Fitzsimons, Tim. 2018. "LGBTQ History Month: The Road to America's First Gay Pride March." NBCNews.com, October 5. https://www .nbcnews.com/feature/nbc-out/lgbtq-history-month-road-america-s-first -gay-pride-march-n917096

Fosburgh, Lacey. 1970. "Thousands of Homosexuals Hold a Protest Rally in Central Park," *New York Times*, June 29. https://www.nytimes.com /1970/06/29/archives/thousands-of-homosexuals-hold-a-protest-rally-in -central-park.html

Johnson, David K. 2006. *The Lavender Scare: The Cold War Persecution of Gays and Lesbians in the Federal Government.* Chicago, IL: University of Chicago Press.

Making History: Kansas City and the Rise of Gay Rights. 2017. UMKC.edu, October 3. https://info.umkc.edu/makinghistory/

Pasulka, Nicole. 2015. "Ladies in the Streets: Before Stonewall, Transgender Uprising Changed Lives." *National Public Radio*, May 5. https://www .npr.org/sections/codeswitch/2015/05/05/404459634/ladies-in-the-streets -before-stonewall-transgender-uprising-changed-lives

Smith, Raymond A., and Donald P. Haider-Markel. 2002. *Gay and Lesbian Americans and Political Participation: A Reference Handbook.* Santa Barbara, CA: ABC-CLIO.

Q9: IS IT TRUE THAT SOME VOCAL OPPONENTS OF LGBTQ RIGHTS ARE CLOSETED GAY PEOPLE?

Answer: Many psychologists and other scholars believe that in some cases, loud expressions of homophobia stem from people denying their own sexual identity, oftentimes to maintain consistency with long-held anti-LGBTQ values or religious beliefs within the culture and/or community in which they live and work. However, many opponents of LGBTQ rights

and equality do so on the basis of genuinely held beliefs that nonheterosexual desires are immoral.

The Facts: One thing is clear: not every person who opposes the rights
of the LGBTQ community secretly harbors same-sex attraction. However,
psychologists have determined that in some cases, those who are vehe-
mently opposed to LGBTQ rights may be suppressing and lashing out
against their own feelings of same-sex attraction or gender identity.

Psychologists have theorized that if an individual who does not support
LGBTQ rights finds themselves feeling same-sex attraction—even if they
do not act on those feelings or identify as a member of the LGBTQ
community—they may become more vocal or strident in their anti-
LGBTQ rhetoric and behavior to feel better about themselves and distance
themselves from those feelings. Similar responses may occur among individuals who do not feel comfortable with the idea of gender as fluid or
nonbinary but find themselves questioning their own gender identity as
assigned at birth.

Research finds that individuals whose sexual identity is at odds with
their implicit sexual attraction—in other words, people who identify as
heterosexual and yet have some degree of same-sex attraction—are much
more frequently raised by parents perceived to be controlling, less accepting, and more prejudiced against homosexuals. Intolerant behavior of
those closest to us (parents, church community, peers, partners) often has
the most profound impact.

A few scales have been developed by psychiatrists and researchers to
measure internalized homophobia. For example, Michael Ross and Simon
Rosser's "Four Dimensions" (1996) measures four key areas of a person's
LGBTQ identity: (1) public identification as being gay; (2) their perception
of stigma associated with being gay; (3) degree of social comfort with other
gay people; and (4) beliefs regarding the religious or moral acceptability of
homosexuality.

Psychologist Netta Weinstein and her colleagues made headlines in
2012 for their paper in the *Journal of Personality and Social Psychology*. In a
New York Times opinion piece that same year titled "Homophobic? Maybe
You're Gay," coauthors Richard M. Ryan and William S. Ryan summarized
the results of six studies the group conducted in the United States and
Germany. They found that some self-identified straight people who har-
bored same-sex desire were more likely to hold discriminatory attitudes.
They pointed to one of their studies that included 784 college students.
Researchers first asked the students to characterize their sexual orientation
on a 10-point scale before asking them to sort words and images that are

"indicative of hetero- and homosexuality." During this sorting, the computer flashed subliminal words of "me" or "other" before each image, designed to reveal implicit bias based on how long it took students to sort the images that did not match their self-avowed sexual identity.

What they found was around 20 percent of self-described "highly straight individuals" subconsciously indicated some degree of same-sex attraction. This subset was "significantly more likely than other participants to favor anti-gay policies; to be willing to assign significantly harsher punishments to perpetrators of petty crimes if they were presumed to be homosexual; and to express greater implicit hostility toward gay subjects."

Netta Weinstein, one of the study's lead authors, wrote that this subset "may be threatened by gays and lesbians because homosexuals remind them of similar tendencies within themselves." In other words, the psychological mechanism behind this subgroup's anti-LGBTQ views is pretty simple: they are taking out their own issues with sexual identity on other people.

An important caveat: obviously not all people who campaign against LGBTQ rights secretly have same-sex attraction. Some are opposed to LGBTQ rights due to their moral values or religious beliefs and most are not transgender and have straight (heterosexual) sexual orientations.

At least some who oppose these rights, however, are people struggling against part of themselves, partly due to the lack of acceptance and homophobic and transphobic views that surround them. This interpretation is evidenced by news reports of anti-LGBTQ elites engaging in same-sex intimacy. For example, Ted Haggard, an evangelical leader who preached that homosexuality was a sin, resigned after a scandal involving a former male prostitute; Larry Craig, a conservative Republican U.S. senator from Idaho who opposed including sexual orientation in hate-crime legislation, was arrested on suspicion of lewd conduct in a men's bathroom; and Glenn Murphy Jr., a leader of the Young Republican National Convention and an opponent of same-sex marriage, pleaded guilty to a lesser charge after being accused of sexually assaulting another man.

There are other instances of conservative lawmakers and religious leaders with long track records of anti-LGBTQ votes and statements secretly engaging in same-sex sexual relations (Avery 2016; Murphy 2017). In the 1990s, in fact, a handful of LGBTQ activists and journalists began to deliberately out "closeted" public officials who were anti-LGBTQ rights (Nichols 2018). In 2004, gay rights activist Mike Rogers founded a blog aimed at outing elected officials and staffers. His first targets included House member Edward L. Schrock (R-Virginia) in 2004, Mark Foley (R-Florida) in 2005, and Senator Craig in 2006. In late 2007, he had

33 names on his blog, all opponents of gay rights. Rogers told the *Washington Post*'s Vargas (2007): "I write about closeted people whose records are anti-gay. If you're a closeted Democrat or Republican and you don't bash gays or vote against gay rights to gain political points, I won't out you." The blog was active until 2011 (Rogers 2014).

FURTHER READING

Avery, Dan. 2016. "20 Republican Politicians Brought Down by Big Gay Sex Scandals." NewNowNext.com, December 30. http://www.newnownext.com/19-republican-politicians-gay-sex/12/2016/

Murphy, Sean. 2017. "Oklahoma GOP Senator's Fall from Power Is Stunningly Fast." Associated Press, March 16. https://apnews.com/63166 633505e4f3c982beded52ec3cc1/oklahoma-gop-senators-fall-power-stunningly-fast

Nichols, James Michael. 2018. "An American Outing: Two Men Who Changed the Face of Our Culture." NewNowNext.com, October 29. http://www.newnownext.com/an-american-outing-two-men-who-changed-the-face-of-our-culture/10/2018/

Rogers, Michael. 2014. "Why I Outed Gay Republicans." *Politico*, June 26. https://www.politico.com/magazine/story/2014/06/mike-rogers-outed-gay-republicans-108368

Ross, Michael W., and B. R. Simon Rosser. 1996. "Measurement and Correlates of Internalized Homophobia: A Factor Analytic Study." *Journal of Clinical Psychology* 52, 1: 15–21.

Ryan, Richard M., and William S. Ryan. 2012. "Homophobic? Maybe You're Gay." *New York Times*, April 29. https://www.nytimes.com/2012/04/29/opinion/sunday/homophobic-maybe-youre-gay.html?auth=login-email

Siegel, Jim. 2017. "'Inappropriate Behavior' with Man in His Office Led to Ohio Lawmaker's Ouster." *Columbus Dispatch*, November 15. https://www.dispatch.com/news/20171115/inappropriate-behavior-with-man-in-his-office-led-to-ohio-lawmakers-ouster

Vargas, Jose Antonio. 2007. "The Most Feared Man on the Hill?" *Washington Post*, September 4. https://www.washingtonpost.com/wp-dyn/content/article/2007/09/03/AR2007090301396.html

Weinstein, Netta, et al. 2012. "Parental Autonomy Support and Discrepancies between Implicit and Explicit Sexual Identities: Dynamics of Self-Acceptance and Defense." *Journal of Personality and Social Psychology* 102, 4: 815–832.

Q10: DO LAWS PROTECTING LGBTQ PEOPLE AFFECT THE FREEDOM OF RELIGIOUS AMERICANS WHO OPPOSE LGBTQ PEOPLE ON RELIGIOUS GROUNDS?

Answer: Yes, but individual rights to religious freedom must be balanced against the rights of LGBTQ people. The idea of "religious freedom" in the United States has become particularly contentious in recent years at it relates to marriage equality, sexuality, and gender identity. One side sees religious freedom as a protection against being forced to do or to accommodate things they do not personally support (e.g., same-sex marriage) because of their moral or religious beliefs. The other side views that argument as discriminatory and a violation of individual civil rights. The complex set of issues is still being considered and decided by executive, legislative, and judicial actors on local, state, and federal levels.

The Facts: Religious freedom is one of the most fundamental rights in the U.S. Constitution and is viewed by many as central to our national identity. It is, after all, in the very first phrase of the First Amendment: "Congress shall make no law respecting an establishment of religion, or prohibiting the free exercise thereof." The Courts have since clarified that laws can regulate action but not belief and that religious practices can be restricted when they might conflict with another legitimate public interest such as promoting order and stability or protecting members of vulnerable populations such as children.

The primacy of religious freedom as a basic civil right is grounded in the nation's founding, which developed in part because individuals facing religious persecution in Europe came to the New World to seek free expression of their beliefs. The United States has traditionally been one of the most religious countries around the world but also one with a strong tradition of allowing for variation in beliefs and practices. Sometimes laws prohibit practices by members of certain religious traditions (such as laws forbidding polygamy) but usually the religious beliefs of members of different groups do not come into direct conflict. This is not the case, however, for a small handful of issues, including whether individuals who believe homosexuality or transgender identity to be a violation of their religious beliefs must be forced to treat LGBTQ people equally. The most common examples of this conflict have tended to concern openly LGBTQ individuals seeking to buy goods or services (flowers, cakes, photography services, etc.) from businesses or individuals who regard such transactions as immoral because homosexuality violates their religious beliefs. Other notable legal battles have centered on whether individual religious beliefs grant people the right to fire or to refuse to hire transgender people.

Attitudes toward the role of religion in civil American life are at the center of the debates about treatment of LGBTQ people and the rights of both gay and straight Americans. One 2019 survey conducted by Pew Research found that 55 percent of respondents felt churches and religious organizations do more good than harm in American society. However, 20 percent felt that religion in public life causes more harm than good while another 24 percent felt that religion does not make much difference either way (Pew Research Center 2019). The same survey also found that many people feel religion is in decline: 74 percent of Democrats and 83 percent of Republicans agreed with the statement that religion is losing influence in American life. Perhaps unsurprisingly, there are stark partisan differences in how Americans responded to a follow-up question about whether this declining influence of religion was "a good thing" or "a bad thing." By a wide margin, Republicans think the loss of religion in American life is a "bad thing" (63 percent) with only 7 percent saying it is a "good thing"; on the other hand, Democrats were more split, with 27 percent reporting the decline was a bad thing and 25 percent saying it was a good thing (Pew Research Center 2019).

It wasn't until 2020 that federal law offered protection from employment discrimination based on sexual orientation or gender identity. In the Supreme Court case *Bostock v. Clayton County* (GA), the Supreme Court decided that Title VII of the Civil Rights Act, which bars discrimination based on sex, applied to gay and transgender people. In his opinion for the majority, Justice Neil Gorsuch wrote, "An employer who fires an individual for being homosexual or transgender fires that person for traits or actions it would not have questioned in members of a different sex. Sex plays a necessary and undisguisable role in the decision, exactly what Title VII forbids" (Supreme Court 2020).

Prior to that 2020 decision, most LGBTQ people did not have protection from employment discrimination because fewer than half of states offer explicit protections for LGBTQ people at the state level. While *Bostock* may eventually extend to other areas of life such as discrimination by private businesses and individuals, there are many examples of instances where LGBTQ people have been evicted from their homes or refused service for no reason other than their sexual orientation and/or gender identity and expression.

For example, in 2012, a gay couple went into Masterpiece Cakeshop in Lakewood, Colorado and requested a cake for their upcoming wedding.

Jack Phillips, the shop owner, declined their order, citing his religious beliefs against same-sex marriage. The couple filed charges of discrimination under the Colorado Anti-Discrimination Act which prohibits discrimination based on sexual orientation. The couple won at the state level but lost on appeal in December 2018 when the United States Supreme Court ruled in *Masterpiece Cakeshop v. Colorado Civil Rights Commission* that the Colorado law violated the baker's religious freedom. The Court noted that the right of the gay couple to not be discriminated against had to be balanced against the cake shop owner's right to freedom of religious expression.

The baker was not the only individual with religious objections to LGBTQ rights to seek to deny service to LGBTQ people. For example, in 2015, a Tennessee hardware store owner posted a "No Gays Allowed" sign in his shop's front window, claiming that his policy was consistent with his Christian beliefs (Robinson 2018). No legal action was taken because unlike Colorado, Tennessee does not have an antidiscrimination law in place to protect LGBTQ people.

On May 4, 2017, President Trump signed an executive order called "Promoting Free Speech and Religious Liberty," directing the IRS to use "maximum enforcement discretion" over the Johnson Amendment, named for its author, then-Senator Lyndon B. Johnson of Texas. This law was passed by Congress in 1954 to prohibit churches, charities, and other nonprofit organizations from engaging in any political activity. Trump's intent was to allow religious organizations to become more involved in U.S. politics. His order also gave regulatory relief to companies objecting to the requirement that they provide contraception coverage in their health-care plans as mandated by the 2010 Affordable Care Act, also known as Obamacare (Vitali 2017).

In 2019, the Trump Department of Justice filed legal briefs claiming that discrimination against LGBTQ people was not a violation of the Civil Rights Act of 1964 as was being argued in the joint cases *Bostock v. Clayton County, GA* and *Altitude Express v. Zarda*. In these cases, gay and transgender individuals claimed that employment discrimination based on their sexual orientation or gender identity was a violation of their civil rights; the Trump Administration argued that it was not. As noted above, on June 15, 2020, the Supreme Court ruled in favor of the plaintiffs in a consolidated decision, finding that the Civil Rights Act of 1964 does extend protections to LGBTQ people (Schmidt 2020).

During the Trump administration, however, new rules at the federal level were put into place that explicitly encouraged religious beliefs to take precedence over concerns about anti-LGBTQ discrimination. For example, on May 24, 2019, the Health and Human Services Office for Civil Rights introduced a new rule that allowed health-care providers to refuse services that conflict with their religious beliefs, including caring for transgender patients (Sanger-Katz 2019). The rule was blocked by a federal judge in August 2020, citing the Supreme Court ruling in *Bostock*, and then reversed by President Joe Biden in April 2021 (Luthi 2020; Goldstein 2021).

The *Bostock* ruling was seen as a loss by religious conservatives who thought the decision would erode their religious freedoms and force Christian organizations to hire LGBTQ people in violation of their religious beliefs. Observers noted that the majority opinion in the case, however, left a window open for religious exemptions because it wrote that protections under the Civil Rights Act could be superseded by religious claims under the free exercise clause of the Constitution (Hollis-Brusky 2020).

The degree to which that is true remains to be seen. The issue of how to balance religious rights against LGBTQ rights again made legal headlines in November 2020, when the Supreme Court heard arguments about a law in Philadelphia, Pennsylvania, that forbids discrimination on the basis of sexual orientation in a case known as *Fulton v. City of Philadelphia*. Catholic Social Services, an organization that had contracted with the city to identify potential foster parents, refused to consider certifying same-sex couples, citing religious objections. The city did not renew its foster placement contract with the group and the conflict over that decision made its way through the courts. The case differs from the Masterpiece Cakeshop case because it involves the government rather than a private business. On June 17, 2021, the Supreme Court unanimously sided with Catholic Social Services, declaring that the private Catholic agency was entitled to renew its contract with the city, even though it violated city law by refusing to consider married LGBTQ couples. However, the victory was a narrow one; the decision left intact a 1990 precedent that held that the free exercise of religion can be restricted by neutral government laws that apply to everyone (Howe 2021; Totenberg 2021).

The Trump administration's policy changes were widely interpreted by both supporters and opponents as encouraging and endorsing discrimination against LGBTQ people. Critics of these laws and policies assert that they threaten the basic dignity and undercut the civil rights of LGBTQ people because they signal that LGBTQ rights and well-being are not valued and are contingent on the goodwill of others. They assert that carving out religious exemptions to stop the advancement of LGBTQ equality sends a powerful signal that members of the community are unequal or undervalued.

Against this backdrop of legal vulnerability, lawmakers who oppose marriage for same-sex couples and recent moves to advance transgender equality have led an anti-LGBTQ charge, pushing for and often succeeding in getting new laws that create religious exemptions for individuals who claim that compliance with particular laws interferes with their religious or moral beliefs. While LGBTQ equality is not the only area where exemptions have been debated—particularly as lawmakers have sought to substantially broaden exemptions related to sexual and reproductive health care—advocates for gay rights contend that these changes constitute a worrying wave of exemptions being introduced to blunt the recognition of LGBTQ rights across the United States.

Detractors of religious exemption laws claim that they send a signal that the state governments enacting them accept and even embrace the dangerous and harmful notion that discrimination against LGBTQ people is a legitimate demand of both conscience and religion. Particularly in states that have no underlying laws prohibiting discrimination against LGBTQ people, critics state that these laws are not "exemptions" as much as they are a license to discriminate—and to deny the civil rights of LGBTQ Americans to equal treatment.

The degree to which protections for LGBTQ people conflict with religious freedom continues to be debated in the courts. In 2013, bakers Melissa and Aaron Klein refused to make a cake for a same-sex marriage of two women, claiming that doing so would violate their religious beliefs. The bakers were fined $135,000 for violating Oregon's antidiscrimination law. The case, *Klein v. Oregon*, was appealed all the way to the U.S. Supreme Court, which ruled in June 2019 that the case should go back to the Oregon court in light of the *Masterpiece Cakeshop* decision it had handed down in 2018. "In doing so, the court kept alive the couple's appeal and left open the question of whether businesses can discriminate against gays and lesbians based on their religious beliefs" (Savage 2019).

FURTHER READING

Bostock v. Clayton County. 2020. Oyez.com, https://www.oyez.org/cases /2019/17-1618

Epps, Garrett. 2018. "Justice Kennedy's *Masterpiece* Ruling." *The Atlantic,* June 4. https://www.theatlantic.com/ideas/archive/2018/06/the-court -slices-a-narrow-ruling-out-of-masterpiece-cakeshop/561986/

Goldstein, Amy. 2021. "Biden Administration Revives Anti-Bias Protections in Health Care for Transgender People." *Washington Post,* May 10.

https://www.washingtonpost.com/health/transgender-protection-hhs
/2021/05/10/0852ce88-b17d-11eb-a980-a60af976ed44_story.html

Hollis-Brusky, Amanda. 2020. "The Supreme Court Closed the Door on
LGBTQ Employment Discrimination. But It Opened a Window."
Washington Post, June 16. https://www.washingtonpost.com/politics
/2020/06/16/supreme-court-closed-door-lgbtq-employment-discrimination
-it-opened-window/

Howe, Amy. 2021. "Court Holds That City's Refusal to Make Referrals
to Faith-Based Agency Violates Constitution." *SCOTUSblog*, June 17.
https://www.scotusblog.com/2021/06/court-holds-that-citys-refusal-to
-make-referrals-to-faith-based-agency-violates-constitution/

Luthi, Susannah. 2020. "Judge Halts Trump's Rollback of Transgender
Health Protections." *Politico*, August 17. https://www.politico.com
/news/2020/08/17/judge-trump-rollback-transgender-health-397332

Masterpiece Cakeshop, Ltd. v. Colorado Civil Rights Commission. 2018. Oyez.
com, https://www.oyez.org/cases/2017/16-111

Pew Research Center. 2012. "Rising Tide of Restrictions on Religion." Pew
Research Center, Religion and Public Life. September 20. https://www
.pewforum.org/2012/09/20/rising-tide-of-restrictions-on-religion-findings
/#america

Pew Research Center. 2019. "Americans Have Positive Views about
Religion's Role in Society, but Want It Out of Politics." Pew Research
Center, Religion and Public Life, November 15. https://www.pewforum
.org/2019/11/15/americans-have-positive-views-about-religions-role
-in-society-but-want-it-out-of-politics/

Robinson, Grant. 2018. "Grainger Co. Shop Owner That Made Headlines
for 'No Gays Allowed' Sign Calls SCOTUS Ruling a Win." *WBIR*, June 4.
https://www.wbir.com/article/news/local/grainger-co-shop-owner-that
-made-headlines-for-no-gays-allowed-sign-calls-scotus-ruling-a-win
/51-561483750

Sanger-Katz, Margot. 2019. "Trump Administration Strengthens 'Conscience Rule' for Health Care Workers." *New York Times*, May 2. https://
www.nytimes.com/2019/05/02/upshot/conscience-rule-trump-religious
-exemption-health-care.html

Savage, David G. 2019. "Supreme Court Passes, for Now, on a New Wedding Cake Dispute." *Los Angeles Times*, June 17. https://www.latimes
.com/politics/la-na-pol-supreme-court-gay-weddings-religion-20190617
-story.html

Schmidt, Samantha. 2020. "Fired After Joining a Gay Softball League,
Gerald Bostock Wins Landmark Supreme Court Case." *Washington
Post*, June 15. https://www.washingtonpost.com/dc-md-va/2020/06/15

/fired-after-joining-gay-softball-league-gerald-bostock-wins-landmark
-supreme-court-case/
Supreme Court. 2020. "Bostock v. Clayton County, Georgia." June 15.
https://www.supremecourt.gov/opinions/19pdf/17-1618_hfci.pdf
Totenberg, Nina. 2021. "Supreme Court Rules for a Catholic Group in a
Case Involving Gay Rights, Foster Care." *National Public Radio*, June 17.
https://www.npr.org/2021/06/17/996670391/supreme-court-rules-for-a
-catholic-group-in-a-case-involving-gay-rights-foster-c
Vitali, Ali. 2017. "Trump Signs 'Religious Liberty' Executive Order Allowing for Broad Exemptions." NBCNews.com, May 4. https://www.nbcnews
.com/news/us-news/trump-signs-religious-liberty-executive-order-allowing
-broad-exemptions-n754786

Q11: DOES GIVING RIGHTS TO LGBTQ PEOPLE LEAD TO THE LEGALIZATION OF PRACTICES LIKE PEDOPHILIA, BESTIALITY, AND NECROPHILIA?

Answer: No. Recognizing the equal rights of LGBTQ people has never resulted in the legalization of practices that are widely considered abnormal variants of human sexuality.

The Facts: Opponents of LGBTQ rights have sometimes made the claim that legal protections for the LGBTQ community will lead to the legalization of other, widely condemned sexual practices, including pedophilia, bestiality, and necrophilia. According to the Southern Poverty Law Center, a nonprofit legal advocacy group focused on civil rights and hate groups, "these fairy tales are important to the anti-gay right because they form the basis of its claim that homosexuality is a social evil that must be suppressed— an opinion rejected by virtually all relevant medical and scientific authorities" (Schlatter and Steinback 2011). In short, there is no truth to these claims; they are not in any way based in reality. Instead, they are meant to diminish the legitimacy of LGBTQ people and their legal rights.

Medical experts, including the American Psychiatric Association, define homosexuality and bisexuality as normal variants of human sexuality. Pedophilia, bestiality, and necrophilia, in contrast, are considered mental disorders, perversions, and paraphilias (Pierce 2015; McDonald 2019). Paraphilia means "love of the unusual" and includes "sexual behaviors that differ from the society's norms" and that have replaced "direct sexual contact with a consenting adult partner" (McDonald 2019).

Pedophilia refers to sexual interest in prepubescent children (age 13 or younger). Bestiality (or zoophilia, the term used in psychiatry) "involves sexual contact between humans and animals as the repeatedly preferred method of achieving sexual excitement. In this disorder, the animal is preferred despite other available sexual outlets. Necrophilia is a rare dysfunction in which a person obtains sexual gratification by looking at or having intercourse with a corpse" (McDonald 2019).

Claims that protecting the rights of LGBTQ people will lead to legalization of paraphilias like pedophilia, bestiality, and necrophilia stem from past classifications of homosexuality and bisexuality as mental disorders. The first issue of the American Psychiatric Association (APA)'s *Diagnostic and Statistical Manual (DSM)*, published in 1952, listed homosexuality as a mental disorder and specifically as a "sociopathic personality disturbance." *DSM-II*, published in 1968, reclassified homosexuality as a "sexual deviation" (Drescher 2015, 568).

In 1973, the APA's Board of Trustees voted to remove homosexuality from the *DSM*, a vote later upheld by a vote of APA members. Instead, the next version of the manual included a new diagnosis, Sexual Orientation Disturbance (SOD), which "regarded homosexuality as an illness if an individual with same-sex attractions found them distressing and wanted to change" (Drescher 2015, 569). In the third edition of the manual in 1980, SOD was replaced by a new category called Ego Dystonic Homosexuality (EDH). EDH was removed by the next revision in 1987; in this edition of the *DSM*, psychologists finally accepted homosexuality as a normal variant of human sexuality (Drescher 2015). These changes in medical understanding of homosexuality, wrote one scholar, were in many ways responses to larger changes taking place in American culture: "The evolution of the status of homosexuality in the classifications of mental disorders highlights that concepts of mental disorder can be rapidly evolving social constructs that change as society changes" (Burton 2015).

In other words, society's perception of homosexuality changed over time, from being a diagnosable mental disorder to being accepted as a normal form of variation in human sexuality. That change signals to some that by this same logic, other variations still considered to be perversions may at some point in the future also become considered appropriate. Claims that protections of gay rights will naturally lead to protections for other, more taboo sexual behaviors also stem from a myth popularized by the antigay American Family Association that the APA recognizes 30 different sexual orientations, including bestiality and necrophilia, as well as other, less known paraphilias.

Similar false claims have been made by other opponents of LGBTQ rights. Following the 2013 Supreme Court decision supporting same-sex marriage, conservative columnist Les Kinsolving declared that the big winners from the ruling weren't just LGBTQ Americans, "but also those who practice pedophilia, incest, polygamy, necrophilia, and bestiality" (Brinker 2013, citing Kinsolving 2013). Similarly, Fox News political analyst Bethany Blankley warned that

> By destroying the institution of marriage, the "gay rights" LBGQTI movement made possible the extension of similar "legal rights" for other "lifestyle choices," including zoophilia, consanguinamorous relationships, necrophilia, pedophilia, polygamy, and every other "fluid" sexual preference or identification—including sologamy and trans-polyamorous relationships. (Blankley 2016)

These and other warnings about how protections of the rights of LGBTQ people will possibly lead to legalization of paraphilias are not solely the province of conservative pundits and religious activists. In a 2003 *amicus* brief filed on behalf of the states of Alabama, South Carolina, and Utah in the Supreme Court's *Lawrence v. Texas* case (on whether homosexual sodomy could constitutionally be legally prohibited), the attorneys general of those states noted:

> Petitioners' protestations to the contrary notwithstanding, a constitutional right that protects "the choice of one's partner" and "whether and how to connect sexually" must logically extend to activities like prostitution, adultery, necrophilia, bestiality, possession of child pornography, and even incest and pedophilia. (Goldberg 2003)

This myth, though, is not true. Normal variations in sexual orientation differ from paraphilias in that they involve consenting adults and the APA recognizes homosexuality as a normal variation in human sexuality. Pedophilia, by definition, does not involve consenting adults and is considered both a mental disorder and a criminal act. Zoophilia and necrophilia are also not considered part of normal variation in human sexuality; they are included among other Paraphilia Not Otherwise Specified (NOS). Paraphilia NOS are defined as "recurrent, intense sexually arousing fantasies, sexual urges or behaviors generally involving nonhuman objects, the suffering or humiliation of oneself or one's partner, or children or other nonconsenting persons that occur over a period of at least 6 months" (Kafka 2010).

Legal distinctions further support psychiatric distinctions between normal variations in human sexuality and paraphilias. "With the exception of prostitution, all sex crimes are based on the twin criteria of lack of consent and harm to the victim" (Ranger and Federoff 2014). In fact, the current (*DSM-5*) version of the APA diagnostic manual does not provide a list of what is or is not considered a paraphilic disorder. The last APA diagnostic manual to provide a paraphilia "list" was *DSM-II*:

> DSM-III defined paraphilia's rather vaguely as "unusual or bizarre imagery or acts necessary for sexual excitement. . . . DSM-III-R and DSM-IV offered no definition whatsoever. . . . In contrast, DSM-5 defines a paraphilia by exclusion by first defining normal foci of sexual arousal . . . and then defining a paraphilia as being intense and persistent sexual interest in anything else.

Hundreds of forms of paraphilia have been described over time but most are clearly distinct from what is considered normal or socially acceptable: sexual preferences focused on nonhuman objects (e.g., zoophilia) and on children (e.g., pedophilia) or other nonconsenting persons (e.g., necrophilia). While the definition of paraphilia remains problematic, it can be described in ways that distinguish it from acceptable sexual behavior (Balon 2016).

In sum, while it is true that societal norms have shifted over time, the extension of legal protections of the equal rights of LGBTQ people does not create a *slippery slope* of extending similar rights to individuals whose sexual behavior causes harm to themselves or others. Arguments about how extending rights that protect LGBTQ people will somehow open the door to forms of sexual attraction and behavior that are considered mental illnesses do not, as stated above, have any factual basis. Instead, societal norms and laws are evolving to recognize the difference between normal variations in sexuality that include consenting adults and those that are diagnosed and criminalized to prevent harm.

FURTHER READING

Balon, Richard. 2016. "Introduction to the Realm of Paraphilias." In Richard Balon, ed., *Practical Guide to Paraphilia and Paraphilic Disorders.* Cham, Switzerland: Springer International Publishing, pp. 1–14.

Blankley, Bethany. 2016. "Next Up: Legalization of Incest, Necrophilia, Pedophilia, Zoophilia and More." *Charisma News*, September 12. https://www.charismanews.com/opinion/59816-next-up-legalization-of-incest-necrophilia-pedophilia-zoophilia-and-more

Brinker, Luke. 2013. "WND Columnist: Marriage Equality Rulings Will Lead to Pedophilia, Bestiality, Necrophilia." *Media Matters*, July 2.

https://www.mediamatters.org/worldnetdaily/wnd-columnist-marriage
-equality-rulings-will-lead-pedophilia-bestiality-necrophilia

Burton, Neel. 2015. "When Homosexuality Stopped Being a Mental Disorder." *Psychology Today*, September 18. https://www.psychologytoday
.com/us/blog/hide-and-seek/201509/when-homosexuality-stopped
-being-mental-disorder

Drescher, Jack. 2015. "Out of DSM: Depathologizing Homosexuality." *Behavioral Sciences* 5, 4: 565–575.

First, Michael B. 2014. "DSM-5 and Paraphilic Disorders." *Journal of the American Academy of Psychiatry and the Law Online* 42, 2: 191–201.

Goldberg, Michelle. 2003. "Defining Judicial Deviancy Down." *Salon*, June 13. https://www.salon.com/2003/06/13/pryor_2/

Kafka, Martin P. 2010. "The DSM Diagnostic Criteria for Paraphilia Not Otherwise Specified." *Archives of Sexual Behavior* 39, 2: 373–376.

Kinsolving, Les. 2013. "I'm with Scalia, Not the Zoophiliacs." *WND*, July 1. https://www.wnd.com/2013/07/im-with-scalia-not-the-zoophiliacs/

McDonald, Deborah R. 2019. "Sexual Variants and Paraphilias." *Salem Press Encyclopedia of Health*. Pasadena, CA: Salem Press.

Pierce, Jessica. 2015. "Sex with Animals: Is It Wrong?" *Psychology Today*, April 24. https://www.psychologytoday.com/us/blog/all-dogs-go-heaven
/201504/sex-animals

Ranger, Rebekah, and Paul Fedoroff. 2014. "Commentary: Zoophilia and the Law." *Journal of the American Academy of Psychiatry and the Law* 42, 4: 421–426.

Ring, Trudy. 2018. "Right-Wing Pundit Says 'B' in 'LGBTQ' Stands for 'Bestiality.'" *Advocate*, July 18, 2018. https://www.advocate.com/media
/2018/7/18/right-wing-pundit-says-b-lgbtq-stands-bestiality

Schlatter, Evelyn, and Robert Steinback. 2011. "10 Anti-Gay Myths Debunked." *Southern Poverty Law Center*, February 27. https://www
.splcenter.org/fighting-hate/intelligence-report/2011/10-anti-gay-myths
-debunked

Q12: HAVE HATE CRIMES AGAINST LGBTQ PEOPLE IN THE UNITED STATES INCREASED OVER TIME?

Answer: Reported hate crimes against LGBTQ people have been increasing in recent years but it is unclear whether this change is because there are more crimes being committed or if it reflects an increase in the reporting of hate crimes to and by law enforcement.

The Facts: According to bias crime data reported by the FBI for 2019, over 19 percent stemmed from anti-LGBTQ bias. The total number of reported incidents increased from 1,217 (in 2017) to 1,347 (2018) to 1,393 (2019). In terms of percentage of total crime, hate crimes went from about 17 percent in 2017 to about 19 percent of all incidents in both 2018 and 2019. The majority of reported incidents were against gay men; however, the increase was most notable for anti-transgender violence: the number of reported incidents increased from 116 (2017) to 168 (2018) to 198 (2019), from about 1.7 percent of all reported hate crimes in 2017 to 2.7 percent in 2019 (FBI: UCR).

These statistics likely do not tell the complete story, in part because reporting is voluntary, and also because many hate crimes are not reported as hate crimes but instead are simply reported as non-bias crimes against people or property (i.e., assault or vandalism). In 2019, only 2,172 law enforcement agencies in the country reported hate crime data to the FBI out of 16,039 possible participants, a participation rate of less than 13 percent. For example, the state of Alabama did not report a single hate crime in 2018 or 2019. An Associated Press investigation in 2016 found that more than 2,700 city police and county sheriff's departments across the country (about 17 percent of law enforcement offices) had not submitted a single hate crime report for the FBI's annual crime tally during the previous six years (Cassidy 2016; FBI: UCR; Fitzsimons 2019).

Using self-reported data on crime from the National Crime Victimization Survey (NCVS), a survey administered by the U.S. Census Bureau, generates much higher rates of hate crime incidents, in part because it includes incidents not reported to police. In 2017, the only year for which NCVS data has been publicly released, the rate of violent victimization of LGBTQ people was 71.1 victimizations per 1,000 people compared to 19.2 victimizations for non-LGBTQ people (Flores et al. 2020). This translates into an estimated 200,000 hate crimes against LGBTQ people each year (Hauck 2019). Again, the difference from the FBI data may be due in part to underreporting: LGBTQ hate crime victims may not report crimes for multiple reasons including fear of retaliation, embarrassment that they were victimized, distrust of law enforcement, fear of being exposed as a member of the LGBTQ community, fear of being re-traumatized by the criminal justice system, or believing the police will not or cannot do anything to help (Ahuja 2016). Documenting hate crimes is also difficult because they are defined by beliefs about the offender's motivation; those seeking to prosecute a crime as a hate crime must often rely on hate speech accompanying the crime as evidence of that motivation (Shanmugasunda-ram 2018).

In his book *Unfinished Lives,* practical theology professor Stephen V. Sprinkle documents the stories of LGBTQ hate crime murder victims. He attributes their deaths to "haters empowered to kill by the heterosexism, misogyny, and homophobia that persistently thrive in our society" (Sprinkle 2011, xvi). These crimes "are perpetrated not just against a single individual. They are message-killings, assassinations meant to terrorize whole populations of queer people" (p. xvii). Documenting the stories of these attacks humanizes the victims and by extension the humanity of all LGBTQ people. The federal law that requires the FBI to collect and report hate crime data is named in part for Matthew Shepard, one of these victims.

On October 7, 1998, Matthew Shepard, a 21-year-old gay student at the University of Wyoming, was beaten, tortured, and tied to a fence and left to die. The brutal attack was prosecuted as a murder but not as a hate crime due to the lack of relevant criminal law. He became a symbol of the need to do more to stop future hate crimes, a movement that culminated in President Obama signing the Matthew Shepard and James Byrd Jr. Hate Crimes Prevention Act (HCPA) in 2009. The law is also named for James Byrd Jr., a Black man who was dragged to his death behind a pickup truck by white assailants earlier that same year. The HCPA increased the jurisdiction of the FBI and Department of Justice to investigate bias-motivated violence and added gender and gender-identity-based violence to the list of hate crimes (Department of Justice, n.d.).

For most of the twentieth century, acts of violence against LGBTQ people were considered "natural" reactions to people perceived to be members of the community. Perpetrators felt justified because they thought their victims were "asking for it," according to psychology professor Dr. Gregory Herek. This view began to change in the 1970s as the gay rights movement demanded that attacks on LGBTQ people be blamed on the perpetrators, not the victims. During the 1980s, hate crime laws in many states were written or revised to include sexual orientation, as was the Hate Crimes Statistics Act of 1990, signed by President George H. Bush. The HCSA was the first federal law to require the federal government to collect data on crimes based on the victim's sexual orientation. The 2009 HCPA built on that law to expand federal definitions of hate crimes to include crimes based on sexual orientation and gender identity; to put them under the jurisdiction of the Department of Justice (DOJ); to authorize the DOJ to assist state and local investigations and prosecutions of hate crimes; and to broaden the FBI's mandate to include collection of statistics about gender and gender identity hate crimes (Herek 2017).

While awareness of LGBTQ hate crimes has increased over time, as has their reporting, it is unclear whether they are becoming more frequent over time due to limitations of available data. Regardless of their true frequency, they are a serious, widespread problem.

FURTHER READING

Ahuja, Harbani. 2016. "The Vicious Cycle of Hate: Systemic Flaws in Hate Crime Documentation in the United States and the Impact on Minority Communities." *Cardozo Law Review* 37, 5: 1882–1883.

Cassidy, Christina A. 2016. "AP: Patchy Reporting Undercuts National Hate Crimes Count." Associated Press, June 4. https://apnews.com /article/race-and-ethnicity-bogalusa-crime-hate-crimes-louisiana -8247a1d2f76b4baea2a121186dedf768

Department of Justice. "The Matthew Shepard and James Byrd, Jr., Hate Crimes Prevention Act of 2009." https://www.justice.gov/crt/matthew -shepard-and-james-byrd-jr-hate-crimes-prevention-act-2009-0

FBI: UCR. Federal Bureau of Investigation, Uniform Crime Reports. "Hate Crimes." https://ucr.fbi.gov/hate-crime

Fitzsimons, Tim. 2019. "Nearly 1 in 5 Hate Crimes Motivated by Anti-LGBTQ Bias, FBI Finds." NBCNews.com, November 12. https://www .nbcnews.com/feature/nbc-out/nearly-1-5-hate-crimes-motivated-anti -lgbtq-bias-fbi-n1080891

Flores, Andrew R., et al. 2020. "Victimization Rates and Traits of Sexual and Gender Minorities in the United States: Results from the National Crime Victimization Survey, 2017." *Science Advances* 6, 40: eaba6910. https://advances.sciencemag.org/content/6/40/eaba6910

Hauck, Grace. 2019. "Anti-LGBT Hate Crimes Are Rising, the FBI Says. But It Gets Worse." *USA Today*, July 1. https://www.usatoday.com/story /news/2019/06/28/anti-gay-hate-crimes-rise-fbi-says-and-they-likely -undercount/1582614001/

Herek, Gregory M. 2017. "Documenting Hate Crimes in the United States: Some Considerations on Data Sources." *Psychology of Sexual Orientation and Gender Diversity* 4, 2: 143–151.

Shanmugasundaram, Swathi. 2018. "Hate Crimes, Explained." SPLC Center, April 15. https://www.splcenter.org/20180415/hate-crimes-explained

Sprinkle, Stephen V. 2011. *Unfinished Lives: Reviving the Memories of LGBTQ Hate Crimes Victims*. Eugene, OR: Resource Publications.

Q13: DO LGBTQ PEOPLE IN THE UNITED STATES STILL SUFFER FROM LEGAL DISCRIMINATION?

Answer: Yes. While discrimination against LGBTQ people has decreased over time and legal protections have increased over time, significant discrimination persists.

The Facts: Most LGBTQ Americans report that they experience harassment and discrimination due to their sexual orientation or gender identity. A 2017 national survey found that 57 percent experienced slurs, 53 percent experienced insensitive or offensive comments, 57 percent reported that they or an LGBTQ friend or family member had been threatened or nonsexually harassed, 51 percent had been sexually harassed, 51 percent experienced violence, and 34 percent were verbally harassed in the bathroom, including being challenged about using the "wrong" bathroom. In terms of workplace discrimination, at least one in five said they had been discriminated against when applying for jobs (20 percent), when seeking equal pay or promotion (22 percent), or when trying to rent a room or apartment or buy a house (22 percent). More than one in four (26 percent) reported unfair treatment by the police or the courts because of their LGBTQ identity (Harvard 2017).

Reported discrimination is even more common among LGBTQ people of color. They are twice as likely as white LGBTQ people to say they have been personally discriminated against when applying for jobs and when interacting with police. The 2017 report documents "how pervasive people's experiences of violence and harassment are," according to Logan S. Casey, one of the researchers for the project. "LGBTQ people's day-to-day experiences are still structured by discrimination, harassment, and prejudice" (Moreau 2017).

Bisexual people are less likely to report discrimination based on their sexual orientation compared with gay and lesbian respondents but bisexuals still experience significant discrimination (Burneson 2018; Mirza 2018). Among women, 36 percent of lesbians reported discrimination based on their sexual orientation in the past year compared to just 19 percent of bisexual women. Among men, 27 percent of gay men reported experiences of discrimination based on their sexual orientation compared to only 10 percent of bisexual men.

Significant discrimination toward transgender and gender-nonconforming people also persists. A large national study conducted by the National Center for Transgender Equality and the National Gay and Lesbian Task

Force found evidence of "pervasive civil rights violations and callous disregard for basic humanity" (Grant et al. 2011). Overall, researchers found that 90 percent of transgender people reported discrimination or harassment or that they hid who they were to avoid discrimination or harassment at work. That report concluded:

> It is part of social and legal convention in the United States to discriminate against, ridicule, and abuse transgender and gender non-conforming people within foundational institutions such as the family, schools, the workplace and healthcare settings, every day. . . . Medical providers and health systems, government agencies, families, businesses and employers, schools and colleges, police departments, jail and prison systems—each of these systems and institutions is failing daily in its obligation to serve transgender and gender nonconforming people, instead subjecting them to mistreatment ranging from commonplace disrespect to outright violence, abuse and the denial of human dignity. (Grant et al. 2011, 8)

A larger follow-up study conducted in 2015 gathered responses from nearly 28,000 transgender people. "Respondents reported high levels of mistreatment, harassment, and violence in every aspect of life." This finding included violence from immediate family members, physical and sexual assaults, and discrimination in the workplace. Nearly 1 in 10 (9 percent) reported being physically attacked in the past year and 47 percent reported attacks during their lifetime. The report also found that transgender people of color reported "deeper and broader patterns of discrimination" (James et al. 2016). The 2017 Harvard study also found discrimination to be more common among transgender people compared to other members of the LGBTQ community: it reported that 38 percent of transgender people experienced slurs, 28 percent were targeted by insensitive or offensive comments, and 18 percent experienced incidents in which people acted afraid of them because of their gender identity (Harvard 2017).

A study conducted in 2016 by the Center for American Progress found that "LGBT people across the country continue to experience pervasive discrimination that negatively impacts all aspects of their lives" (Singh and Durso 2017). They note:

> LGBT people still face widespread discrimination: Between 11 percent and 28 percent of LGB workers report losing a promotion simply because of their sexual orientation, and 27 percent of transgender

workers report being fired, not hired, or denied a promotion in the past year [because of their gender identity]. Discrimination also routinely affects LGBT people beyond the workplace, sometimes costing them their homes, access to education, and even the ability to engage in public life.

Data from a nationally representative survey of LGBT people conducted by CAP shows that 25.2 percent of LGBT respondents have experienced discrimination because of their sexual orientation or gender identity in the past year. The January 2017 survey shows that, despite progress, in 2016 discrimination remained a widespread threat to LGBT people's well-being, health, and economic security.

In sum, discrimination against LGBTQ people is persistent and pervasive. However, as of June 2020 it is illegal. In June 2020, the U.S. Supreme Court ruled in *Bostock v. Clayton County* that the 1964 Civil Rights Act protects gay, lesbian, and transgender employees from workplace discrimination (including firing and other adverse employment decisions) made on the basis of their sexual orientation or gender identity (see Q10). Until that decision, it was legal in more than half of the states to fire workers for being gay, bisexual, or transgender. However, the ruling noted that federal law also includes protections for religious groups and employers which may give them latitude to discriminate against LGBTQ people in their employment decisions (Liptak 2020).

FURTHER READING

Burneson, Elizabeth Childress. 2018. "The Invisible Minority: Discrimination against Bisexuals in the Workplace." *University of Richmond Law Review* 52: 63–82.

Grant, Jaime M., et al. 2011. *Injustice at Every Turn: A Report of the National Transgender Discrimination Survey.* Washington, DC: National Center for Transgender Equality and National Gay and Lesbian Task Force.

Harvard Opinion Research Program. 2017. "Discrimination in America." https://www.hsph.harvard.edu/horp/discrimination-in-america/

James, Sandy E., et al. 2016. *Executive Summary of the Report of the 2015 U.S. Transgender Survey.* Washington, DC: National Center for Transgender Equality. https://www.ustranssurvey.org/

Liptak, Adam. 2020. "Civil Rights Law Protects Gay and Transgender Workers, Supreme Court Rules." *New York Times*, June 15. https://www.nytimes.com/2020/06/15/us/gay-transgender-workers-supreme-court.html

Mirza, Shabab Ahmed. 2018. "Disaggregating the Data for Bisexual People." Center for American Progress, September 24. https://www .americanprogress.org/issues/lgbtq-rights/reports/2018/09/24/458472 /disaggregating-data-bisexual-people/

Moreau, Julie. 2017. "Most LGBTQ Americans Experience Harassment, Discrimination, Harvard Study Finds." NBCNews.com, November 26. https://www.nbcnews.com/feature/nbc-out/most-lgbtq-americans -experience-harassment-discrimination-harvard-study-finds-n823876

Singh, Sejal, and Laura E. Durso. 2017. "Widespread Discrimination Continues to Shape LGBT People's Lives in Both Subtle and Significant Ways." Center for American Progress, May 2. https://www .americanprogress.org/issues/lgbtq-rights/news/2017/05/02/429529 /widespread-discrimination-continues-shape-lgbt-peoples-lives-subtle -significant-ways/

3

Public Visibility of
LGBTQ People

In general, public opinion doesn't change very quickly on an aggregate level. People have strong individual incentives to keep their attitudes consistent over time, which usually means that it takes something substantial to change the opinions of a big group of people. There have been exceptions, however, and support for LGBTQ rights has been one of those exceptions. According to Gallup polls, only 27 percent of Americans supported legalizing same-sex marriage in 1996 while 68 percent of Americans were opposed. Just a few decades later, attitudes had nearly flipped: surveys in 2020 found support had increased to 67 percent of Americans with only 31 percent opposed (Gallup 2020).

Chapter 3 investigates this rapid change and related issues, including potential causes of these attitudinal shifts and various effects. Q14 provides an overview of public opinion toward LGBTQ relationships and marriage over time and Q15 focuses on public opinion toward LGBTQ people being parents. Q16 provides an overview of increased support for LGBTQ individuals among some religious organizations and leaders over time. Q17 identifies the overall effect of more people coming out as LGBTQ and Q18 discusses the increase of openly LGBTQ elected officials. Finally, Q19 looks into media coverage of LGBTQ people in television and movies as a potential catalyst for opinion change.

Q14: HAS THE PUBLIC BECOME MORE SUPPORTIVE OF SAME-SEX RELATIONSHIPS AND MARRIAGES?

Answer: Yes. From the first major poll asking about same-sex marriage in 1996 to today, support for same-sex relationships and marriage (often called marriage equality) has increased dramatically.

The Facts: Attitudes are usually very slow to change, even over time. People like to feel that they have consistent beliefs and it usually takes something significant to make them change their mind about something and have that change last over time. Typically, if there is a sudden, significant change in what people think about a particular political topic (e.g., in response to a news event), opinions tend to revert back to where they were after a short while. For example, attitudes toward gun control laws usually change dramatically after a highly publicized mass shooting but tend to return to previous levels after the media coverage dies down.

On the other hand, sometimes public opinion changes so dramatically, it takes everyone a bit by surprise. After decades and even centuries of discrimination and harassment, attitudes toward same-sex relationships and marriage began to undergo a dramatic shift in the mid- to late 1990s. In 1996, Gallup, one of the most well-known pollsters in the United States, asked the question of its respondents, "Do you think marriages between same-sex couples should or should not be recognized by the law as valid, with the same rights as traditional Americans?" (Gallup 2020). The results, according to Gallup, were that 68 percent of Americans opposed legalizing gay marriage/same-sex marriage and only 27 percent thought such unions should be legally recognized as valid. From that point forward, however, support for gay marriage steadily increased over time, per Gallup—to 37 percent in 2005, 46 percent in 2007, 53 percent in 2011, 60 percent in 2015, and 63 percent in 2019. The movement in attitudes toward marriage equality, even across different identity groups, does not follow the typical pattern of opinion change. From 27 percent support for marriage equality in 1996 to 63 percent support in 2019 is simply remarkable.

In addition to changes in attitudes toward marriage for same-sex couples, attitudes toward the legality and morality of gay or lesbian relationships between consenting adults changed dramatically as well (Gallup 2020). Scholars point to several factors that contributed to this change, including that we simply have a longer span of time with measured opinion on these sets of issues. First, in terms of legality, opinion changed a lot in the mid- to late 1980s, probably related to the HIV/AIDS crisis of the 1980s and 1990s and to Supreme Court decisions that were significant legal setbacks for the LGBTQ community, such as *Bowers v. Hardwick* in 1986. Opinion was pretty stable throughout the 1990s, though there were not many surveys asking this question. However, starting in 2003, pollsters reported a large increase in support for providing legal protections for gay and lesbian relationships. Some observers speculate that this increase in support could be related to the Supreme Court ruling in *Lawrence v. Texas* that same year. In that 6–3 decision, the Court ruled that laws prohibiting private sexual activities between consenting gay adults were unconstitutional.

There is another set of questions about the morality (not legality) of gay and lesbian relationships. A common survey question asks, "Regardless of whether or not you think it should be legal, please tell me whether you personally believe that in general" gay and lesbian relations are "morally acceptable or morally wrong" (Gallup 2020). Again, the change in American attitudes on this question over a relatively short period of time is remarkable. In 2001, 53 percent of people reported they thought gay and lesbian relations were morally *wrong*; in 2019, 63 percent of people reported that gay or lesbian relations were morally *acceptable*. Again, this magnitude of change toward support (or tolerance, at minimum) of the LGBTQ community over a short period of time is unprecedented in the modern history of public opinion measurement.

Gallup polls comparing data from 1999 and 2019 show an increase in overall support for marriage equality from 35 to 63 percent during the course of those two decades, an increase of 28 percentage points. Among Democrats, the increase was even larger, from 42 percent to 79 percent (a shift of 37 percentage points), but Republicans also shifted their attitudes, doubling their level of support from 22 percent to 44 percent. Young people (age 18–29) became much more supportive, from 52 percent to 83 percent (a shift of 31 percentage points), but older people also changed their minds, including a massive shift among those over age 65 from 11 percent to 47 percent (a 36 percentage-point change). Attitudes were changed among all ages, among both men and women, and across all major regions of the United States. Although Americans living in the South remain the least supportive of marriage equality of any region of the country (57 percent in 2019), even that level of support is more than double what it was in 1999 (27 percent) (McCarthy 2018).

There are many reasons why such a dramatic change took place in a relatively short period of time. Three major causes frequently cited are the increased visibility of LGBTQ people in American public life; messaging shifts in LGBTQ outreach and advocacy; and increased diversity in the voices of people speaking out in support of gay rights and marriage equality (Harrison 2020). From labor leader Dolores Huerta and President Barack Obama to musician and producer Jay-Z, people from many different identity groups—heterosexual people, BIPOC (Black, Indigenous, and other people of color), religious leaders, professional athletes and other sports leaders—began to speak out in favor of LGBTQ people and rights.

First, visibility. A 2015 Pew Research Poll found that 88 percent of Americans reported that they knew someone gay or lesbian, a significant change from the 61 percent who gave the same answer in 1993 (Pew Research 2015). This increase was the result of a deliberate strategy by members of the gay community to come out to their friends and family, to show them that they already knew and loved people who were gay. As more people made the brave decision to come out, more of their friends, family, coworkers, and neighbors were moved to reconsider their previous opposition to same-sex rights and relationships. The same 2015 survey showed that almost 75 percent of people who said they knew a lot of gay and lesbian people supported marriage equality, as did two-thirds of people who had gay or lesbian family members. People who had few or no gay or lesbian friends or family members, however, were much less supportive (32 percent and 44 percent, respectively).

Secondly, the messaging of LGBTQ advocacy changed over time, from a focus on rights to a focus on love. In other words, the public was encouraged to see same-sex couples not as asking for "special rights" but as people who fall in love just like straight people. Individuals and groups advocating for LGBTQ rights made increased use of personal stories of people in their outreach and persuasion campaigns instead of more abstract concepts. For example, when activists campaigned to increase support for marriage equality in Massachusetts, they focused their outreach campaign on LGBTQ families and couples. As Marc Solomon, national campaign director for Freedom to Marry, wrote:

> We knew that the one thing that could break through the fear was allowing lawmakers to get to know [same-sex] married couples and their families. When they did, they would understand viscerally that these families were not much different from their own and that they should treat gay families as they'd want their own family to be treated. (Solomon 2014, 79)

Finally, having diversity among those speaking out in favor of LGBTQ people was a big part of the change in opinion. People who are seen as identity group leaders can have a huge effect in changing hearts and minds

(Harrison and Michelson 2017). One notable example of this concept came on May 9, 2012, when President Barack Obama decided to endorse same-sex marriage: "I've just concluded that for me personally it is important for me to go ahead and affirm that I think same-sex couples should be able to get married." It was definitely a risk for the president to make such a statement in an election year (Touré 2012). While many Black leaders—especially religious leaders (NPR 2012)—did not follow Obama's lead on LGBTQ rights, many others did, including former chairman of the Joint Chiefs of Staff (and Republican) Colin Powell, Jesse Jackson, Al Sharpton, then-Newark mayor Cory Booker, then-Massachusetts governor Deval Patrick (at the time, the nation's only Black governor), most of the Congressional Black Caucus, and entertainers 50 Cent, Jay-Z, and Will Smith (Thrasher 2012). Black public sentiment toward gay marriage warmed markedly in the days and weeks following Obama's declaration.

While LGBTQ people have been discriminated against throughout U.S. history, there has been a remarkable shift in how the American public views and supports the relationships between gay and lesbian people. Public opinion typically does not move quickly over time; this example, however, can give hope for other identity groups who hope to increase their level of support and visibility in American political and social life.

FURTHER READING

Gallup. 2020. "Gay and Lesbian Rights." http://www.gallup.com/poll/1651/gay-lesbian-rights.aspx

Harrison, Brian F. 2020. *A Change Is Gonna Come: How to Have Effective Political Conversations in a Divided America*. New York: Oxford University Press.

Harrison, Brian F., and Melissa R. Michelson. 2017. *Listen, We Need to Talk: How to Change Attitudes about LGBT Rights*. New York: Oxford University Press.

McCarthy, Justin. 2018. "Two in Three Americans Support Same-Sex Marriage." Gallup, May 23. https://news.gallup.com/poll/234866/two-three-americans-support-sex-marriage.aspx

NPR. 2012. "Obama's Gay Marriage Stance Stirs Black Community." NPR, *All Things Considered*, May 11. https://www.npr.org/2012/05/11/152520955/obamas-gay-marriage-stance-stirs-black-community

Pew Research. 2015. "Support for Same-Sex Marriage at Record High, but Key Segments Remain Opposed." Pew Research Center, June 8. https://www.pewresearch.org/wp-content/uploads/sites/4/2015/06/6-8-15-Same-sex-marriage-release1.pdf

Pew Research. 2017. "Support for Same-Sex Marriage Grows, Even Among Groups That Had Been Skeptical." Pew Research Center, June 26. http://www.people-press.org/2017/06/26/support-for-same-sex-marriage-grows-even-among-groups-that-had-been-skeptical/

Siddiqui, Sabrina. 2012. "Ohio's Black Voters Support Same-Sex Marriage After Obama's Endorsement, Poll Finds." Huffington Post, July 3. http://www.huffingtonpost.com/2012/07/03/ohio-black-voters-same-sex-marriage-obama_n_1646189.html

Silver, Nate. 2015. "Change Doesn't Usually Come This Fast." *FiveThirtyEight*, June 26. https://fivethirtyeight.com/features/change-doesnt-usually-come-this-fast/

Solomon, Marc. 2014. *Winning Marriage: The Inside Story of How Same-Sex Couples Took on the Politicians and Pundits—and Won.* New York: ForeEdge Publishers, 79.

Thrasher, Steven. 2012. "Obama Finally Loses Support of a Black Leader Over Gay Marriage, And It's . . . Farrakhan!" *The Village Voice Blogs*, May 31. https://www.villagevoice.com/2012/05/31/obama-finally-loses-support-of-a-black-leader-over-gay-marriage-and-its-farrakhan/

Touré. 2012. "Will Black Voters Punish Obama for His Support of Gay Rights? The President Might Be on the Right Side of History, but He's on the Wrong Side of a Crucial Voting Bloc." *Time*, May 9. http://ideas.time.com/2012/05/09/will-black-voters-punish-obama-for-his-support-of-gay-rights/#ixzz2nkqVBoLZ

Vedantam, Shankar, Parth Shah, Tara Boyle, and Jennifer Schmidt. 2019. "Radically Normal: How Gay Rights Activists Changed the Minds of Their Opponents." *National Public Radio*, April 8. https://www.npr.org/2019/04/03/709567750/radically-normal-how-gay-rights-activists-changed-the-minds-of-their-opponents

Q15: HAS THE PUBLIC BECOME MORE SUPPORTIVE OF SAME-SEX PEOPLE BEING PARENTS?

Answer: Yes. Public opinion polls show that attitudes toward same-sex parenting have shifted dramatically over the past few decades, with clear majorities of Americans voicing support for same-sex couples having the right to adopt a child.

The Facts: Surveys show that support for same-sex couples adopting children has increased dramatically since Gallup first asked the public about the issue in 1977. While same-sex couples can become parents through other means, including donor insemination and surrogacy, most survey data focus on attitudes toward same-sex adoption.

In the first survey conducted by Gallup in 1977, only 14 percent of Americans said that gay and lesbian people should be allowed to adopt children. Attitudes have since shifted considerably. In 1994, 28 percent of Americans favored adoption by same-sex couples; twenty years later, that proportion had increased to 63 percent. More recent surveys find that support has continued to climb to a high of 75 percent as of May 2019 (McCarthy 2019; Montero 2014).

Although it is clear that support for same-sex parenting has increased dramatically over the past four decades, not all public opinion polls can be compared directly due to changes in survey question wording. The 1977 Gallup question asked, "Do you think homosexuals should or should not be allowed to adopt children?" In 1992, the question was amended to ask, "Do you think that homosexual couples should be legally permitted to adopt children?" In 2003, the Gallup item was amended again to ask, "Do you think same-sex couples should or should not have the legal right to adopt a child?" Finally, in 2019, Gallup asked, "Do you think gays and lesbians should or should not be allowed to adopt children?" (McCarthy 2019).

This shift not only reflects overall increases in public support for LGBTQ rights but has even often outpaced support for same-sex marriage. This broad acceptance of gay adoption rights may in part reflect evidence that children raised by same-sex parents often do just as well as and sometimes better than peers raised by different-sex parents. A European study of 1,200 children raised by same-sex couples and more than 1 million kids raised by different-sex couples from 1995 until 2005 found that children raised by same-sex couples performed better in school and were more likely to graduate from high school (Long 2019). Some of these differences were due to socioeconomic status—same-sex couples had higher levels of income and wealth—but they persisted even when the researchers controlled for those differences.

A study of 315 same-sex parents and 500 children in Australia found that children raised by same-sex couples scored higher than their peers on physical health and social well-being but also reported that they were more likely to experience some form of stigma due to their parents' sexual orientation, with negative effects on their mental and emotional well-being (Crouch et al. 2014). Public health researcher Simon Crouch, the lead researcher of that study, noted that the findings may be due to the lack of strict gender roles and stereotypes in same-sex couple homes. "Same-sex parents, for instance, are more likely to share childcare and work responsibilities more equitably than heterosexual-parent families. . . . Our research suggests that abandoning such gender stereotypes might be beneficial to child health" (Crouch et al. 2014; see Q7).

In 2013, the National Health Interview Survey estimated there were 690,000 same-sex couples in the United States, more than 124,000 (18 percent) of whom were married. The survey also found that up to 2.2 million children were being raised by same-sex couples or by lesbian, gay, or bisexual parents (Gates 2014).

Same-sex couples are more likely to raise adopted or foster children compared to different-sex couples. According to a 2018 study from the Williams Institute at the UCLA School of Law, more than one in five (21 percent) of same-sex couples are raising adopted children compared to just 3 percent of different-sex couples; 2.9 percent of same-sex couples have foster children compared to just 0.4 percent of different-sex couples (Goldberg and Conron 2018).

Attitudes about same-sex parenting, like other attitudes about LGBTQ people, have tended to be split along partisan lines. In 2008, Republican presidential candidate John McCain, himself an adoptive father, told the *New York Times* that he didn't support "gay adoption." His stance reflected Republican orthodoxy at the time. Democrats tend to be more supportive of same-gender couples adopting—85 percent in 2012—compared to Republicans (23 percent) (Montero 2014). Younger people tend to be more supportive than older people and women tend to be more supportive than men. A June 2018 survey found that most Americans (55 percent) believe same-sex and different-sex couples can be equally good parents, a view shared by 49 percent of men and 61 percent of women (Ballard 2018).

In February 2019, the U.S. Supreme Court agreed to hear *Fulton v. Philadelphia*. The case originated in March 2018, when the City of Philadelphia learned that two of the agencies it hires to provide foster care services would not license same-sex couples to be foster parents. The agencies claimed that their refusal to consider same-sex couples was based on the religious beliefs of their owners. One of the agencies agreed to comply with the city's request to change its policy but the other agency, Catholic Social Services (CSS), sued, claiming that the request was a violation of their right to free exercise of religion. In June 2021, the court ruled in favor of CSS that the city's decision to terminate their contract was unconstitutional. The somewhat complex ruling in favor of CSS left intact a precedent from 1990, *Employment Division v. Smith*, that "neutral and generally applicable" laws comply with the free exercise of religion so long as they don't target religious conduct. The result was not a clear win for either party. Observers expect future challenges to *Smith* to further clarify how to balance conflicts between religious freedom and LGBTQ rights (Howe 2021; Totenberg 2021).

The nuances of the *Fulton* case mirror the patchwork nature of laws regarding same-sex parenting. In some states, adoption agencies are prohibited from discriminating based on sexual orientation while in others, laws allow agencies to claim religious objections to doing so. Some states require a non-biological parent to go through legal adoption to be recognized as the child's second parent. This process can be both lengthy and expensive (Harris 2017).

Overall, public opinion has shifted since the 1970s to be more supportive of same-sex parents adopting children, increasing from just 14 percent in 1977 to 75 percent in May 2019. While some Americans are still opposed, most Americans now believe that same-sex and different-sex couples can be equally good parents.

FURTHER READING

Ballard, Jamie. 2018. "What Americans Think about Gay Couples and Adoption." YouGov.com, June 26. https://today.yougov.com/topics/lifestyle/articles-reports/2018/06/26/most-americans-support-gay-couples-adopting-childr

Crouch, Simon R., et al. 2014. "Parent-Reported Measures of Child Health and Wellbeing in Same-Sex Parent Families: A Cross-Sectional Survey." *BMC Public Health* 14: 635.

Gates, Gary J. 2014. "LGB Families and Relationships: Analyses of the 2013 National Health Interview Study." Williams Institute, UCLA School of Law, September. https://williamsinstitute.law.ucla.edu/wp-content/uploads/lgb-families-nhis-sep-2014.pdf

Goldberg, Shoshana K., and Kerith J. Conron. 2018. "How Many Same-Sex Couples in the US Are Raising Children?" Williams Institute, UCLA School of Law, July 31. https://williamsinstitute.law.ucla.edu/press/same-sex-parenting/

Harris, Elizabeth A. 2017. "Same-Sex Parents Still Face Legal Complications." *New York Times*, June 20. https://www.nytimes.com/2017/06/20/us/gay-pride-lgbtq-same-sex-parents.html

Howe, Amy. 2021. "Court Holds That City's Refusal to Make Referrals to Faith-Based Agency Violates Constitution." *SCOTUSblog*, June 17. https://www.scotusblog.com/2021/06/court-holds-that-citys-refusal-to-make-referrals-to-faith-based-agency-violates-constitution/

Liptak, Adam. 2021. "Supreme Court Backs Catholic Agency in Case on Gay Rights and Foster Care." *New York Times*, June 17. https://www .nytimes.com/2021/06/17/us/supreme-court-gay-rights-foster-care.html

Long, Heather. 2019. "Children Raised by Same-Sex Couples Do Better in School, New Study Finds." *Washington Post*, February 6. https://www .washingtonpost.com/business/2019/02/06/children-raised-by-same-sex -couples-do-better-school-new-study-finds/

McCarthy, Justin. 2019. "Gallup First Polled on Gay Issues in '77. What Has Changed?" gallup.com, June 6. https://news.gallup.com/poll/258065 /gallup-first-polled-gay-issues-changed.aspx

Montero, Darrel M. 2014. "America's Progress in Achieving the Legalization of Same-Gender Adoption: Analysis of Public Opinion, 1994 to 2012." *Social Work* 59, 4: 321–328.

Supreme Court. 2020. *Fulton v. City of Philadelphia, PA.* https://www .supremecourt.gov/qp/19-00123qp.pdf

Totenberg, Nina. 2021. "Supreme Court Rules for a Catholic Group in a Case Involving Gay Rights, Foster Care." *National Public Radio*, June 17. https://www.npr.org/2021/06/17/996670391/supreme-court-rules-for-a -catholic-group-in-a-case-involving-gay-rights-foster-c

Q16: ARE MAJOR RELIGIONS IN THE UNITED STATES MORE SUPPORTIVE OF LGBTQ PEOPLE THAN THEY USED TO BE?

Answer: Yes. In general, religious organizations and leaders are becoming more supportive of LGBTQ people and rights over time. While some institutions maintain opposition to same-sex marriage and other LGBTQ rights, many other spiritual communities and faith leaders and their followers have changed their opinions and policies in ways that have positively impacted LGBTQ people, both those who are religious and those who are not.

The Facts: During a 2019 interview with a Mexican broadcaster, Pope Francis endorsed civil unions for same-sex couples, saying, "What we have to create is a civil union law. . . . That way they are legally covered." The pope's comment aired in October 2020 when the documentary *Francesco* made its debut at the Rome Film Festival. The pope reiterated in the interview that he believes gay people are "children of God" (Horowitz 2020). This was a watershed moment: it was the first time a pope, the leader of an estimated 1.2 billion Roman Catholics worldwide, had expressed an opinion supportive of LGBTQ rights. However, it was just one comment in a series of mixed messages from the Catholic church. In March 2021, the Vatican issued a report saying it would not bless same-sex unions. The directive said individuals with "homosexual inclinations" could be blessed but only if they agree to not have sex; the report also included incendiary language like "sin" and "disordered" when referring to LGBTQ Catholics (Picheta and Gallagher 2021; Schlumpf 2021).

Traditionally, the Abrahamic religions of Judaism, Christianity, and Islam forbid nonheterosexual and non-vaginal sexual intercourse, typically labeled as sodomy, deriving a belief that this kind of behavior is sinful from the story of Sodom and Gomorrah. This common interpretation of the story of the cities of Sodom and Gomorrah, two notoriously sinful cities destroyed by God, was for centuries understood as based on an interpretation of those sinful acts as sexual relations between men. Today, however, many biblical scholars believe this reference is flawed. Biblical studies professor Perry Kea believes the true lesson of these passages is that mob violence against outsiders—not homosexual behavior—is the true sin of Sodom (Kea 2018). According to history and gender studies professor Linda McClain, most religious scholars now believe Sodom and Gomorrah were being punished by God for arrogance and the lack of charity and hospitality, not for any sexual acts (McClain 2019).

Regardless, many denominations within Christianity and Judaism accept LGBTQ members and some permit ordination of openly LGBTQ candidates for ministry. LGBTQ-affirming denominations include the Reconstructionist, Conservative, and Reform branches of Judaism; the United Church of Christ, United Church of Canada, the Episcopal Church in the United States; the Evangelical Lutheran Church in America; the Presbyterian Church; Community of Christ; and Metropolitan Community Church. In Europe, several Lutheran, Reformed United, and Old Catholic churches have adopted increasingly supportive policies toward LGBTQ members. Leaders of other groups like Orthodox Jewish people and followers of African American churches that have traditionally opposed LGBTQ people and rights are making incremental changes to be more supportive than they were in the past (Lazewatsky 2011, 2012). Many faith groups are developing rituals and rites to be inclusive of LGBTQ people (Latimer 2012) and to address important issues like LGBTQ youth homelessness (Murray 2012).

It isn't just religious leaders who are becoming more supportive of LGBTQ rights: followers of these religions are also changing their views as well. According to research from PRRI, white evangelical Protestants remain the only major religious group with a majority of members who oppose marriage equality (34 percent in favor, 63 percent in opposition) (PRRI 2020). Ninety percent of religiously unaffiliated Americans support LGBTQ marriage equality, as do a majority of adherents of every other major religious group in the United States: 79 percent of white mainline Protestants, 78 percent of Hispanic Catholics, 72 percent of non-Christian religious groups, 68 percent of Hispanic Protestants, 67 percent of white Catholics, 57 percent of Black Protestants, and 56 percent of what the survey identifies as "other Christian religious groups" (PRRI 2020). Support extends beyond marriage equality as well, with large majorities supportive of nondiscrimination laws protecting LGBTQ people, ranging from 59 percent among white evangelical Protestants to 92 percent of religiously unaffiliated Americans. With the exception of Americans who are white evangelical Protestants, majorities of Americans from all religious groups oppose religion-based refusals to serve gay or lesbian people. This includes white mainline Protestants (65 percent), white Catholics (69 percent), Black Protestants (71 percent), and Hispanic Catholics (72 percent). In contrast, only 34 percent of white evangelical Protestants oppose this policy (PRRI 2020).

Americans from a broad range of religious traditions also oppose policies that discriminate against LGBTQ people. Majorities of Americans from most major religious groups favor transgender people serving openly in the U.S. military, including 73 percent of white Catholics, 67 percent of Hispanic Catholics, 60 percent of Black Protestants, and 58 percent of white mainline Protestants. In contrast, only 46 percent of white evangelical Protestants favor allowing transgender people to serve openly in the military (PRRI 2020).

Overall, 70 percent of Americans oppose allowing religiously affiliated agencies that receive taxpayer funding to refuse to accept qualified gay and lesbian couples as foster parents while only 28 percent favor this policy. Opposition comes from Catholics (82 percent), white mainline Protestants (70 percent), Hispanic Catholics (65 percent), and Black Protestants (62 percent). In contrast, only 42 percent of white evangelical Protestants agree while a majority (53 percent) support the discriminatory policy against gay and lesbian parents (PRRI 2020).

Many religious leaders in the United States are not supportive of LGBTQ people or the rights and recognition the community seeks. The breadth of this opposition, however, may be exaggerated due at least in part to media interviews that disproportionately cite those in opposition. GLAAD reports that the proportion of media reports including interviews with evangelical Christians is higher than their proportion of the population (34 percent of media coverage compared to 26 percent of the U.S. population). Similarly, over half of Roman Catholics who were featured in media coverage presented negative messages about LGBTQ rights, even though a clear majority of American Catholics support both marriage equality (71 percent) and antidiscrimination laws that protect LGBTQ people in the workplace and in public accommodations (73 percent). Finally, GLAAD's analysis finds that mainstream media cites fewer religious sources from groups like mainline Protestants and Jewish people who are predominantly supportive of LGBTQ rights (GLAAD n.d.).

In addition, there are reasons to think that it is partisanship, not just religious identity, that drives some opposition to LGBTQ rights. For example, PRRI surveys that asked people about religious-based refusals to serve gay and lesbian people found that support for nondiscrimination protections for LGBTQ people edged up between 2015 and 2019 (Fitzsimons 2020). However, there was also an increase in the percentage of respondents who agreed that a small business owner in their state should be allowed to refuse to provide products or services to gay or lesbian people if doing so violates their religious beliefs, from 16 percent to 30 percent (Greenberg et al. 2019). When the data are broken down by partisan identity, it is clear most of the change came from Republicans. Between 2014 and 2019, the percentage of people who agreed that business owners should be able to deny goods and services to LGBTQ people based on individual religious belief increased among Democrats (from 11 percent to 18 percent) and Independents (16 percent to 24 percent). The increase among Republicans, however, was far more dramatic, from 21 percent to 47 percent in the same time period. In other words, while support for so-called religious objections increased over the last several years, attitudes are closely correlated with partisan identity, not just religious identity.

Another important thing to consider is that many LGBTQ people themselves identify as religious, underscoring the idea that some members of religious communities are more likely to come into contact with LGBTQ people as a part of their worship. A 2020 study by the Williams Institute found that there are about 5.3 million LGBTQ adults who are religious, including roughly 3.1 million who consider themselves moderately religious and 2.2 million who consider themselves highly religious (Conron, Goldberg, and O'Neill 2020). Religious LGBTQ adults spanned across age categories and racial and ethnic groups, among married and single people, among those who are parenting or not, and among people who live in both rural and urban areas. Scholars believe that the presence and visibility of LGBTQ people among religious groups and communities has been important in changing the hearts and minds of people of faith in the United States.

While the relationship between religious identity and the LGBTQ community can sometimes be complicated, many religious leaders and people of faith are becoming more supportive of LGBTQ people being open and active members of their faith community. In addition, religious groups and people of faith are, generally speaking, becoming more supportive of key LGBTQ campaigns to secure equal rights in areas like marriage equality, parenting laws, and nondiscrimination laws; however, surveys show that religious Americans are also becoming more supportive of claims by business owners that the rights of LGBTQ people can be limited by religious freedom.

FURTHER READING

Al-Fitrah Foundation. n.d. http://www.al-fitrah.org.za/index.html

Conron, Kerith J., Shoshana K. Goldberg, and Kathryn O'Neill. 2020. "Religiosity among LGBT Adults in the US." Williams Institute, UCLA School of Law, October. https://williamsinstitute.law.ucla.edu/publications /lgbt-religiosity-us/

Fitzsimons, Tim. 2020. "More Americans OK with Businesses Not Serving Gays Based on Religion, Survey Finds." NBCNews.com, April 14. https://www.nbcnews.com/feature/nbc-out/more-americans-ok-businesses -not-serving-gays-based-religion-survey-n1183866

GLAAD. n.d. "Religion, Faith, and Values." https://www.glaad.org /programs/faith

Greenberg, Daniel, Maxine Najle, Natalie Jackson, Oyindamola Bola, and Robert P. Jones. 2019. "Increasing Support for Religiously Based Service Refusals." PRRI, June 25. https://www.prri.org/research/increasing -support-for-religiously-based-service-refusals/

Horowitz, Jason. 2020. "In Shift for Church, Pope Francis Voices Support for Same-Sex Civil Unions." *New York Times*, October 21. https://www .nytimes.com/2020/10/21/world/europe/pope-francis-same-sex-civil -unions.html

Kea, Perry. 2018. "Sodom and Gomorrah: How the 'Classical' Interpretation Gets It Wrong." *Westar Institute* (blog), September 19. https://www .westarinstitute.org/blog/sodom-and-gomorrah-how-the-classical -interpretation-gets-it-wrong/

Keshet. n.d. "Community Inclusion Guides." https://www.keshetonline .org/resources-and-events/community-inclusion-guides/

Latimer, Nichole. 2012. "Faith Communities Develop More LGBT-Inclusive Liturgical Rites." GLAAD, March 5. https://www.glaad.org/blog/faith -communities-develop-more-lgbt-inclusive-liturgical-rites

Lazewatsky, Miriam. 2011. "Orthodox Communities Struggle with LGBT Acceptance." GLAAD, December 8. https://www.glaad.org/blog/orthodox -communities-struggle-lgbt-acceptance

Lazewatsky, Miriam. 2012. "African American Pastors Support Marriage Equality." GLAAD, February 12. https://www.glaad.org/blog/african -american-pastors-support-marriage-equailty

McClain, Lisa. 2019. "A Thousand Years Ago, the Catholic Church Paid Little Attention to Homosexuality." The Conversation, April 10. https:// theconversation.com/a-thousand-years-ago-the-catholic-church-paid -little-attention-to-homosexuality-112830

Murray, Ross. 2012. "Homeless LGBT Youth and the Focus of 'Weekend of Prayer and Learning.'" GLAAD, January 19. https://www.glaad.org/blog /homeless-lgbt-youth-focus-weekend-prayer-and-learning

Picheta, Rob, and Delia Gallagher. 2021. "Vatican Says It Will Not Bless Same-Sex Unions, Calling Them a 'Sin.'" CNN, March 15. https:// www.cnn.com/2021/03/15/europe/vatican-same-sex-unions-decision -intl/index.html

PFLAG. n.d. "Faith in Our Families." https://pflag.org/resource/faith-our -families

PRRI. 2020. "Americans Are Broadly Supportive of a Variety of LGBTQ Rights." PRRI, October 30. https://www.prri.org/spotlight/americans-are -broadly-supportive-of-a-variety-of-lgbtq-rights/

Schlumpf, Heidi. 2021. "The Pope's Openness to LGBTQ Catholics Hits a Wall." March 15. CNN. https://www.cnn.com/2021/03/15/opinions /pope-ruling-on-lgbtq-catholics-schlumpf/index.html

Trevor Project. n.d. "LGBTQ + Religion." https://www.thetrevorproject .org/trvr_support_center/lgbtq-religion/

Q17: ARE MORE PEOPLE COMING OUT AS LGBTQ?

Answer: Yes. Since the 1980s, people have been more likely to "come out" as LGBTQ.

The Facts: "Coming out" refers to when people who are LGBTQ reveal their sexual orientation and/or non-cisgender gender identity. Coming out is often more than a single event; instead, it is a repeated, ongoing process that takes place over an extended period of time as individuals choose to communicate their identity to others in their lives. This process includes coming out to their families and close friends, coworkers, and people they meet. Some people choose to come out to some people but not to others;

for example, someone might choose to come out to their close friends but not to their coworkers.

The likelihood of people choosing to come out as LGBTQ has increased significantly over the past fifty years, since the launch of the modern gay rights movement in 1969. At the first Gay Liberation March in New York City in 1970, one of the organizers said, "We'll never have the freedom and civil rights we deserve as human beings unless we stop hiding in closets and in the shelter of anonymity" (Saguy 2020).

In 1978, Harvey Milk, one of the first openly gay elected officials in the country when he was elected to the San Francisco Board of Supervisors in 1977, issued a call to his community that they must come out but cautioned that they should "come out only to the people you know, and who know you."

> Gay brothers and sisters, you must come out. Come out to your parents. I know that it is hard and will hurt them, but think about how they will hurt you in the voting booth! Come out to your relatives. Come out to your friends, if indeed they are your friends. Come out to your neighbors, to your fellow workers, to the people who work where you eat and shop. Come out only to the people you know, and who know you, not to anyone else. But once and for all, break down the myths. Destroy the lies and distortions. For your sake. For their sake. (Milk 1978)

While acknowledging the potential hardship and hurt that can result from coming out, Milk understood that many people would respond positively to coming-out stories from people that they knew and loved. Research has subsequently confirmed Milk's optimism. National Coming Out Day was first celebrated on October 11, 1988, exactly one year after the historic Second March on Washington for Lesbian and Gay Rights that drew half a million participants. National Coming Out Day events are now held in all 50 states and in many countries around the world. The event was organized by psychologist Robert Eichberg and activist Jean O'Leary. In 1993, echoing Milk's words, Eichberg explained their motivation: "Most people think they don't know anyone gay or lesbian, and in fact everyone does. It is imperative that we come out and let people know who we are and disabuse them of their fears and stereotypes" (Associated Press 1995).

Members of Queer Nation, an activist group created by HIV/AIDS activists in New York City in 1990, used coming out as a political strategy in the 1990s, visiting heterosexual bars and suburban shopping malls while wearing T-shirts with LGBTQ pride slogans, staging kiss-ins, and chanting "we're here, we're queer" slogans. Similar tactics were used by ACT UP (AIDS Coalition to Unleash Power) in the 1980s and 1990s. The groups used social movement strategies combined with coming out publicly as a way to build visibility and political power for the LGBTQ community (Sugay 2020; Aizenman 2019).

A 2013 survey of lesbian, gay, and bisexual people found that a vast majority of gay men (90 percent) and lesbians (94 percent) were out to at least some of their family and friends while bisexual people were less likely to be out (60 percent). Differences were even more stark within the bisexual community, with bisexual men far less likely to have told a close friend or family member about their sexual orientation. The same study reported that 70 percent of gay men and 67 percent of lesbians had come out to their mother; however, only 47 percent of bisexual women and 22 percent of bisexual men had done the same. Similarly, while 53 percent of gay men and 45 percent of lesbians had come out to their father, only 29 percent of bisexual women and only 8 percent of bisexual men had done so (Pew Research Center 2013).

LGBTQ people are much less likely to be out at work. This state of affairs reflects the reality that until recently, it was legal to fire someone for their sexual orientation or gender identity in many parts of the United States. A 2018 survey by the Human Rights Campaign Foundation found that 38 percent of LGBTQ people hid their sexuality from coworkers to avoid being stereotyped, 36 percent did so because they did not want to make people uncomfortable, and 31 percent were worried about losing connections or relationships with work colleagues. Finally, 13 percent of respondents said they worried that they would be fired if their sexual orientation became known at their workplace (Paul 2019). Discrimination against transgender people is more widespread and thus there are more likely to be negative consequences for them if they choose to come out. A 2009 survey found that more than one in four transgender people had lost a job due to their gender identity and more than three-fourths of transgender people had been mistreated at work in some way. Mistreatment at work was almost universally reported (97 percent) by transgender people of color (Grant et al. 2011).

In *Bostock v. Clayton County*, a historic decision handed down in June 2020, the U.S. Supreme Court ruled that the 1964 Civil Rights Act protects gay, lesbian, and transgender employees from discrimination based on sex (see Q10 and Q13). Justice Neil Gorsuch, President Trump's first appointee to the Supreme Court, wrote the majority opinion. It was a 6–3 ruling, with Chief Justice John Roberts and the court's four liberal justices agreeing. Gorsuch wrote, in part, "Today, we must decide whether an employer can fire someone simply for being homosexual or transgender. The answer is clear." The ruling relied on the text of the 1964 law that bans discrimination in employment due to race, national origin, religion, and sex. "It is impossible to discriminate against a person for being homosexual or transgender without discriminating. . . . based on sex," wrote Gorsuch. He gave the example of two employees attracted to men—one male, the other female. "If the employer fires the male employee for no reason other than the fact that he is attracted to men," but not the woman who is attracted to men, that is clearly a firing based on sex (Totenberg 2020).

A 2017 Gallup survey found that more adults identified as LGBTQ compared to similar data collected in 2012, although it is unclear whether this also means that more people are coming out. Gallup found that 4.1 percent of respondents identified as LGBTQ, up from 3.5 percent in 2012. Most of the increase was among millennials, defined as those born between 1980 and 1998; LGBTQ identification also increased among women, non-Latinx Asians, and Latinx Americans (Gates 2017).

FURTHER READING

Aizenman, Nurith. 2019. "How to Demand a Medical Breakthrough: Lessons from the AIDS Fight." NPR, February 9. https://www.npr.org/sections/health-shots/2019/02/09/689924838/how-to-demand-a-medical-breakthrough-lessons-from-the-aids-fight

Associated Press. 1995. "Robert Eichberg, 50, Gay Rights Leader." *New York Times*, August 15. https://www.nytimes.com/1995/08/15/obituaries/robert-eichberg-50-gay-rights-leader.html

Gates, Gary. 2017. "In U.S., More Adults Identifying as LGBT." Gallup, January 11. https://news.gallup.com/poll/201731/lgbt-identification-rises.aspx

Grant, Jaime M., et al. 2011. *Injustice at Every Turn: A Report of the National Transgender Discrimination Survey*. Washington, DC: National Center for Transgender Equality and National Gay and Lesbian Task Force.

Milk, Harvey. 1978. "That's What America Is." *Speech given at Gay Freedom Day Parade of June 25, 1978*, San Francisco, CA. Transcript provided in Schilts, Randy. 1982. *The Mayor of Castro Street: The Life and Times of Harvey Milk*. New York: St. Martin's Press.

Paul, Kari. 2019. "Nearly 50% of LGBTQ Americans Are in the Closet at Work." MarketWatch, October 11. https://www.marketwatch.com/story/half-of-lgbtq-americans-are-not-out-to-co-workers-2018-06-27

Pew Research Center. 2013. "A Survey of LGBT Americans: Attitudes, Experiences and Values in Changing Times." Pew Research Center,

June 13. https://www.pewsocialtrends.org/wp-content/uploads/sites/3
/2013/06/SDT_LGBT-Americans_06-2013.pdf

Saguy, Abigail C. 2020. *Come Out, Come Out, Whoever You Are.* New
York: Oxford University Press.

Salam, Maya. 2017. "If You're Asking, 'Am I Gay? Lesbian? Bi? Trans?
Queer?' Here's a Start." *New York Times*, May 17. https://www.nytimes
.com/2017/05/17/smarter-living/gay-lesbian-bisexual-transgender.html

Totenberg, Nina. 2020. "Supreme Court Delivers Major Victory to LGBTQ
Employees." NPR, June 15. https://www.npr.org/2020/06/15/863498848
/supreme-court-delivers-major-victory-to-lgbtq-employees

Q18: ARE THERE MORE OPENLY LGBTQ ELECTED OFFICIALS THAN THERE USED TO BE?

Answer: Yes. There were almost no openly gay elected officials in the United States until the 1980s but as of May 2021, there are 987 openly LGBTQ elected officials nationwide, an estimated 0.19 percent of all elected officials (LGBTQ Victory Institute 2021). This statistic represents a huge increase over time and a giant step forward from the first electoral victories by openly LGBTQ candidates in the 1970s and 1980s.

The Facts: The number of openly LGBTQ elected officials has blossomed in recent years, inspiring headlines about a "Rainbow Wave" in 2018, when 300 of over 700 openly LGBTQ candidates won their elections. Great strides have been made in this regard since 1973 when Kathy Kozachenko, who won a seat on the city council in Ann Arbor, Michigan, became the first openly LGBTQ candidate elected to public office. Despite this trend, however, openly LGBTQ people make up only 0.19 percent of all elected officials, far below their proportion of the total U.S. population.

Pete Buttigieg, former mayor of South Bend, Indiana, became the first openly gay candidate to be a major contender for a U.S. party's presidential nomination in 2019 and the first to win a state's nominating primary or caucus. He came out as gay in 2015 while running for reelection in South Bend. While his bid for the Democratic nomination was not successful, his candidacy was a notable step forward for LGBTQ Americans with political aspirations. After the 2020 election, president-elect Joe Biden nominated Buttigieg to be Secretary of Transportation and on February 3, 2021, he became the first openly LGBTQ person to serve in a cabinet position.

Buttigieg's candidacy also marked a milestone in the efforts of the LGBTQ community to accrue more political clout and to get more LGBTQ people elected to public office. For many years, homophobic attitudes among American voters had made many LGBTQ people feel that running for office was a waste of time. But a few candidates made successful bids in progressive areas of the country and their example and encouragement proved vital in inspiring the next generation of LGBTQ candidates.

Perhaps the most famous openly LGBTQ politician was Harvey Milk, the first openly gay elected official in the history of California when he was elected to the San Francisco Board of Supervisors in 1977. He served nearly 11 months in office, during which he sponsored bills banning discrimination on the basis of sexual orientation in public accommodations, housing, and employment. He also encouraged fellow members of the LGBTQ community to run for elected office. "It's not my victory, it's yours and yours and yours," he said to LGBTQ supporters after his election victory. "If a gay can win, it means there is hope that the system can work for all minorities if we fight. We've given them hope" (Fitzsimons 2018). Milk was assassinated in 1978 by a disgruntled fellow council member who had clashed with Milk over LGBTQ issues. While Milk was only in office a short time, his story inspired many other LGBTQ people to run for public office.

The Victory Fund, founded in 1991 by LGBTQ activists Vic Basile and William Waybourn as a nonpartisan political action committee, has a stated mission of electing "LGBTQ people to positions at all levels of government." The 2018 midterm election saw record numbers of LGBTQ candidates running for office (Stack 2018b) and a record number of those candidates won (Caron 2018). According to the Victory Fund, at least 399 LGBTQ candidates in all levels of government, including 22 for Congress and four for governor, were on the ballot in states across the country, the highest ever recorded in the fund's history. Most were Democrats though there were 18 Republicans and seven independents. Overall, of 802 LGBTQ elected officials serving in 2020, only 21 identify as Republican.

While being openly LGBTQ may have been an obstacle to winning elective office in the past, it has become an asset in many areas of the country. As Annise Parker, president and CEO of the Victory Fund and former mayor of Houston, said after the 2018 victories, "We're not going out and pleading with people to run. These are people who say, 'I want to go out and do this and bring my whole self to the campaign'" (Caron 2018). For example, until 2018, Kansas was one of seven states that had never elected an openly LGBTQ state legislator. In the midterm elections that year, Brandon Woodard, who identifies as gay, and Susan Ruiz, a lesbian, were elected state representatives (Caron 2018). Sharice Davids also won a seat in the U.S. House of Representatives in Kansas's 3rd district, becoming the first lesbian elected to Congress from the state. Also in 2018, several notable incumbents were reelected, including Oregon governor Kate Brown, who is bisexual, and Wisconsin senator Tammy Baldwin, a lesbian who was the first openly LGBTQ person ever elected to the U.S. Senate.

LGBTQ people of color won several state legislative seats in 2018, including Sonya Jaquez Lewis of Colorado, a Latina lesbian; Shevrin Jones of Florida, a Black gay man who became the first LGBTQ person of color elected to the Florida legislature; and Malcolm Kenyatta, a Black gay man and the first openly LGBTQ person of color ever elected to the Pennsylvania state legislature (Caron 2018). Also in 2018, Democratic congressman Jared Polis of Colorado became the first openly gay man ever elected as governor of a U.S. state.

The campaign trail in 2018 was not without difficulty, however. Many candidates faced bias, discrimination, and threats. For example, Gina Ortiz Jones, a Democratic candidate in Texas's 23rd Congressional District, was forced to acknowledge her sexual orientation after being asked onstage by an opponent to tell voters that she was a lesbian so it would not be "revealed later." She narrowly lost the election to incumbent Republican Will Hurd (R-TX).

In 2017, Danica Roem, then 33 years old, became the first openly transgender person elected to the Virginia legislature, defeating an incumbent Republican, Bob Marshall, who had served 14 terms and was hostile to transgender people and rights. During the campaign, Marshall repeatedly misgendered Ms. Roem, using male pronouns to refer to her (Siddiqui 2017). Roem's victory inspired other transgender people to run for office in subsequent years.

At the time, there had only been one other openly transgender person elected to a state legislature in the United States: Democrat Stacie Laughton won a seat in the New Hampshire House in 2012 but never took office because of an undisclosed felony conviction. Althea Garrison, elected to the Massachusetts House in 1992, came out as transgender during her term in office; she subsequently lost every election after coming out (Astor 2017). Roem's victory, then, was a notable one. But it was not the only 2017 race won by transgender candidates. Andrea Jenkins and Phillipe Cunningham won races to join the Minneapolis City Council; Jenkins is the first openly transgender African American person to be elected to office in the United States. Other transgender candidates elected in 2017 included Lisa Middleton, who won a seat on the Palm Springs City Council, and Tyler Titus, elected to the Erie School Board.

In what some have called the "Year of the Lesbian Mayor," 2019 election victories include Lori Lightfoot, the first lesbian, first woman, and first Black person ever to be elected mayor of Chicago. Other notable mayoral victories by LGBTQ candidates included Jane Castor's bid to become mayor of Tampa, Florida, and Satya Rhodes-Conway's triumph in Madison, Wisconsin (Ring 2019).

As of early 2020, openly LGBTQ elected officials included two governors, nine members of Congress, seven statewide officials, 43 mayors, 156 state legislators, 474 other local officials, and 107 judicial members across the United States. This represents a huge increase in representation since the early victories of Kathy Kozachenko and Harvey Milk in the 1970s. In the November 2020 election, at least 1,006 LGBTQ candidates ran for office in the United States, more than ever before. The 2020 results marked a 41 percent increase over the 2018 midterms, according to the LGBTQ Victory Fund (Bussey 2020). In New York, attorney Mondaire Jones and City Councilman Ritchie Torres won their races to become the first gay Black men elected to the U.S. House; Torres identifies as Afro Latino (Crary 2020).

The year 2020 brought a flurry of firsts at the state level as well. Delaware elected Democrat Sarah McBride as its first transgender state senator. McBride is the first openly transgender person to serve in a state senate anywhere in the country. Two other transgender women—Taylor Smalls and Stephanie Byers—won notable state-level races in Vermont and Kansas, respectively. Shevrin Jones won his race to become the first LGBTQ person to win a seat in the Florida state Senate (moving up from the Florida House of Representatives); Michele Rayner won her seat in the Florida House to become the first openly LGBTQ woman of color elected to the Florida legislature. In Tennessee, Republican Eddie Mannis, who is gay, and Democrat Torrey Harris, who identifies as bisexual, won their seats to become the first openly LGBTQ members of the Tennessee state House (Crary 2020). These are just some of many notable firsts throughout the country in terms of electing LGBTQ people into political office (Out.com 2020).

Overall, voters in the 2020 election chose hundreds of LGBTQ candidates in local, state, and federal races. Now, all 50 states have been served in some capacity by an openly LGBTQ elected politician and 47 states have elected an openly LGBT politician to one or both houses of their state legislature, according to the LGBTQ Victory Fund. Only Alaska, Louisiana, and Mississippi have never elected an openly LGBTQ legislator (Crary 2020). LGBTQ advocates assert that this representation has been vital in communicating to LGBTQ people that they have a place in the mainstream of American political life and that their concerns and priorities are being heard and respected.

FURTHER READING

Allen, Samantha. 2018. "Brianna Titone Just Made Transgender History in Colorado." Daily Beast, November 13. https://www.thedailybeast .com/brianna-titone-just-made-transgender-history-in-colorado

Astor, Maggie. 2017. "Danica Roem Wins Virginia Race, Breaking a Barrier for Transgender People." *New York Times*, November 7. https://www .nytimes.com/2017/11/07/us/danica-roem-virginia-transgender.html

Bussey, Timothy R. 2020. "'Rainbow Wave' of LGBTQ Candidates Run and Win in 2020 Election." The Conversation, November 4. https:// theconversation.com/rainbow-wave-of-lgbtq-candidates-run-and-win -in-2020-election-149066

Buttigieg, Pete. 2015. "South Bend Mayor: Why Coming Out Matters." *South Bend Tribune*, June 16. https://www.southbendtribune.com/news /local/south-bend-mayor-why-coming-out-matters/article_4dce0d12 -1415-11e5-83c0-739eebd623ee.html

Caron, Christina. 2018. "In 'Rainbow Wave,' L.G.B.T. Candidates Are Elected in Record Numbers." *New York Times*, November 7. https:// www.nytimes.com/2018/11/07/us/politics/lgbt-election-winners-midterms .html

Crary, David. 2020. "In Blue and Red States, Milestone Wins for LGBTQ Candidates." AP, November 4. https://apnews.com/article/lgbtq-candidates -milestone-election-f33555c8fd1a8d2c31417cc60bf0022c

Dison, Denis. 2012. "Victory Fund Celebrates Huge Night for Gay Candidates." Gay Politics, November 7. Archived at https://web.archive.org /web/20121108175351/http:/www.gaypolitics.com/2012/11/07/victory -fund-celebrates-huge-night-for-gay-candidates/

Fitzsimons, Tim. 2018. "Forty Years After His Death, Harvey Milk's Legacy Still Lives On." NBCNews.com, November 27. https://www.nbcnews .com/feature/nbc-out/forty-years-after-his-death-harvey-milk-s-legacy -still-n940356

Johnson, Chris. 2019. "Lesbian Candidate Wins Big in Tampa Mayoral Race." *Washington Blade*, April 23. https://www.washingtonblade.com /2019/04/23/lesbian-candidate-wins-big-in-tampa-mayoral-race/

LGBTQ Victory Institute. 2021. "Out for America." https://outforamerica .org

Out.com. 2020. "Rainbow Wave 2020: LGBTQ+ Candidates Who Won on Election Night." *Out.com*, November 3. https://www.out.com /politics/2020/11/03/all-lgbtq-candidates-won-2020-election#media -gallery-media-2

Reese, Phil. 2012. "2012 Proving Busy Year for Victory Fund." *Washington Blade*, April 26. https://www.washingtonblade.com/2012/04/26/2012 -proving-busy-year-for-victory-fund/

Reynolds, Andrew. 2018. *The Children of Harvey Milk: How LGBTQ Politicians Changed the World*. New York: Oxford University Press.

Ring, Trudy. 2019. "The Top LGBTQ Stories of the 2010s." *The Advocate*, December 31. https://www.advocate.com/politics/2019/12/31/top-lgbtq -stories-2010s#media-gallery-media-8

Shilts, Randy. 1982. *The Mayor of Castro Street*. New York: St. Martin's Griffin.

Siddiqui, Faiz. 2017. "Campaign Flier Paid for by Virginia GOP 'Misgenders' Democratic Candidate." *Washington Post*, October 28. https://www .washingtonpost.com/local/virginia-politics/campaign-flier-paid-for-by -virginia-gop-misgenders-democratic-candidate/2017/10/28/91e28e6c -bc1d-11e7-9e58-e6288544af98_story.html

Stack, Liam. 2018a. "Christine Hallquist Would Like to Talk about the Power Grid." *New York Times*, October 17. https://www.nytimes .com/2018/10/17/us/politics/christine-hallquist-vermont.html

Stack, Liam. 2018b. "Facing Threats and Bias, L.G.B.T. Candidates Are Running in Record Numbers." *New York Times*, November 5. https:// www.nytimes.com/2018/11/05/us/politics/lgbt-candidates.html

Q19: ARE THERE MORE LGBTQ PEOPLE ON TV AND IN MOVIES THAN THERE USED TO BE?

Answer: Yes, there has been a significant increase in the number of openly LGBTQ people in both television and movies. Having more representation for LGBTQ people can be a powerful force in eliminating stereotypes and reducing prejudice, provided the media portrayals are realistic and fair.

The Facts: Research suggests that fictional characters we see in the media can have a significant impact on the way individuals perceive real people in the world around them. Some watchers of television and movies can even come to feel that they are in a sort of relationship with those characters. This is also known as parasocial contact or parasocial interaction (Horton and Wohl 1956). These relationships can work in different

ways. When there are increased numbers of diverse identity groups represented on TV and movies, there are more opportunities for connections to
be made with people with whom viewers might not interact on a regular
basis. On the other hand, negative media portrayals can also perpetuate
stereotypes and create more distance between different socioeconomic and
demographic groups.

Starting in 1996, GLAAD has issued a report tracking the number of
LGBTQ characters on television. In the 1996–1997 season, the group
found 34 LGBTQ characters on television. In its 2020–2021 report,
GLAAD found that over the 773 regular, recurring characters in broadcast
scripted prime-time television, 70 (9.1 percent) are LGBTQ, a decrease
from a record high of 10.2 percent in 2019–2020. (Regular characters are
defined as those who appear in every episode or the majority of episodes in
a series.) They also found an additional 31 LGBTQ recurring characters on
broadcast, 95 regular LGBTQ characters on original scripted series, and 46
LGBTQ recurring characters on streaming services Amazon, Hulu, and
Netflix, all decreases from the prior year. In total, they report 141 LGBTQ
characters, down from 153 in 2019–2020. The GLAAD report notes that
these decreases were expected due to the COVID-19 pandemic stopping or
slowing production and negatively impacting the creation of new shows.

Across all three platforms (broadcast, cable, and streaming), GLAAD's
report documented a 2 percentage-point increase in bisexual characters in
2020–2021, finding the numbers still lean toward women (65 women and
33 men) and only one character who is nonbinary. There are 29 regular and
recurring transgender characters (15 trans women, 12 trans men, and 2 trans
characters who are nonbinary); 26 of the 29 characters are either played or
voiced by transgender actors (Townsend and Deerwater 2021).

Pioneering Gay and Lesbian Characters

On April 30, 1997, actress Ellen DeGeneres made history in what is called
"the puppy episode"—a deliberately misleading title chosen to throw off
folks who had heard rumors of what was coming—when she came out as
gay on her *Ellen* sitcom. The episode aired two weeks after she publicly
came out on the cover of *Time* magazine. While the show lost viewers and
was soon cancelled, it paved the way for future shows with prominent
LGBTQ characters and personalities like *Will & Grace* (1998–2006), *Buffy
the Vampire Slayer* (1997–2003), *Queer as Folk* (2000–2005), *Six Feet Under*
(2001–2005), *Queer Eye for the Straight Guy* (2003–2007), *Brothers and
Sisters* (2006–2011), *True Blood* (2008–2014), *Glee* (2009–2015), *Modern
Family* (2009–2020), and *American Gods* (2017–present).

The inclusion of gay and lesbian characters in mainstream television shows and movies took a major step forward with the show *Will & Grace*. Premiering the year after Ellen's coming-out episode, the show about a gay man (Will) living with his straight best friend (Grace) was notable because it prominently featured gay men during a primetime sitcom on a major network and because that portrayal was largely positive (Framke 2017). Because the highly acclaimed show also garnered strong viewership ratings, gay lead characters Will and Jack became a staple of many American living rooms. Their characters changed many American minds about gay people and about marriage equality (Garretson 2018). In his May 2012 remarks endorsing same-sex marriage, Vice President Joe Biden commented, "I think 'Will & Grace' probably did more to educate the American public than almost anything anybody has ever done so far" (Borden 2017).

The ability of gay and lesbian characters in television and media to create positive attitudes toward gay men and lesbians more broadly is predicated on positive, reinforced exposure to those characters. In other words, while previous shows included occasional or minor gay characters, they were often portrayed in negative ways that did not build connections to viewers. Television shows like *Ellen* and *Will & Grace* broke that norm. Additional shows followed, as did public opinion. Similarly, mainstream movies with compelling gay and lesbian roles also became much more common in the twenty-first century. Examples of these influential films— some of which included well-known Hollywood leading men playing the roles of gay men—include *Brokeback Mountain* (2005), *The Kids Are All Right* (2010), and the Oscar-winning best picture *Moonlight* (2016).

Transgender Characters

Transgender characters tend to be portrayed less positively than gay men and lesbians, resulting in less positive (and less accurate) media exposure. In 2012, GLAAD documented 102 episodes and nonrecurring storylines of scripted television from the previous decade that contained transgender characters. The group found that 54 percent of the story lines contained "negative representations at the time of their airing," with an additional 35 percent ranging from problematic to good. Only 12 percent were considered fair and accurate by the organization (GLAAD 2012). GLAAD also found that 40 percent of transgender characters were cast in a "victim role"; 21 percent of transgender characters were either killers or villains, and the most common profession of transgender characters was sex worker (20 percent of the sample). Anti-transgender slights, language, and dialogue were present in roughly 60 percent of the episodes and story lines. In 2014, GLAAD issued an updated report that acknowledged that depictions of transgender characters had improved; nonetheless, the organization claimed that nearly half (45 percent) of all portrayals of transgender people were based on negative, damaging stereotypes (Townsend 2014). The most recent GLAAD report from 2020–2021 does not characterize the portrayals of transgender characters in media.

Until fairly recently, it was unlikely that Americans would experience any parasocial contact with a transgender person or that that exposure would include transgender characters in film and television who were portrayed positively. Until a few years ago, transgender characters portrayed in media were frequently cartoonish in nature, often depicted as deviant, predatory, and/or mentally ill.

Another limitation of parasocial contact with transgender people is that transgender characters have historically been played by cisgender actors. For example, in one of the earliest portrayals of a transgender person, Tim Curry (a cisgender man) famously played the character Dr. Frank N. Furter in *The Rocky Horror Picture Show* (1975), an over-the-top, self-proclaimed "sweet transvestite from Transsexual, Transylvania." In 1992, Jaye Davidson (also a cisgender male) played the character Dil, a transgender woman who hid her gender identity in the film *The Crying Game*. Even contemporary portrayals that attempted to accurately tell the stories of transgender people have fallen short. For example, the 1999 movie *Boys Don't Cry* was a dramatization of real-life events surrounding the murder of Brandon Teena, a transgender man who was sexually assaulted and murdered. Teena was portrayed by Hilary Swank, a cisgender female. Similarly, cisgender actors like Jared Leto in *The Dallas Buyers Club* and Jeffrey Tambor in *Transparent* have increased the visibility of the transgender population, though with backlash from those who would have preferred casting of transgender actors.

There has been some progress, however, as some transgender characters have become more multidimensional and sympathetic than in previous years. For example, transgender actress Laverne Cox depicted Sophia Burset, a transgender woman of color, on the Netflix series *Orange Is the New Black* from 2013 to 2019. Cox earned a 2014 Emmy award nomination for the role in recognition of the complexity and depth of her portrayal. GLAAD has recognized episodes of shows like *Grey's Anatomy* (ABC), *Cold Case* (CBS), and *Two and a Half Men* (CBS) with GLAAD Media Award nominations for their realistic and positive depictions of transgender people. It has also praised shows like *The Education of Max Bickford* (CBS), *Degrassi* (Teen Nick), *The Riches* (FX), and *Ugly Betty* (ABC) for

their "fully-formed and complex representations of transgender people"
(GLAAD 2012). In 2018, this list expanded even further, including the FX
series *Pose*, which includes five transgender actors of color cast in regular
roles, setting a record for a scripted series (Goldberg 2017). The third episode was directed by Janet Mock, marking the first time an openly transgender woman of color had written and directed any television episode
(Gemmill 2018). Other additions, in 2019, included characters on *Supergirl*
(on the CW), where transgender actor Nicole Maines plays a transgender
superhero named Dreamer, and on *The Chilling Adventures of Sabrina*
(Netflix), which includes as a story line the transition of nonbinary actor
Lachlan Wilson from Susie to Theo. In 2020–2021, transgender characters
and actors were featured in a wide variety of shows, from scripted broadcast
shows like ABC's *Grey's Anatomy* and *The Conners* and Fox's *9-1-1: Lone
Star* to cable shows like *Pose*, *Billions*, and *The Chi*. As transgender characters are portrayed more positively and more frequently in the media, particularly on shows that attract a widespread audience, transgender
Americans hope that those representations will help them in the same way
that *Ellen* and *Will & Grace* helped lesbian and gay Americans gain greater
social acceptance.

FURTHER READING

Borden, Jane. 2017. "'Will & Grace' Reduced Homophobia, but Can It Still
    Have an Impact Today?" *Washington Post*, September 15. https://www
    .washingtonpost.com/entertainment/will-and-grace-reduced-homophobia
    -but-can-it-still-have-an-impact-today/2017/09/14/0e6b0994-9704-11e7
    -82e4-f1076f6d6152_story.html
Framke, Caroline. 2017. "Will & Grace Is Back, and So Is the Debate over
    Its Place in LGBTQ History." Vox.com, September 29. https://www.vox
    .com/fall-tv/2017/9/29/16360962/will-and-grace-history-controversy
Garretson, Jeremiah. 2018. *The Path to Gay Rights: How Activism and Com-
    ing Out Changed Public Opinion.* New York: New York University Press.
Gemmill, Allie. 2018. "Janet Mock Wrote and Directed an Episode of
    'Pose' and Made TV History." *Teen Vogue*, July 9. https://www.teenvogue
    .com/story/janet-mock-wrote-directed-episode-of-pose-made-tv-history
GLAAD. 2012. "Victims or Villains: Examining Ten Years of Transgender
    Images on Television." GLAAD, November 20. https://www.glaad.org
    /publications/victims-or-villains-examining-ten-years-transgender
    -images-television

Goldberg, Lesley. 2017. "Ryan Murphy Makes History with Largest Cast of Transgender Actors for FX's 'Pose.'" *Hollywood Reporter*, October 25. https://www.hollywoodreporter.com/live-feed/ryan-murphy-makes -history-largest-cast-transgender-actors-fxs-pose-1051877

Horton, Donald, and R. Richard Wohl. 1956. "Mass Communication and Para-Social Interaction." *Psychiatry: Interpersonal and Biological Processes* 19, 3: 215–229.

Michelson, Melissa. R., and Brian F. Harrison. 2020. *Transforming Prejudice: Identity, Fear, and Transgender Rights.* New York: Oxford University Press.

Serano, Julia. 2013. "Skirt Chasers: Why the Media Depicts the Trans Revolution in Lipstick and Heels." In Susan Stryker and Aren Z. Aizura, eds., *The Transgender Studies Reader 2.* New York: Routledge, pp. 226–233.

Townsend, Megan. 2014. "GLAAD's Third Annual Trans Images on TV Report Finds Some Improvement." GLAAD, November 18. https:// www.glaad.org/blog/glaads-third-annual-trans-images-tv-report-finds -some-improvement

Townsend, Megan, and Raina Deerwater. 2021. "Where We Are on TV 2020–2021." GLAAD Media Institute, https://www.glaad.org /whereweareontv20.

4

Gender Identity, Performance, and Dynamics

Expectations for how people behave and act are closely linked to how people think and feel about LGBTQ people. In particular, a belief that there are only two genders (male and female) as well as gender norms and expectations can lead people to adhere to stereotypes and myths that simply aren't true.

Chapter 4 discusses these dynamics in more detail, explaining how misconceptions about gender and sex can limit a complete understanding of LGBTQ identity. Q20 tackles the question of relationship dynamics and the misconception that in any relationship, regardless of the gender of the people, one person needs to act as the man and one as the woman. This expectation can perpetuate harmful ideas of how people should behave and look. Q21 addresses the question of whether lesbians have fundamentally different views toward men than other women while Q22 addresses the parallel myth about how gay men feel about women and about lesbians in particular. Q23 addresses the myth that bisexuals are confused people who are either straight or gay but can't make up their mind.

Q24 and Q25 investigate expectations of masculinity and femininity in gay men and lesbians, respectively, and how these expectations are based on outdated stereotypes of the LGBTQ community. Q26 explains why people with nonheterosexual sexual orientation and non-cisgender gender identities are grouped together in the LGBTQ community. Finally, Q27 outlines the differences between cross-dressing, drag, and transgender identity, confronting the myth that men who enjoy cross-dressing and/or drag are really transgender people.

Q20: DO LGBTQ RELATIONSHIPS HAVE THE SAME DYNAMICS THAT STRAIGHT RELATIONSHIPS DO?

Answer: Not necessarily, no. Some individuals in LGBTQ relationships align themselves with notions of "husband" or "wife" that are similar to straight gender dynamics while others adopt more egalitarian, non-gendered, or nonnormative gender roles.

The Facts: The mistaken belief that individuals in LGBTQ relationships (relationships among gay, lesbian, bisexual, and transgender people) inevitably reproduce straight gender dynamics stems from the outdated and inaccurate theory that LGBTQ attraction is a result of skewed gender roles, an idea endorsed by Sigmund Freud. However, modern science finds no evidence that this societal stereotype is true.

Overall, when compared to roles in heterosexual couples, relationship patterns among LGBTQ people tend to not follow a stereotypical masculine/feminine pattern. In other words, LGBTQ couples do not generally include one partner who is the "man" and one who is the "woman." It is true that same-sex lesbian couples are more likely to include one femme-identifying partner (one partner who performs gender in more stereotypically feminine ways); one butch-identifying partner (one partner who performs gender in more stereotypically masculine ways); or two androgynous partners rather than two butch-identifying partners or two femme-identifying partners. However, these self-identifications do not predict roles in those relationships such as who does a larger share of the housework (Rothblum, Balsam, and Wickham 2018). Rather than mimicking traditional husband-wife relationship and household responsibility patterns, many of these couples establish more egalitarian relationships that value equity in responsibility and influence. Of course, some heterosexual relationships do not abide by traditional gender roles either. LGBTQ couples tend to minimize traditional notions of role-playing; even when inequality exists in divisions of household work or in sexual intimacy issues, these inequalities are unrelated to masculinity or femininity (Lev 2010; Doan and Quadlin 2019; Geist and Ruppanner 2018; Reczek 2020).

Researchers have acknowledged that "traditional culturally constructed gender roles are presumed to be both desirable and consistent across the spectrum of human sexual identities" (Felmlee, Orzechowicz, and Fortes 2010, 227). However, in a study of romantic attractions among gay men and lesbians, sociologist Diane Felmlee and her colleagues found little evidence that members of same-sex partnerships were "attempting to reconstruct a purportedly typical heterosexual relationship model in which one partner is supposed to be primarily masculine in gender role orientation while the other is expected to be feminine" (Felmlee et al. 2010, 237). This is consistent with older studies conducted in the 1970s, 1980s, and 1990s (see Peplau and Spalding 2000, 113–114).

While traditional gender roles are less common in LGBTQ couples, they do still occur. This can be attributed in part to exposure to models of gender role-playing among opposite-sex couples in cultural representations (books, television, religious texts, etc.). In other words, because everyone is exposed to these same cultural norms, they can choose to reproduce these roles in their own relationships to some extent. However, those normative models are less internalized among LGBTQ couples because they do not see themselves in those representations of how to behave as a couple. In addition, they may see their relationship as a unique form of relationship. They are also more likely to understand gender as existing along a spectrum (rather than as a binary including male and female only) and thus be less likely to see their own gender identity as necessarily linked to a particular gender role (Marecek, Finn, and Cardell 1982; Nagoshi et al. 2014).

Related to how they experience relationship dynamics, LGBTQ people are less likely to define themselves on an individual level as exclusively masculine or feminine. They are more likely than heterosexual and cisgender people to understand that gender roles can be expressed in ways that do not always correspond to traditional gender identities—that masculinity and femininity are social constructs and that there are many ways to perform gender that are separate from being male or female (Nagoshi et al. 2014). Social work researchers Julie Rosenzweig and Wendy Lebow attribute some of this flexibility in gender roles among lesbians to the sexual revolution and the women's movement of the 1970s, when traditional gender roles began to loosen (Rosenzweig and Lebow 1992). Their survey found that far more lesbians perceive themselves to be androgynous or of a neutral gender compared to those who see themselves as feminine or masculine.

Gender roles are more fluid in LGBTQ relationships because they are not bound by the same cultural expectations. Heterosexual, cisgender men and women in opposite-sex relationships usually conform to traditional cultural norms about how to be part of a couple and there is relatively little conflict over these roles. In LGBTQ couples, in contrast, there is more freedom for the partners to build their roles in the relationship based on talents, skills, personal interests, and employment schedules. Thus, rather than conforming to traditional norms about it being more appropriate for the woman in a relationship to take primary responsibility for housework, members of a same-sex couple may divide up the housework duties based on each individual's preferences and skills and in ways that are mutually satisfying (Mackey, O'Brien, and Mackey 1997).

FURTHER READING

Doan, Long, and Natasha Quadlin. 2019. "Partner Characteristics and Perceptions of Responsibility for Housework and Child Care." *Journal of Marriage and Family* 81, 1: 145–163.

Felmlee, Diane, David Orzechowicz, and Carmen Fortes. 2010. "Fairy Tales: Attraction and Stereotypes in Same-Gender Relationships." *Sex Roles* 62, 3–4: 226–240.

Geist, Claudia, and Leah Ruppanner. 2018. "Mission Impossible? New Housework Theories for Changing Families." *Journal of Family Theory & Review* 10, 1: 242–262.

Lev, Arlene Istar. 2010. "How Queer!—The Development of Gender Identity and Sexual Orientation in LGBTQ-Headed Families." *Family Process* 49, 3: 268–290.

Mackey, Richard A., Bernard A. O'Brien, and Eileen F. Mackey. 1997. *Gay and Lesbian Couples: Voices from Lasting Relationships*. Westport, CT: Praeger Publishers.

Marecek, Jeanne, Stephen E. Finn, and Mona Cardell. 1982. "Gender Roles in the Relationships of Lesbians and Gay Men." *Journal of Homosexuality* 8, 2: 45–49.

Nagoshi, Julie L., Heather K. Terrell, Craig T. Nagoshi, and Stephanie Brzuzy. 2014. "The Complex Negotiations of Gender Roles, Gender Identity, and Sexual Orientation among Heterosexual, Gay/Lesbian, and Transgender Individuals." *Journal of Ethnographic & Qualitative Research* 8, 4: 205–221.

Peplau, Letitia Anne, and Leah R. Spalding. 2000. "The Close Relationships of Lesbians, Gay Men, and Bisexuals." In Clyde Hendrick and Susan S. Hendrick, eds., *Close Relationships: A Sourcebook*. Thousand Oaks, CA: Sage Publications, pp. 111–124.

Reczek, Corinne. 2020. "Sexual- and Gender-Minority Families: A 2010 to 2020 Decade in Review." *Journal of Marriage and the Family* 82, 1: 300–325.

Rosenzweig, Julie M., and Wendy C. Lebow. 1992. "Femme on the Streets, Butch in the Sheets?" *Journal of Homosexuality* 23, 3: 1–20.

Rothblum, Esther D., Kimberly F. Balsam, and Robert E. Wickham. 2018. "Butch, Femme, and Androgynous Gender Identities within Female Same-Sex Couples: An Actor-Partner Analysis." *Psychology of Sexual Orientation and Gender Diversity* 5, 1: 72–81.

Q21: DO LESBIANS AND STRAIGHT WOMEN HARBOR DIFFERENT VIEWS AND ATTITUDES TOWARD MEN?

Answer: Lesbians have often been stereotyped as man-haters but studies indicate that they are no more likely to have negative attitudes toward men than straight women. The only difference is that lesbians are not sexually attracted to men.

The Facts: In the 1970s, some prominent radical feminists in the United States spoke of their hatred of men. Since then, misandry—the hatred of men—has often been attributed to feminists who are labeled "lesbians and man-haters." These stereotypes persist even today but overall, there is no evidence that lesbians hate men more than straight women do or that all feminists are secretly lesbians. These falsehoods are often perpetuated by heterosexual, cisgender men (and some women) who rely on stereotypes of angry, irrational women to discredit the true intent behind the societal changes that they seek.

In the 1970s and early 1980s, there was a movement led by lesbian feminists, cultural feminists, and lesbian separatists to create all-female communities that were physically, economically, and politically separate from wider society. Early separatists in San Francisco, Berkeley, New York, and Seattle tried to live lives entirely free from interaction with men, male values, and male culture. Some sects held radical beliefs inconsistent with mainstream feminism; for example, some lesbian separatists were drawn to "mutant male theory," believing men to be mutants and genetically inferior (Rensenbrink 2010). The most radical separatists even rejected mothering of male children, arguing that "these boys would inevitably grow up to be incorporated into the patriarchy as oppressors of women" (Rivers 2013, 158). The lesbian separatist movement waned in the early 1980s due to issues that included criticism from other feminists for an ideology that some considered racist and divisions related to separationist rejection of boy children (Rivers 2013; Rensenbrink 2010).

Women of color who lived in these lesbian separatist collectives agreed with the need to push back against patriarchy and sexism; however, they sometimes found the white lesbians who comprised the bulk of those collectives unwilling to recognize the need to also push back against white supremacy or their own racism or to address the way in which racism and sexism created intersectional challenges for women of color (Rensenbrink 2010). Divisions also stemmed from the presence of lesbian mothers with male children. Some separatists believed these children should be excluded (perhaps sent to their fathers or other relatives to be raised) while others felt that including sons of lesbians might cause those male children to learn to respect women; still others saw the anti–boy children policies as oppressive of mothers of sons. Disagreements also centered on the age at which boy children should be excluded, if at all, from lesbian communal spaces (Rivers 2013).

While lesbian separatism faded in the 1980s, stereotypes about lesbians as man-haters persisted. Media scholars attribute the persistence of the "lesbians hate men" stereotype to how lesbians were commonly portrayed in movies and television. Generally invisible in television and film until the early 1990s when they finally began appearing in mass media, lesbians were presented "for the pleasure of a carefully targeted consumer audience: straight men" (Streitmatter 2008, 81). In many cases, media portrayed lesbians as exemplars of pornography geared toward straight men's pleasure, suggesting lesbianism was fake or performative. In 1992, for example, Sharon Stone's lesbian character in *Basic Instinct* portrayed this exact stereotype, with Stone a promiscuous, homicidal lesbian who plunges an ice pick into her male lover. Her character played right into stereotypes since she had sex with men yet also had homicidal feelings toward them. Similar stereotypical descriptions of lesbians—as simultaneously homicidal and as man-haters—were common in newspaper descriptions of Aileen Wuornos, "the nation's first female serial killer," who was put on death row in Florida in 1992 (Bremmers 2020).

At the same time, it is true that lesbians have different attitudes compared to straight women about whether they find men to be sexually attractive. In other words, the concern with how to present oneself to men is often eliminated for lesbians because they have no interest in being found attractive or desirable by men. Author (and lesbian) Ariel Schrag put it this way:

The people who consistently complain about men are straight women. Lesbians don't care. If we want to be friends with a man, we will. If we don't, we, unlike straight women, have no needs that can be met only by men. In general, people hate others when they need something they're not getting from them. Anything else is just finding someone annoying. (Schrag 2014)

Numerous authors have noted the inaccuracy of the stereotype that lesbians are man-haters. Anna Redman, a contributor to *Gayly* magazine, wrote in a 2018 column that the stereotype is "rooted in misogyny and is largely baseless. . . . Frankly, lesbianism has nothing to do with men" (Redman 2018). Nonetheless, scholars have noted that negative attitudes toward men have long been a common stereotype attributed to lesbians (Simon 1998).

FURTHER READING

Adamski, Kim. 2014. "A History of Man-Hating: Separatism, Lesbianism, and Misrepresentation." WHUS.org, December 5. https://whus.org/2014/12/a-history-of-man-hating-separatism-lesbianism-and-misrepresentation-2/

Bremmers, I. A. M. 2020. *A Feminist Reconsideration of the Story of Aileen Wuornos: Hidden in the Shadows of the Media*. MS thesis, Utrecht University. https://dspace.library.uu.nl/handle/1874/398232

Redman, Jordan. 2018. "Being a Lesbian Has Nothing to Do with Men." *Gayly*, April 26. https://www.gayly.com/being-lesbian-has-nothing-do-men

Rensenbrink, Greta. 2010. "Parthenogenesis and Lesbian Separatism: Regenerating Women's Community through Virgin Birth in the United States in the 1970s and 1980s." *Journal of the History of Sexuality* 19, 2: 288–316.

Rivers, Daniel Winunwe. 2013. *Radical Relations: Lesbian Mothers, Gay Fathers, and Their Children in the United States since World War II*. Chapel Hill: University of North Carolina Press.

Schrag, Ariel. 2014. "9 Lesbian Myths, Debunked: Breaking Down the Common Misconceptions People Have about Lesbians." *Cosmopolitan*, January 15. https://www.cosmopolitan.com/entertainment/celebs/news/a5359/9-lesbian-myths-debunked/

Simon, Angela. 1998. "The Relationship between Stereotypes of and Attitudes toward Lesbians and Gays." In Gregory M. Herek, ed., *Stigma and Sexual Orientation: Understanding Prejudice against Lesbians, Gay Men and Bisexuals*. Thousand Oaks, CA: Sage Publications, pp. 62–81.

Streitmatter, Rodger. 2008. *From Perverts to Fab Five: The Media's Changing Depiction of Gay Men and Lesbians*. New York: Routledge.

Q22: DO GAY MEN HATE WOMEN, ESPECIALLY LESBIANS?

Answer: No. It is not true that gay men hate women in general or lesbians in particular; in fact, many men identify as feminists. At the same time, men of all sexual orientations—including gay and bisexual men—can be misogynists (prejudiced against women). This prejudice stems from their socialization as men in a culture that privileges men.

The Facts: The relationship between gay men and lesbians has been difficult at times. In the early 1970s, as the gay liberation movement was beginning, lesbians sometimes broke off from the first activist organizations due to the sexism exhibited by some gay men in the movement. "Frustrated with the male leadership of most gay liberation groups, lesbians influenced by the feminist movement of the 1970s formed their own collectives" (Morris 2009). Most men, regardless of their sexual orientation, were raised from birth with the privilege that stems from their biological gender. With that privilege comes a sense that they are preferred by society and are better than women, creating internal and/or external misogyny for men of any sexual orientation.

Charges of misogyny have been raised against gay men for decades. In a podcast interview in 2014, actor Rose McGowan, known for her role as an activist in the Me Too movement against sexual assault and harassment, sparked headlines for her comment that "gay men are as misogynistic as straight men, if not more so" (quoted in Blumell and Rodriguez 2020). This claim of gay misogyny—that gay men hate women—is rooted in theories about masculinity and masculine norms. Masculine norms refer to the desire by men regardless of their sexual orientation to be perceived as masculine in their mannerisms, dress, and other expressions, including the norm of having dominance over women. In addition, many men are raised to believe that anything feminine is inferior, leading to internalized misogyny and internalized homophobia, particularly toward effeminate men. These norms can also lead gay men to strongly prefer masculinity in themselves and their partners and to hold negative attitudes toward effeminacy (feminine behaviors, mannerisms, and styles) when exhibited by other men (Murgo et al. 2017). This preference for masculine norms, also known as hegemonic masculinity, naturalizes men's dominance over women and encourages men to engage in traditional masculine behavior, also known as performing masculinity. This can lead gay men to compensate for their sexuality (and thus deviance from dominant sexual norms) by "mascing"— emphasizing their masculine presentation of gender, enacting hypermasculine manners and behaviors to reject stereotypes about gay men or at least reduce the risk that those stereotypes might be employed against them (Rodriguez, Huemmer, and Blumell 2016). Men are privileged over women and masculinity is privileged over femininity; these privileges can, in turn, manifest as misogyny.

In other words, preference for masculine norms can lead gay men both to prefer masculinity in themselves and in their partners and to believe that men are superior to women. Researchers believe that gay men may exhibit sexism to compensate for their loss of status in the hegemonic hierarchy; they are lower in the social hierarchy than straight men but they can still be higher in the hierarchy than women (Blumell and Rodriguez 2020). According to scholars Sadie Hale and Tomás Ojeda, "gay male misogyny reinforces white male dominance over women and queer femininities specifically," reinforcing the existing gender and racial hierarchy (Hale and Ojeda 2018). Journalist Monica Rodman notes in an op-ed in the *Advocate* magazine, "Gay men—like the rest of us—are products of a patriarchal social structure, which feminist theorists believe is the root cause of female oppression in cultures throughout the world" (Rodman 2018). Harvard professor Michael Bronski notes: "In our culture of binary, heterosexual dysfunction, men hate women. It just so happens that some of them are gay" (quoted in O'Flynn 2018).

Author Rich Benjamin argues that misogyny by gay men is often overlooked due to stereotypes of gay men as more sensitive than straight men. This stereotype enables many gay men to get away with "scandalous chauvinism" while internalized sexism "still lards our interactions with women" (Benjamin 2019). Similarly, journalist Nico Lang wrote in 2017 that "when it comes to treating women like whole people, not objects or accessories, a lot of queer men have work to do.

> Because gay men, first and foremost, are men. We're not immune to the cultural conditioning that comes with growing up in a society that views femininity as "weak" and "lesser." Even if your best friends are women, that programming is difficult to break. Sexism among gay men persists because many of us don't feel the need to change, especially when the hierarchy that glorifies maleness seems to benefit us. (Lang 2017)

Gay author and journalist Michael Musto noted in a 2014 op-ed for *Out* magazine that this has not always been true. In the 1980s, particularly during the fight against the AIDS epidemic, lesbians and gay men often worked together. Contemporary political battles have provided multiple opportunities for gay men and lesbians to work in common cause for issues related to LGBTQ rights, like marriage equality, parenting and adoption, employment discrimination, and hate crimes. "Rather than gays versus lesbians, it became gays and lesbians versus the homophobic other" (Musto 2014).

FURTHER READING

Benjamin, Rich. 2019. "Op-Ed: Gay Men Need to Be Feminists, Too." *Los Angeles Times*, June 23. https://www.latimes.com/opinion/op-ed/la-oe -benjamin-gay-men-need-to-be-feminists-20190623-story.html

Blumell, Lindsey E., and Nathian Shae Rodriguez. 2020. "Ambivalent Sexism and Gay Men in the US and UK." *Sexuality & Culture* 24: 209–229.

Hale, Sadie E., and Tomás Ojeda. 2018. "Acceptable Femininity? Gay Male Misogyny and the Policing of Queer Femininities." *European Journal of Women's Studies* 25, 3: 310–324.

Lang, Nico. 2017. "Sorry, Gay Guys, I'm Not Here for Your Casual Misogyny." NewNowNext.com, March 8. http://www.newnownext.com/casual -misogyny/03/2017/

Morris, Bonnie J. 2009. "History of Lesbian, Gay, Bisexual and Transgender Social Movements." American Psychological Association. https:// www.apa.org/pi/lgbt/resources/history

Murgo, Michael A. J., et al. 2017. "Anti-Effeminacy Moderates the Relationship between Masculinity and Internalized Heterosexism among Gay Men." *Journal of LGBT Issues in Counseling* 11, 2: 106–118.

Musto, Michael. 2014. "Why Don't Gays and Lesbians Get Along Better?" *Out*, June 30. https://www.out.com/entertainment/michael-musto/2014 /06/30/why-don%E2%80%99t-gays-and-lesbians-get-along-better

O'Flynn, Brian. 2018. "'They Just Wanted to Silence Her': The Dark Side of Gay Stan Culture." *The Guardian*, September 4. https://www .theguardian.com/music/2018/sep/04/they-just-wanted-to-silence-her -the-dark-side-of-gay-stan-culture

Rodman, Monica. 2018. "Gay Men Can Be Misogynists Too." *Advocate*, July 20. https://www.advocate.com/commentary/2018/7/20/gay-men-can -be-misogynists-too

Rodriguez, Nathian Shae, Jennifer Huemmer, and Lindsey E. Blumell. 2016. "Mobile Masculinities: An Investigation of Networked Masculinities in Gay Dating Apps." *Masculinities and Social Change* 5, 3: 241–267.

Q23: ARE BISEXUAL PEOPLE JUST CONFUSED GAY (OR STRAIGHT) PEOPLE WHO CAN'T MAKE UP THEIR MIND?

Answer: No. Bisexuality is a valid identity that is distinct from other identities like heterosexuality and homosexuality. In addition, a person can be pansexual (sexually attracted to people regardless of their gender, gender identity, or sexual orientation).

The Facts: The term *bisexual* (or bi) describes people who have the capacity for emotional, romantic, and/or physical attraction to more than one sex or gender. Bisexual people can be in different-sex relationships, same-sex relationships, or, of course, no relationship at all.

Bisexuality is not the same thing as identifying as gay or lesbian. Many people deny the existence of bisexuality and assume that everyone who identifies as bisexual is secretly gay; however, several studies have revealed that bisexuality involves a distinct pattern of sexual interest and arousal. For example, researchers have conducted studies to track responses to photos of men and women. The results revealed that bisexual people spent similar amounts of time looking at photos of both men and women while gay men and lesbians spent far longer looking at photos of their desired sex. Other research has found that bisexual men exhibit high levels of genital and psychological arousal in response to both men and women whereas gay men only show strong arousal in response to men. In fact, several studies have found strong evidence that bisexuality involves distinct patterns of attraction, sexual interest, and arousal.

Bisexuality is not dependent on how many relationships someone has with people of each gender or how strong their feelings are. Being bisexual does not necessarily mean that someone is *equally* attracted to both men and women. Being bisexual involves a *capacity* for attraction to men and women but attraction to each sex does not necessarily have to be equally strong. For instance, research has found that bisexual men usually demonstrate more genital arousal to one sex over the other, although it isn't necessarily the same for each person (i.e., some show more arousal to women, others to men). Research on bisexual women has found that they do not exhibit equal levels of arousal to both sexes either. Some bisexual people may experience equally high attraction to men and women but equal levels of attraction to both genders is not an essential or defining feature of bisexuality. In other words, anyone who is interested in more than one gender may have a preference in that they prefer one gender more than another, even if it is by a small margin. These preferences are completely normal regardless of the gender of the person.

According to GLAAD, bisexual people make up more than half of the LGBTQ community. Research also finds that a growing percentage of Americans experience attraction to or have been involved with individuals of more than one gender, even if they don't identify as bisexual. People of color are more likely than white people to identify as bisexual: a 2012 Gallup poll found that bisexual women of color comprise 36 percent of bisexual women, compared to 26 percent of heterosexual women. Bisexual people are more likely to be parents than gay and lesbian people (Gates and Newport 2012).

It is important to distinguish between sexual orientation and gender identity since they are distinctive identities. Recall that sexual orientation is about attractions and relationships with other people; gender identity is about how an individual defines themselves (see Q1). For example, surveys that ask people to identify as LGBTQ can conflate a person's gender identity with their sexual orientation, leading to inaccurate data. Some surveys include the term transgender in survey questions because it is part of the LGBTQ acronym, resulting in questions asking whether someone is lesbian, bisexual, gay, or transgender. This question type can result in inaccurate data since a transgender person can be heterosexual and a cisgender person can be nonheterosexual. Conflating gender identity and sexual orientation can lead to undercounts of transgender people who identify as bisexual, lesbian, gay, or straight.

One of the reasons people may not identify as bisexual is that they don't feel comfortable being open about their attractions. In 2013, a Pew Research survey showed that only 28 percent of people who identified as bisexual did so openly. This has been the case so often that the San Francisco Human Rights Commission recently called bisexual people "an invisible majority," one in need of support and additional resources. Bisexual youth in particular are often told that bisexuality doesn't exist, that it is just a phase, or that they are just being indecisive about embracing their true sexuality. Ellen Kahn, director of the Human Rights Campaign Foundation's Children, Youth, and Families Program has said that some young people identify as queer or pansexual rather than as bisexual because those self-identifiers are less likely to be dismissed as illegitimate (Cruz 2014).

The invisibility of and prejudice against bisexual people persists both in the general public *and* within the LGBTQ community (Allen 2017). In a 2018 survey, both gay men and lesbians said they believed bisexual men and women were primarily attracted to men (Matsick and Rubin 2018). Statistics show that bisexual people are less likely than gay men and lesbians to come out: in a 2016 survey, only 28 percent of bisexuals interviewed said that all the important people in their life know they are bisexual compared to 77 percent of gay men and 71 percent of lesbians (Movement Advancement Project 2016). LGBTQ Americans face higher rates of poverty, unemployment, and negative health outcomes than straight Americans and bisexual people face even higher rates of these negative outcomes than lesbians and gay men (Movement Advancement Project 2016).

One 2014 analysis found that approximately 25 percent of bisexual men and 30 percent of bisexual women live in poverty compared to 15 percent and 21 percent of heterosexual men and women and 20 percent and 23 percent of gay men and lesbians. Bisexual women are also more likely to depend on public financial assistance such as SNAP (food stamps). Finally, 20 percent of bisexual people report experiencing a negative employment decision based on their sexuality and almost 60 percent of bisexual people report hearing anti-bisexual jokes and comments on the job. Nearly half (49 percent) of bisexual people report that they are not out to any of their coworkers compared to just 24 percent of lesbian and gay people (Movement Advancement Project 2014).

There are ample data that show how bisexual people differ from those who identify as gay and lesbian. One interesting finding has to do with age: younger people (particularly between the ages of 18 and 29) are much more likely to say they are not "entirely gay, lesbian, or heterosexual" than older age groups; in other words, they feel some level of attraction to more than one gender. In a 2015 survey, 29 percent of people between the ages of 18 and 29 identified as something other than gay, lesbian, or heterosexual compared to 24 percent of people between 30 and 44 years old; 8 percent of people between 45 and 64; and 7 percent of people 65 years or older (Moore 2015). Younger generations seem to be more in tune with their capacity for attraction to more than one gender or are at least more likely to admit their attraction to researchers, likely due to several factors. First, societal norms around sexual behavior have changed in many different ways over time, likely affecting younger generations during their formative years. More specific to LGBTQ identity, the representation of sexuality among LGBTQ identifiers likely increases attention to sexual behavior. The internet and new apps also allow for additional information and exploration, including access to a wide range of pornography; however, additional access can have negative effects as well.

FURTHER READING

Allen, Samantha. 2017. "Are Bisexuals Shut Out of the LGBT Club?" *Daily Beast*, April 13. https://www.thedailybeast.com/are-bisexuals-shut -out-of-the-lgbt-club

Andre, A., et al. 2014. "Supporting and Caring for Our Bisexual Youth." The Human Rights Campaign Foundation. HRC.org, September 23. https://assets2.hrc.org/files/assets/resources/Supporting_and_Caring _for_Bisexual_Youth.pdf

Cruz, Eliel. 2014. "HRC Report: Bi Youth Face Greater Challenges than Gay & Lesbian Peers." *Advocate*, September 23. https://www.advocate .com/bisexuality/2014/09/23/hrc-report-bi-youth-face-greater-challenges -gay-lesbian-peers

Denizet-Lewis, Benoit. 2014. "The Scientific Quest to Prove Bisexuality Exists," *New York Times*. March 23. https://www.nytimes.com/2014/03/23 /magazine/the-scientific-quest-to-prove-bisexuality-exists.html

Gates, Gary J., and Frank Newport. 2012. "Special Report: 3.4% of U.S. Adults Identify as LGBT." Gallup, October 18. https://news.gallup.com /poll/158066/special-report-adults-identify-lgbt.aspx

Matsick, Jes L., and Jennifer D. Rubin. 2018. "Bisexual Prejudice among Lesbian and Gay People: Examining the Roles of Gender and Perceived Sexual Orientation." *Psychology of Sexual Orientation and Gender Diversity* 5, 2: 143–155.

Moore, Peter. 2015. "A Third of Young Americans Say They Aren't 100% Heterosexual." YouGov, August 20. https://today.yougov.com/topics /lifestyle/articles-reports/2015/08/20/third-young-americans-exclusively -heterosexual

Movement Advancement Project. 2016. *Invisible Majority: The Disparities Facing Bisexual People and How to Remedy Them*. https://www.lgbtmap .org/policy-and-issue-analysis/invisible-majority

Movement Advancement Project, BiNet USA, and Bisexual Resource Center. 2014. "Understanding Issues Facing Bisexual Americans." https:// www.lgbtmap.org/understanding-issues-facing-bisexual-americans

Q24: ARE GAY MEN LESS MASCULINE THAN STRAIGHT MEN?

Answer: No. The belief that all gay men have characteristics perceived as feminine is a false stereotype and not based in fact. Some gay men present themselves as more feminine and some don't. Any way a gay man wants to express himself is valid whether that is more feminine, masculine, or androgynous.

The Facts: Studies have shown that it is impossible to determine one's sexual orientation simply based on physical characteristics, behavior, or the way a person dresses. In other words, gender expression varies from person-to-person regardless of sexual orientation. However, certain segments of the population *are* more comfortable expressing traits and behaviors that fall outside traditionally accepted gender norms and expectations. Specifically, gay men in the United States are more likely to be comfortable with aspects of their personality, behaviors, mannerisms, styles, or gender roles more often associated with women. The term *effeminate* is often used to describe these characteristics by people who believe that males should display traditionally masculine traits and behaviors and it is often used to imply criticism or ridicule of this behavior (as opposed to merely describing a man as feminine).

Overall, however, expectations are different depending on the person and the situation. For example, many people don't have the expectation that gay men should behave in a traditionally masculine manner. In fact, for some gay men, a more feminine personality and flamboyant dress are a signifier for being gay and an explicit rejection of traditional gender norms. Norms also change by the setting; gay men in particular may change their mannerisms and behaviors depending on their perception of the acceptance level of those around them.

Prior to the Stonewall Riots in 1969, gay men took defiant pleasure in flouting traditional conventions about how men should look, dress, and behave. Many in the pre-Stonewall "closet" culture—that is, those who identified as and may have behaved like LGBTQ people but had not acknowledged the identity publicly—embraced the connection between homosexuality and gender-nonconforming or stereotypically feminine behavior (also known by terms like camp, drag, or swish) and interests in fashion and decorating. Other gay men, however, engaged in stereotypically masculine behavior, even after the HIV/AIDS crisis became an urgent concern for personal and public health. Masculine behavior was stereotyped as being unconcerned about safe sex practices while engaging in promiscuous sexual behavior. Early reports from New York City when the AIDS crisis emerged indicated that more women had themselves tested for HIV/AIDS than men, though those rates changed as perceptions about the virus changed.

Many studies have examined gender-typed behavior in children (whether they prefer to play with dolls than with trucks, or if they prefer rough-and-tumble play to playing house) and whether this performance of gender in children is a predictor of sexual orientation. The overall conclusion of this work is that there is a connection between gendered play in childhood and sexual orientation as adults. Early studies tended to be retrospective, meaning that they asked adults to recall their childhood behavior; in these studies, gay men and lesbians were more likely than heterosexual men and women to recall gender-nonconforming behavior (Alanko et al. 2010).

More recent research has confirmed those early findings with more rigorous methodology. Using childhood home videos that were rated by independent viewers, psychologist Gerulf Rieger and his colleagues (2008) found large and significant differences in gender-typed behavior between children who later identified as gay or lesbian. A more recent and more rigorous study assessed the gender-typed behavior of over 14,000 children born in 1991 or 1992 at three time points during the preschool period (at ages 2.5, 3.5, and 4.75) and then surveyed the children at age 15 about their sexual behavior and orientation. The researchers found large and statistically significant differences in behavior between "pre-lesbian/gay children" and their heterosexual peers, with higher levels of gender-nonconforming behavior by boys starting at age 2.5 and by girls starting at age 3.5 (Li, Kung, and Hines 2017).

The *masculine overcompensation thesis* suggests that when men are concerned about the social implications of losing their masculinity (e.g., being seen as gay or otherwise lacking masculine traits), they tend to overcompensate by exhibiting extreme masculine behaviors and attitudes to create the impression that they are, indeed, masculine in socially desirable ways (Adams, Wright, and Lohr 1996). Masculine overcompensation has been cited as the cause of relatively benign behaviors like buying sports cars at the onset of "mid-life crises" all the way up to escalation of the Vietnam War by President Johnson (Kimmel 1996). Antigay hate crimes "are tied closely to rigid and hierarchical ideas about masculinity that depend on differentiating 'real' men from women as well as gay and bisexual men" (Wade 2016). Introducing rigid, masculine stereotypes from a young age increases the likelihood that boys will be more defensive or aggressive if their masculinity is ever threatened in some way.

Men who are heavily invested in masculinity at extreme levels—a phenomenon known as *toxic masculinity*—are more likely to engage in domestic violence against their female partners, to sexually harass women, and even to commit mass shootings (Karner 1996; Wade 2016). As many boys grow into men, "they learn that they are entitled to feel like a real man, and that they have the right to annihilate anyone who challenges that sense of entitlement" (Kimmel 2012, quoted in Wade 2016).

In a 2013 experiment led by sociologist Robb Willer, men in the study who were told that they are feminine were more supportive of war, more homophobic, and more interested in purchasing an SUV than were men who were told that they were masculine. The researchers also found that when their masculinity was threatened in this way, men were more supportive of the ideas that men were meant to be dominant in society and that men were superior to women (Willer et al. 2013). Interestingly, they did not find the same effect among women: there were no differences in attitudes about gender roles or increased support for traditionally feminine behaviors between women who were told that they were masculine and women who were told that they were feminine. A 2016 experiment found that threatening the masculinity of men increased their transphobia while threatening the femininity of women had no effect (Michelson and Harrison 2020).

Attitudes toward transgender people are a contemporary example of how masculine overcompensation can lead to negative attitudes about others. People who are transgender often, by definition, challenge the traditional conceptualization of gender identity as binary and immutable (Burdge 2007). Studies and polls have repeatedly found that men are less supportive of transgender people and transgender rights than women. Gay men can also express negative attitudes toward effeminate behavior among other men. This includes overt statements on dating sites by men who do not want effeminate partners and instead express a preference for masculine self-presentation among potential partners (Bailey et al. 1997). Scholars have also found consistent evidence that most gay men wish to be more masculine and less feminine, preferences that many researchers attribute to internalized homophobia (Sánchez and Vilain 2012).

In short, gay men are not inherently more feminine than straight men. There is natural variance in people along the traditional feminine and masculine spectrum; however, gay men are more likely than their straight counterparts to feel comfortable not conforming to rigid gender stereotypes, even as young boys.

FURTHER READING

Adams, Henry E., Lester W. Wright Jr., and Bethany Lohr. 1996. "Is Homophobia Associated with Homosexual Arousal?" *Journal of Abnormal Psychology* 105, 3: 440–445.

Alanko, Katarina, et al. 2010. "Common Genetic Effects of Gender Atypical Behavior in Childhood and Sexual Orientation in Adulthood: A Study of Finnish Twins." *Archives of Sexual Behavior* 39, 1: 81–92.

Ashe, Fidelma. 2006. *The New Politics of Masculinity: Men, Power and Resistance.* New York: Routledge.

Bailey, J. Michael, Peggy Y. Kim, Alex Hills, and Joan A. W. Linsenmeier. 1997. "Butch, Femme, or Straight Acting? Partner Preferences of Gay

Men and Lesbians." *Journal of Personality and Social Psychology* 73, 5: 960–973.

Bergling, Tim. 2001. *Sissyphobia: Gay Men and Effeminate Behavior.* New York: Routledge.

Burdge, Barb J. 2007. "Bending Gender, Ending Gender: Theoretical Foundations for Social Work Practice with the Transgender Community." *Social Work* 52, 3: 243–250.

Duberman, Martin Bauml, Martha Vicinus, and George Chauncey, eds. 1990. *Hidden from History: Reclaiming the Gay & Lesbian Past.* New York: New American Library.

Halperin, David M. 2002. *How to Do the History of Homosexuality.* Chicago: University of Chicago Press.

Karner, Tracy. 1996. "Fathers, Sons, and Vietnam: Masculinity and Betrayal in the Life Narratives of Vietnam Veterans with Post Traumatic Stress Disorder." *American Studies* 37, 1: 63–94.

Kimmel, Michael. 2012. "Masculinity, Mental Illness, and Guns: A Lethal Equation?" CNN.com, December 19. http://www.cnn.com/2012/12/19/living/men-guns-violence/

Kimmel, Michael S. 1996. *Manhood in America: A Cultural History.* New York: Free Press.

Levine, Martin P. 1998. *Gay Macho.* New York: New York University Press.

Li, Gu, Karson T. F. Kung, and Melissa Hines. 2017. "Childhood Gender-Typed Behavior and Adolescent Sexual Orientation: A Longitudinal Population-Based Study." *Developmental Psychology* 53, 4: 764–777.

McDermott, Monika L. 2016. *Masculinity, Femininity, and American Political Behavior.* New York: Oxford University Press.

Michelson, Melissa R., and Brian F. Harrison. 2020. *Transforming Prejudice: Fear, Identity, and Transgender Rights.* New York: Oxford University Press.

Rieger, Gerulf, et al. 2008. "Sexual Orientation and Childhood Gender Nonconformity: Evidence from Home Videos." *Developmental Psychology* 44, 1: 46–58.

Sánchez, Francisco J., and Eric Vilain. 2012. "'Straight-Acting Gays': The Relationship between Masculine Consciousness, Anti-Effeminacy, and Negative Gay Identity." *Archives of Sexual Behavior* 41, 1: 111–119.

Serano, Julia. 2007. *Whipping Girl.* Berkeley: Seal Press.

Wade, Lisa. 2016. "The Hypermasculine Violence of Omar Mateen and Brock Turner." *New Republic*, June 14. https://newrepublic.com/article/134270/hypermasculine-violence-omar-mateen-brock-turner

Willer, Robb, Christabel L. Rogalin, Briget Conlon, and Michael T. Wojnowicz. 2013. "Overdoing Gender: A Test of the Masculine Overcompensation Thesis." *American Journal of Sociology* 118, 4: 980–1022.

Q25: ARE LESBIANS LESS FEMININE THAN STRAIGHT WOMEN?

Answer: No. Presentations of gender roles differ widely among both lesbians and heterosexual women as well as among bisexual women and people of other sexual orientations and gender identities who identify as women. While lesbians are often stereotyped as masculine, their approaches to gender roles vary significantly depending on a broad array of factors. Gender and gender performance are fluid identities, varying from person-to-person.

The Facts: People are socialized to understand gender identities to correspond to particular sets of traits and behaviors, with men expected to be more masculine and women expected to be more feminine. The ways in which men and women perform gender—the ways that they conform to cultural expectations of how to be a man or a woman—are widespread and constantly reinforced by society. For example, as mentioned in Q24, men are expected to be less emotional while women are expected to be more nurturing. Some individuals choose to reject these traditional ways of performing gender, particularly members of the LGBTQ community: gay men tend to be more comfortable exhibiting behaviors more traditionally associated with women and perceived as feminine while lesbians tend to be more comfortable behaving in ways that result in them being perceived as masculine.

The truth is that masculinity and femininity exist as continua, not as two distinct categories. According to social psychologist Bobbi Carothers, "Sex is not nearly as confining a category as stereotypes and even some academic studies would have us believe" (Ferro 2013). The stereotype of a lesbian is of a butch or masculine woman. Lesbians who are more feminine are less visible, in part because they are more likely to be perceived as heterosexual. At the same time, the few lesbian characters in television and film tend to be portrayed as "lipstick lesbians"—as traditionally attractive and extremely feminine. These characters are sexualized and sometimes even are intimate with men, reflecting society's "male gaze" preference that women in the visual arts should be attractive to men (Sanders 2014).

The truth is that some lesbians are more feminine-presenting, some are more masculine-presenting, and some are androgynous; there is wide variation within each of these broader categories (Manders 2020). Lesbians perform gender in a wide diversity of ways across the gender expression spectrum. Femme-identifying lesbians cultivate a more traditionally feminine appearance and behavior, butch lesbians present gender closer to the masculine end of the gender spectrum, and individual lesbians may also exhibit characteristics (clothing style, hairstyle, mannerisms) across the butch/femme continuum at different points in time. While these labels are linked to societal norms about masculinity and femininity, these individual presentations of self do not necessarily correspond to more masculine or feminine behaviors or attitudes (Walker et al. 2012). As sociologist Rhea Ashley Hoskin notes, the authenticity of femme queer people—including femme bisexuals and transgender women—is often called into question, a state of affairs that stems in part from the stereotype that "real" lesbians are more masculine (Hoskin 2019).

According to clinical psychologists Heidi Levitt and Kathleen Collins, femme lesbians have been a recognizable group since the 1940s, when many American men were sent overseas to fight in World War II. As women took on employment positions previously reserved for men, they also began to wear pants and earn salaries, shifting societal expectations about presentations of gender. While some women took this opportunity to embrace a more masculine (butch) gender expression, others adopted a femme gender expression, wearing heels and bright lipstick and modeling themselves after popular Hollywood stars of the era (Levitt and Collins 2019). Historically, however, femme lesbians found their legitimacy as lesbians questioned (Harris and Crocker 1997). Since the 1990s, there has been increased support for femme lesbians, reflecting an affirmative embrace of the wide diversity of gender expression by the LGBTQ community—especially among younger cohorts (Kenneady and Oswalt 2014). Femininity is often associated with being desirable to men, a trait more commonly associated with being heterosexual; as a result, femme lesbian women continue to face questions of legitimacy as valid lesbians and are often mistakenly assumed to be heterosexual (Hoskin 2019).

Surveys by psychologist Richard Lippa find that lesbian women display more variation in their self-reported masculinity or femininity compared to straight women but those results have not always been confirmed by other studies. For example, work by psychologist Gerulf Rieger finds that lesbians are more likely to perform gender in ways that are gender nonconforming but do not self-report as more masculine or feminine compared to straight women (Lippa 2015; Rieger et al. 2016).

The bottom line is that men and women can perform gender in a variety of ways along the masculine-feminine continuum. The ways in which individuals express their gender are independent of their sexual orientation and gender identity. Expectations that women who are more masculine must be lesbians or that feminine women must be heterosexual are based on outdated stereotypes.

FURTHER READING

Blair, Karen L., and Rhea Ashley Hoskin. 2015. "Experiences of Femme Identity: Coming Out, Invisibility and Femmephobia." *Psychology & Sexuality* 6, 3: 229–244.

Ferro, Shaunacy. 2013. "Science Confirms the Obvious: Men and Women Aren't That Different." *Popular Science*, February 6. https://www.popsci.com/science/article/2013-02/science-confirms-obvious-men-and-women-arent-different/

Harris, Laura, and Elizabeth Crocker, eds. 1997. *Femme: Feminists, Lesbians and Bad Girls*. New York: Routledge.

Hoskin, Rhea Ashley. 2019. "Femmephobia: The Role of Anti-Femininity and Gender Policing in LGBTQ+ People's Experiences of Discrimination." *Sex Roles* 81, 11–12: 686–703.

Kenneady, Donna Ann, and Sara B. Oswalt. 2014. "Is Cass's Model of Homosexual Identity Formation Relevant to Today's Society?" *American Journal of Sexuality Education* 9, 2: 229–246.

Levitt, Heidi M., and Kathleen M. Collins. 2020. "Making Intelligible the Controversies over Femme Identities: A Functionalist Approach to Conceptualizing the Subversive Meanings of Femme Genders." *Journal of Lesbian Studies*. https://doi.org/s10.1080/10894160.2019.1694788

Lippa, Richard A. 2015. "Assessing Sexual Orientation and Category Specificity in a Representative Sample of 2,825 United States Adults." Paper presented at The Puzzle of Sexual Orientation meeting, Lethbridge, Alberta, Canada, July.

Manders, Kerry. 2020. "The Renegades." *New York Times Magazine*, April 13. https://www.nytimes.com/interactive/2020/04/13/t-magazine/butch-stud-lesbian.html

Rieger, Gerulf, et al. 2016. "Sexual Arousal and Masculinity-Femininity of Women." *Journal of Personality and Social Psychology* 111, 2: 265–283.

Sanders, Tasha. 2014. "Why the Media Still Doesn't Get Lesbianism Right." Adios Barbie, November 5. http://www.adiosbarbie.com/2014/11/why-the-media-still-doesnt-get-lesbianism-right/

Walker, Ja'nina J., et al. 2012. "Butch Bottom—Femme Top? An Exploration of Lesbian Stereotypes." *Journal of Lesbian Studies* 16, 1: 90–107.

Q26: WHY ARE LGB PEOPLE (PEOPLE WITH NONHETEROSEXUAL SEXUAL ORIENTATIONS) GROUPED TOGETHER WITH T PEOPLE (NON-CISGENDER GENDER IDENTITIES) INTO ONE LGBTQ COMMUNITY?

Answer: While sexual orientation and gender identity are separate concepts, all members of the LGBTQ community, including LGB (lesbian, gay, bisexual) people, transgender and nonbinary people, and queer people, actively defy traditional gender roles and expectations and have often faced discrimination and prejudice as a result. These shared experiences and identities have historically brought the community together into one group under a common identity umbrella.

The Facts: Sexual orientation and gender identity minorities fit together as a community because all LGBTQ people do not conform to gender norms and expectations. If the norm is for a person to be cisgender and heterosexual, the LGBTQ community as a whole represents a place of acceptance for anyone who doesn't fit within the constructs of social expectations. As transgender author and activist Brynn Tannehill notes, "LGB people break one of the most fundamental stereotypes and expectations of gender, namely women should fall in love with men, and vice versa. Transgender people violate other gender stereotypes, sometimes including who we are supposed to fall in love with and marry. At some point in their lives, many transgender people will either be seen as LGB by others, or see themselves as LGB" (Tannehill 2016).

Psychiatrist Jack Drescher notes that "many cultures routinely conflate homosexuality with transgender identities because they rely upon several beliefs that use conventional heterosexuality and cisgender identities as a frame of reference. Once regarded as synonymous, it is only relatively recently that *sexual orientation* (defined as an individual's erotic response tendency or sexual attractions) and *gender identity* (defined as one's sense of oneself as being either male or female) have been regarded as separate categories" (Drescher 2010, 430) (see Q1).

One common question is whether LGBTQ people categorized themselves together or if this grouping was imposed from outside by gender and sexual traditionalists. One classic piece along these lines, "How Did the T Get in LGBT?" was written in 2007 by John Aravosis, a longtime gay rights advocate and blogger:

> In simpler times we were all gay. But then the word "gay" started to mean "gay men" more than women, so we switched to the more

inclusive "gay and lesbian." Bisexuals, who were only part-time gays, insisted that we add them too, so we did (not without some protest), and by the early 1990s we were the lesbian, gay and bisexual, or LGB community. Sometime in the late '90s, a few gay rights groups and activists started using a new acronym, LGBT—adding T for transgender/transsexual. And that's when today's trouble started. (Avarosis 2007)

The "trouble" to which he was referring was the contentious politics and intra-LGBTQ conflict over the Employment Non-Discrimination Act (ENDA), a bill crafted to add legal protections against employment discrimination. It has been introduced to Congress nearly every year since 1994, most recently in 2019 as part of a broader Equality Act, though it has never passed. The closest it came to passage was in 2007, when Aravosis wrote his piece. Between 1974, when the earliest form of ENDA was introduced, and 2007, the protections only extended to sexual orientation, never gender identity. Gender identity was added to the bill in 2007, the same year it had a real chance of passing both the House and the Senate. It gradually became clear, however, that the bill's prospects for passage were greater if gender identity was dropped from the bill. As a result, the bill's author, openly gay representative Barney Frank (D-MA), dropped gender identity from the bill with the endorsement of the Human Rights Campaign (HRC), the largest LGBTQ advocacy organization in the country.

Many other activists, including more than 200 national and local gay rights groups, angrily demanded that gender identity be put back in the bill and vowed to fight against any version of ENDA that left gender identity out. This coalition convinced House Democratic leaders to delay action on ENDA until later in October, deciding they would rather have no bill at all than pass one that didn't include protections for gender identity. The transgender community, too, reacted with anger, and the only transgender member of the HRC Board of Directors resigned. Ultimately, the bill never passed. The episode is considered by some as part of a pattern of "betrayal of transgender rights to gay and lesbian causes" (Talusan 2014). More recent versions of the Equality Act, including the version passed by the House in 2020, prohibit discrimination based on an individual's sexual orientation or gender identity.

Opponents of transgender rights have at times sought to "divide and conquer" by separating out transgender issues. At the 2017 meeting of the Values Voter Summit (an annual networking event for Christian conservatives), for example, "speakers wrapped their opposition to nondiscrimination measures in rhetoric passing as progressive: transgender rights were depicted as anti-feminist, hostile to minorities, and even disrespectful to LGB individuals. This seems to be part of a larger strategy intended to weaken transgender rights advocates by attempting to separate them from allies like feminists and gay and lesbian rights advocates." One speaker noted, "Trans and gender identity are a tough sell, so focus on gender identity to divide and conquer. . . . If we separate the T from the alphabet soup we'll have more success" (Barthélemy 2017). In 2020 and 2021, social conservatives continued this strategy by attacking transgender people with state legislation criminalizing participation of transgender participation in sports and gender-confirming care for children (Yurcaba 2021).

Transgender people have always existed but they have not always been included as equal members of the LGBTQ community. Overall, the gay liberation movement has expanded—especially since transgender people began to come out publicly in the late 1980s and early 1990s—to include transgender identities. "Sexual orientation and transgender identities, once conflated, and only recently separated from each other as discrete categories, now found common political cause" (Drescher 2010, 442).

FURTHER READING

Aravosis, John. 2007. "How Did the 'T' Get in LGBT?" Salon.com, October 6. https://www.salon.com/2007/10/08/lgbt/

Barthélemy, Hélène. 2017. "Christian Right Tips to Fight Transgender Rights: Separate the T from the LGB." SPLC, October 23. https://www.splcenter.org/hatewatch/2017/10/23/christian-right-tips-fight-transgender-rights-separate-t-lgb

Drescher, Jack. 2010. "Queer Diagnoses: Parallels and Contrasts in the History of Homosexuality, Gender Variance, and the *Diagnostic and Statistical Manual*." *Archives of Sexual Behavior* 39, 2: 427–460.

Talusan, Meredith. 2014. "45 Years After Stonewall, the LGBT Movement Has a Transphobia Problem." American Prospect, June 26, 2014. https://prospect.org/power/45-years-stonewall-lgbt-movement-transphobia-problem/

Tannehill, Brynn. 2016. "Why 'LGB' and 'T' Belong Together." Huffington Post, February 2. https://www.huffpost.com/entry/why-lgb-and-t-belong-together_b_2746616

Yurcaba, Jo. 2021. "'State of Crisis': Advocates Warn of 'Unprecedented' Wave of Anti-LGBTQ Bills." *NBC News*, April 25, 2021. https://www.nbcnews.com/feature/nbc-out/state-crisis-advocates-warn-unprecedented-wave-anti-lgbtq-bills-n1265132

Q27: ARE MEN WHO ENJOY CROSS-DRESSING OR DRAG TRANSGENDER?

Answer: No. Dressing in clothes typically worn by a different gender is known as cross-dressing or, if for a public performance, as performing in drag. These activities are behaviors, not necessarily an expression of a person's gender identity. Most drag queens and cross-dressers are cisgender (i.e., not transgender) gay men, although those activities are also performed by individuals of other sexual orientations and gender identities, including transgender men and women. Transgender is a gender identity.

The Facts: A *transgender* person is someone whose gender identity does not correspond to the sex they were assigned at birth—for example, someone who is assigned as male or female when they are born but later identifies as another gender. Other gender identities that fall under the nonbinary umbrella include someone who identifies with neither gender (agender); both genders (bigender or genderfluid); genderqueer (someone who identifies neither male nor female and outside the gender spectrum); and pangender (someone whose gender identity is not limited to one gender and who may feel like a member of more than one gender at a time). These and other identities, including intersex people, are about gender *identity:* the way someone sees themselves either in and of themselves or in relation to those around them. They are *not* about the way a person dresses, acts, or otherwise behaves. (For more on this topic, see Q1.)

Many gay cisgender men enjoy playing with gender norms in ways that violate conventional norms and expectations. They have done so for decades despite the fact that it was illegal in the United States for a man to appear in public wearing women's clothing for the majority of the twentieth century. This kind of play can include wearing single or multiple pieces of women's clothing, wearing makeup and nail polish, or otherwise engaging in behaviors that conventionally are associated with women. There is also a long-standing and deep tradition in the gay male community of performing in drag, either with the idea of creating an illusion of female impersonation or in a more campy, over-the-top style that exaggerates female stereotypes. Many drag performers identify as gay men, not as transgender women. That said, drag culture includes people of many gender identities and sexual orientations and several famous transgender women began their careers as drag performers, including Aleshia Brevard and Laverne Cox (Fitzgerald and Marquez 2020). Experimenting with gender and gender identity can be a pertinent point in many trans people's lives, illustrating the broader phenomenon that dressing or performing in drag can facilitate shifts in sexual and gender identities (Rupp and Taylor 2003). However, this experimentation does not necessarily mean a person identifies as transgender; it may reflect an effort to process one's own gender identity.

Drag performers are just that—performers. They generally do not appear in drag except when they are performing in front of audiences. These performances often include lip-synching and are usually performed in bars, nightclubs, and at organized drag competitions (Moncrieff and Lienard 2017). While initially invisible to the mass public, drag has gradually gone mainstream. It has been depicted in hit movies of the 1990s including *The Adventures of Priscilla, Queen of the Desert* (1994), *The Birdcage* (1996), and *To Wong Foo: Thanks for Everything, Julie Newmar* (1995); and since 2009, drag has been featured on the television show *RuPaul's Drag Race* (Fitzgerald and Marquez 2020). Over the years, the show has included mostly gay cisgender men as contestants but it has also occasionally featured transgender and nonbinary people as well. One of the constants in the show is the drawing of distinctions between performing drag (a behavior) and sexual orientation and the show is a celebration of both.

Linguistics professor Rusty Barrett notes that as the drag community has become more aware of transgender women, performers have "come to draw on more exaggerated looks that make it clear that the performer is indeed a drag queen and not a (cisgender or transgender) woman" (Barrett 2017, 36). While drag performers use female pronouns to refer to themselves and each other, they do not identify as women; the pronouns are part of the gender performance. "Perhaps the strongest distinction between drag queens and trans women is the distinction between performance and identity, in that trans women typically maintain a gender identity that corresponds to their gender performance (but may not correspond to their anatomically assigned sex), whereas the gender performance of drag queens typically does not correspond to either gender identity or anatomical sex" (Barrett 2017, 41). Drag can also include drag kings, typically cisgender women performing exaggerated masculine behaviors, as well as bio queens, women who embellish the gender they were assigned at birth when they participate as drag performers (Miller 2016).

On the other hand, a cross-dresser is a person who dresses in and acts in the style of the gender opposite to the one they were assigned at birth. An example of cross-dressing is a man who wears female panties underneath his work clothes or in the privacy of his home. This behavior, too, is not necessarily about how the person identifies and more about how the person acts. Cross-dressing is more common than many realize, for it is often done in secret out of fear that the activity will result in societal rejection or humiliation. Researchers have documented instances of cross-dressing by business professionals, doctors, lawyers, and blue-collar and white-collar workers. Cross-dressing does not exclude based on profession or financial status. Although it is often socially acceptable for women to wear men's clothes, it is generally less socially acceptable for men to wear women's clothes. Therefore, men who are cross-dressers are often viewed by others as deviants to avoid or to fear.

Some cross-dressers are gay or bisexual but many cross-dressers are heterosexual men. Those men often report they enjoy the feel of women's clothes, the excitement of pushing the limits of societal acceptance, and/or enjoy the thrill of risk-taking (e.g., they could be caught). Similar to drag performance, cross-dressing does not necessarily have a sexual component at all: some cross-dressers only do it for the enjoyment and the feeling they get. For others, cross-dressing can be part of a sexual fetish. Cross-dressing males commonly report they remember as far back as early childhood enjoying dressing in female clothes. Frequency and visibility of cross-dressing tend to increase with age.

Finally, not all cross-dressers are transgender. Some transgender people want to engage in behavior that blurs the lines of gender, including cross-dressing; many do not. Again, transgender is a term used for a person who experiences a difference of internal fit between their own gender identity and the sex they were assigned at birth. The key difference to keep in mind is between identity and behavior: one person may identify one way and conform to traditional gendered behavior and another person may not. The desire to engage in cross-dressing does not suggest or infer anyone's gender identity.

Performing in drag or cross-dressing is something that people *do*. Being LGBTQ is something that people *are*.

FURTHER READING

Barrett, Rusty. 2017. *From Drag Queens to Leathermen: Language, Gender, and Gay Male Subcultures.* New York: Oxford University Press.

Chess, Simone. 2016. *Male-to-Female Crossdressing in Early Modern English Literature: Gender, Performance, and Queer Relations.* London: Routledge.

Fitzgerald, Tom, and Lorenzo Marquez. 2020. *Legendary Children: The First Decade of RuPaul's Drag Race and the Last Century of Queer Life.* New York: Penguin.

Miller, Shaeleya. 2016. "Drag." In Nancy A. Naples, ed., *The Wiley Blackwell Encyclopedia of Gender and Sexuality Studies.* https://doi.org/10.1002/9781118663219.wbegss657

Moncrieff, Michael, and Pierre Lienard. 2017. "A Natural History of the Drag Queen Phenomenon." *Evolutionary Psychology: An International Journal of Evolutionary Approaches to Psychology and Behavior* 15, 2.

Nissim, Mayer. 2018. "Transvestite, Transsexual, Transgender: Here's What You Should Actually Call Trans People." Pink News, March 19. https://www.pinknews.co.uk/2018/03/19/transsexual-transgender-transvestite-what-should-you-call-trans-people/

Rodger, Gillian M. 2018. *Just One of the Boys: Female-to-Male Cross-Dressing on the American Variety Stage.* Urbana: University of Illinois Press.

Rupp, Leila J., and Verta Taylor. 2003. *Drag Queens at the 801 Cabaret.* Chicago: University of Chicago Press.

Sasson, Eric. 2014. "Why Are Americans More Accepting of Gays and Lesbians than Bisexuals and Cross Dressers?" *New Republic*, April 27. https://newrepublic.com/article/117526/bisexuals-and-cross-dressers-lag-gays-and-lesbians-wider-acceptance

5

Transgender and Nonbinary Identity

Transgender and nonbinary people have been an important part of the LGBTQ community for a very long time; however, transgender and nonbinary identity and rights have traditionally been overlooked, possibly because transgender and nonbinary people constitute a relatively small part of the overall community. At the same time, they are particularly vulnerable to explicit discrimination, bigotry, and violence. Chapter 5 addresses several myths and misconceptions about transgender and nonbinary people and identity that are sometimes catalysts for negative attitudes and behavior toward them.

Q28 gets at the heart of transgender and nonbinary identity: the concept of a gender binary. Many people incorrectly believe that there are only two sexes that a person can be assigned at birth: male and female. Further, many people incorrectly believe that their gender assigned at birth is the same as the gender identity they will have the rest of their lives. Gender, however, is much more nuanced than that. Q29 looks at how medical and psychological professionals address transgender and nonbinary identities and how views have changed over time to shift away from treating those identities as signs of mental illness. Q30 addresses the common question of whether children can know they are transgender or nonbinary at a young age. Q31 looks at the physicality of being transgender, making the point that not all transgender people want to alter their body surgically or any other way. Some transgender and nonbinary individuals feel they were born into the wrong body but others do not. Q32 looks at the increasingly common practice of asking people their pronouns. Q33 discusses the overlap between sexual orientation and gender identity, debunking the myth that all transgender men are former lesbians and all transgender women are former gay men. Finally, Q34 addresses the tensions surrounding the inclusion of transgender women and nonbinary people in the feminist movement.

Q28: IS IT TRUE THAT GENDER IS NOT BINARY?

Answer: Yes. Neither sex nor gender are binary concepts; many people define themselves in ways that do not fit into the traditional two categories of male or female.

The Facts: Cultures like ours where gender is generally recognized with only two options—male and female—embrace what is known as a "gender binary" because binary means "having two parts."

Most people, including most transgender people, see themselves as either male or female. However, many people don't fit so neatly into the categories of "man" or "woman," "male" or "female." For example, some identify with a gender that has elements of being both a man and a woman; others identify with a gender that is different than either male or female. Some don't identify with any gender; others' gender identity changes over time.

There are a variety of terms that people use to describe themselves if they don't identify in a traditional binary way, including bigender, agender, and genderqueer, among others; each means something slightly different, but all speak to an experience of gender that is not exclusively male or female. *Nonbinary* is the most common way for people to identify if they don't fall into one of the two categories of male and female and the nonbinary umbrella term includes a variety of different gender identities. Gender identities that are, temporarily or permanently, neither exclusively male nor female are also sometimes referred to as *genderfluid*; identities that are situated outside the gender binary are often called *genderqueer* or *agender*.

Some, but not all, nonbinary people undergo medical procedures to make their bodies more congruent with their gender identity. While not all nonbinary people need medical care to live a fulfilling life, it's critical and even lifesaving for many people.

Nonbinary people are nothing new. Nonbinary people aren't confused about their gender identity or following a new fad. To the contrary, nonbinary identities have been recognized for millennia by cultures and societies around the world. For example, many Native American tribes recognize people now referred to as two-spirit—an umbrella term for nonbinary definitions of gender and sexuality that are part of some Indigenous traditions and predate colonization (Davis-Young 2019). Nonbinary people have been recognized by other precolonial societies around the world, including in India, where a third gender, *hijira*, has been recognized as far back as the early eighth century BCE (McNabb 2018). Precolonial societies on multiple continents have also recognized and celebrated fluid genders; for example, holy people known as Bissu in the Bugis society of Southern Sulawesi in Indonesia are seen as powerful due to their ability to shift between genders (Ibrahim 2019; Hegarty, Ansara, and Barker 2018).

Nonbinary people are not the same as intersex people. *Intersex* is a socially constructed category that reflects real biological and/or genetic variation. It is a term for conditions where a person is born with a reproductive or sexual anatomy that doesn't fit the typical definitions of female or male. For example, someone may appear to be female on the outside at birth but have mostly male-typical anatomy on the inside. A person could be born with genitals that seem to be in-between the typical male-female anatomy—a girl may be born with a noticeably large clitoris or lacking a vaginal opening; a boy may be born with a notably small penis or with a scrotum that is divided so that it has formed more like labia. Finally, a person may be born with what is known as *mosaic genetics* so that some of their cells have XX chromosomes and some of them have XY.

Genetically, sexuality is determined by X and Y chromosomes. Females inherit an X chromosome from each parent, giving them XX chromosomes, while males inherit an X chromosome from their mother and a Y chromosome from their father, giving them XY chromosomes. Most people have XX or XY chromosomes but some individuals (a few births per thousand) are born with a single sex chromosome (X or Y) or with three or more sex chromosomes (XXX, XYY, XXY, etc.). Because Y chromosomes are dominant inducers of male phenotype, individuals with at least one Y chromosome tend to present as phenotypically male (with male genitalia and likely to be assigned male gender at birth). In addition, some males are born XX due to the translocation of a section of the Y chromosome, and some females are born XY due to mutations in the Y chromosome (WHO Gender and Genetics n.d.).

Though intersex is often considered an inborn condition, intersex anatomy doesn't always show up at birth. Sometimes a person isn't found to have intersex anatomy until they reach the age of puberty, find themselves an infertile adult, or die of old age and are autopsied. Some people live and die with intersex anatomy without anyone (including themselves) ever knowing. Estimates of the number of intersex people vary widely, ranging from 1 in 5,000 to 1 in 60, because experts dispute which of the myriad conditions to include and how to tally them accurately (Padawer 2016).

Being nonbinary is not the same thing as being intersex: again, intersex people have anatomy or genes that don't fit typical definitions of male and female. Nonbinary people are usually not intersex: they're usually born with anatomies that fit typical definitions of male and female but their innate gender identity is something other than male or female (e.g., genderfluid or genderqueer). At the same time, it is also true that some intersex people identify as nonbinary.

For generations, the false perception that there are two distinct biological sexes has had many negative effects. This worldview has muddied historical archaeological records and it has caused humiliation for athletes around the globe who are closely scrutinized. In the mid-1940s, female Olympic athletes went through a degrading process of having their genitals inspected to receive "femininity certificates" (Padawer 2016). Chromosome testing became more common in the late 1960s and eventually, hormone testing became the norm. However, instead of rooting out imposters for athletic purposes, these tests helped to illustrate the complexity of human sex and gender.

Two governing bodies have vigorously tried to determine who counts as a woman for the purpose of athletic competitions: World Athletics (formerly known as the International Amateur Athletic Federation) and the International Olympics Committee (IOC). The testing regimens carried out by these organizations have been justified as attempts to catch male athletes masquerading as women. Not one imposter has ever been discovered; however, the sex of many athletes has been challenged due to the conflating of genetics and anatomy. One prominent example was Ewa Klobukowska, a Polish sprinter who in 1968 was among the first to be disqualified from Olympic competition because her chromosome test found both XX and XXY chromosomes, leading her to be identified as "not female." (Typically, genetic females have XX chromosomes and genetic males have XY chromosomes. Individuals with Klinefelter syndrome have XXY chromosomes; despite the extra X chromosome, they are considered genetically male.)

A 1968 editorial in the *I.O.C.* (International Olympic Committee) magazine insisted the chromosome test "indicates quite definitely the sex of a person" but many geneticists and endocrinologists disagreed, pointing out that sex was determined by a confluence of genetic, hormonal, and physiological factors, not any one factor alone. In 1999, compulsory gender identification in Olympic competitions was abandoned, reflecting an increased understanding of the complexity of gender and sexual identity within the athletic community (Ritchie, Reynard, and Lewis 2008).

The United States has a mixed record of policies affirming that gender is not binary. The Obama administration loosened the legal definition of gender in federal programs, including education and health care, recognizing gender as an individual conceptualization not determined by sex assigned at birth (Green, Benner, and Pear 2018). In 2018, the Trump administration reversed course, pushing the U.S. Department of Health and Human Services to codify a binary definition of sex, establishing a person "as male or female based on immutable biological traits identifiable by or before birth." The new definition essentially eradicated federal recognition of the estimated 1.4 million Americans who have opted to recognize themselves—surgically or otherwise—as a gender other than the one they were assigned at birth. The policy was reversed again by the Biden administration via an executive order on his first day in office in January 2021. The order directed the federal government to interpret all sex nondiscrimination policies to include protection from discrimination based on sexual orientation, gender identity, or gender expression (Yurcaba 2021).

It might be more convenient for the U.S. federal government to have a binary system for determining legal sex; many U.S. laws and customs are built on such an assumption. Critics of such a stance, however, contend that just because it's a convenient system of classification doesn't mean it's right. Some countries like Canada and some states in the United States, including Oregon (the first state to do so), Arkansas, California, Colorado, Illinois, Maryland, New Mexico, Pennsylvania, and Virginia, as well as the District of Columbia, allow people to declare a nonbinary gender identity on their driver's license or other identification documents.

FURTHER READING

Bergner, Daniel. 2019. "The Struggles of Rejecting the Gender Binary." *New York Times*, June 4. https://www.nytimes.com/2019/06/04/magazine/gender-nonbinary.html

Davis, Heath Fogg. 2017. *Beyond Trans: Does Gender Matter?* New York: New York University Press.

Davis-Young, Katherine. 2019. "For Many Native Americans, Embracing LGBT Members Is a Return to the Past." *Washington Post*, March 29. https://www.washingtonpost.com/national/for-many-native-americans-embracing-lgbt-members-is-a-return-to-the-past/2019/03/29/24d1e6c6-4f2c-11e9-88a1-ed346f0ec94f_story.html

Green, Erica L., Katie Benner, and Robert Pear. 2018. "'Transgender' Could Be Defined Out of Existence under Trump Administration." *New York Times*, October 21. https://www.nytimes.com/2018/10/21/us/politics/transgender-trump-administration-sex-definition.html

Hegarty, Peter, Y. Gavriel Ansara, and Meg-John Barker. 2018. "Nonbinary Gender Identities." In Nancy Dess, Jeanne Marecek, and Leslie Bell, eds., *Gender, Sex, and Sexualities: Psychological Perspectives*. New York: Oxford University Press, pp. 53–76.

Ibrahim, Farid M. 2019. "Homophobia and Rising Islamic Intolerance Push Indonesia's Intersex Bissu Priests to the Brink." Australian Broadcasting Company, February 26. https://www.abc.net.au/news/2019-02-27/indonesia-fifth-gender-might-soon-disappear/10846570

Joseph, Rebecca. 2017. "Canadian Passports to Have 'X' Gender Starting August 31." *Global News*, August 25. https://globalnews.ca/news/3694753/canadian-passports-x-gender/

Kralick, Alexandra. 2018. "We Finally Understand That Gender Isn't Binary. Sex Isn't Either." Slate, November 13. https://slate.com/technology/2018/11/sex-binary-gender-neither-exist.html

McNabb, Charlie. 2018. *Nonbinary Gender Identities: History, Culture, Resources*. Lanham, MD: Rowman & Littlefield.

Moreau, Julie. 2017. "Federal Civil Rights Law Doesn't Protect Transgender Workers, Justice Department Says." NBCNews.com, October 5. https://www.nbcnews.com/feature/nbc-out/federal-civil-rights-law-doesn-t-protect-transgender-workers-justice-n808126

National Center for Transgender Equality. 2018. "Understanding Non-Binary People: How to Be Respectful and Supportive." October 5. https://transequality.org/issues/resources/understanding-non-binary-people-how-to-be-respectful-and-supportive

Padawer, Ruth. 2016. "The Humiliating Practice of Sex-Testing Female Athletes." *New York Times*, July 3. https://www.nytimes.com/2016/07/03/magazine/the-humiliating-practice-of-sex-testing-female-athletes.html

Parks, Casey. 2019. "Oregon Becomes First State to Allow Nonbinary on Drivers License." *Oregonian*, Jan. 9. https://www.oregonlive.com/portland/2017/06/oregon_becomes_first_state_to.html

Ritchie, Robert, John Reynard, and Tom Lewis. 2008. "Intersex and the Olympic Games." *Journal of the Royal Society of Medicine* 101, 8: 395–399.

WHO Gender and Genetics. n.d. "Genetic Components of Sex and Gender." World Health Organization, Genomic Resource Centre. https://www.who.int/genomics/gender/en/index1.html

Yurcaba, Jo. 2021. "Biden Issues Executive Order Expanding LGBTQ Non-Discrimination Protections." *NBC News*, Jan. 21. https://www.nbcnews.com/feature/nbc-out/biden-issues-executive-order-expanding-lgbtq-nondiscrimination-protections-n1255165

Q29: DO MEDICAL AND PSYCHOLOGICAL AUTHORITIES REGARD TRANSGENDER OR NONBINARY GENDER IDENTITY AS A MENTAL ILLNESS?

Answer: While transgender or nonbinary gender identity is still considered a mental illness in some countries, that is no longer the case in the United States or according to the United Nations.

The Facts: In the past, people whose gender identity did not conform to the gender they had been assigned at birth were considered to be mentally ill. However, medical and psychological experts in the United States and many other countries no longer consider this to be true.

Medical professionals have changed their classification of transgender identity over time. In 1968, transgender identity was initially considered a *sexual deviation*. In 1980, it was reclassified as a *psychosexual disorder* and in 1994, it was listed as a *gender identity disorder*. In 2007, the American Medical Association recognized gender dysphoria as a medical condition that could be treated by transitioning: by allowing the individual to live as the gender with which they identify rather than as the gender they were assigned at birth. In 2013, the term *gender identity disorder* was dropped and replaced with *gender dysphoria*. Gender dysphoria is defined by the American Psychiatric Association (APA) as "a conflict between a person's physical or assigned gender and the gender with which he/she/they identify" (American Psychiatric Association n.d.).

Until 2013, being transgender was still considered a form of mental illness, a definition the APA claims it made to increase access to trans-related medical care. Insurance eligibility for some medical care, including gender confirmation surgery, often requires a diagnosis from a doctor of a mental or physical illness. "If we took conditions related to gender identity out of the [DSM-5] classification altogether, it would undermine the access to health services that transgender people have," stated psychology professor Geoffrey Reed. "They wouldn't have a diagnostic code that conveyed eligibility." When the APA decided to end its classification of transgenderism as a disorder in the *Diagnostic and Statistical*

Manual of Mental Disorders, Fifth Edition (*DSM-5*) in 2013, transgender advocates were split in their reactions. Some saw the change to the manual, the primary guide used by psychiatrists to diagnose mental illness, as a step toward removing stigma against transgender people. Others, however, noted that the change might create new barriers to people seeking to access trans-related medical care (Love 2016).

According to Norman Spack, a pediatric endocrinologist at Boston Children's Hospital, the *DSM-5* change shifted the emphasis in treatment to resolving distress over the mismatch that some individuals feel between their identities and their bodies. The change also reflected a recognition that a mismatch is not necessarily a disorder or must have a pathological basis (Russo 2017).

Clinical psychologist Robin Rosenberg noted at the time of the *DMS-5* change that many transgender people are not distressed by their cross-gender identification (Parry 2013). Their dysphoria is a condition that can be treated by living as a transgender person, sometimes but not necessarily while also making use of hormone therapy and gender-affirming surgeries (APA 2013). Other transgender and nonbinary people may not have gender dysphoria at all but feel comfortable with their bodies despite the gender identity they feel internally. For example, a nonbinary individual may be comfortable with their body because they consider themselves to be a combination of female and male and those body parts represent one aspect of their gender identity.

Medical experts note that while not all transgender people suffer from gender dysphoria, those individuals who do have severe, untreated gender dysphoria can experience severe mental health issues, including debilitating depression, anxiety, and suicidal ideation. The APA noted at the time of the change:

> DSM-5 aims to avoid stigma and ensure critical care for individuals who see and feel themselves to be a different gender than their assigned gender. It replaces the diagnostic name "gender identity disorder" with "gender dysphoria," as well as makes other important clarifications in the criteria. It is important to note that gender nonconformity is not in itself a mental disorder. The critical element of gender dysphoria is the presence of clinically significant distress associated with the condition. (APA 2013)

Transgender people are more likely than cisgender people to suffer from mental health issues, including depression and anxiety, and are more likely to attempt suicide. However, these issues stem not from their gender identity but from gender dysphoria and from "the discrimination, stigma, lack of acceptance, and abuse they face on an unfortunately regular basis," and even from the stress resulting from the anticipation of discrimination (Schreiber 2016). Reed notes that suffering and distress among transgender people are caused by external factors such as experiences of social rejection or violence, not from gender incongruence itself (Love 2016).

Several other countries and international organizations have made changes similar to those within the U.S. medical community. On May 25, 2019, the World Health Organization (WHO), the health agency of the United Nations, agreed to adopt a new version of the WHO's International Classification of Diseases (ICD-11) by January 1, 2022. The new version removes *gender identity disorder* from the chapter on mental disorders and reclassifies transgender identity as *gender incongruence*, an entry in the chapter on sexual health. This change means that United Nations member states that currently classify transgender identity as a mental disorder, including Japan, Kazakhstan, Ukraine, and Indonesia, must revise their policies by January 1, 2022 (Haynes 2019; WHO 2018).

While transgender identity is not a mental illness, transgender people are more likely to suffer from mental illness as a result of the discrimination and stigma they face from modern society. Gender dysphoria is still listed in the handbook used by the medical community to diagnose mental disorders but not all transgender people suffer from gender dysphoria.

FURTHER READING

American Psychiatric Association (APA). n.d. "What Is Gender Dysphoria?" https://www.psychiatry.org/patients-families/gender-dysphoria/what-is-gender-dysphoria

American Psychiatric Association (APA). 2013. "Gender Dysphoria Fact Sheet." https://www.psychiatry.org/psychiatrists/practice/dsm/educational-resources/dsm-5-fact-sheets

Haynes, Suyin. 2019. "The World Health Organization Will Stop Classifying Transgender People as Having a 'Mental Disorder,'" *Time*, May 28. https://time.com/5596845/world-health-organization-transgender-identity/

Love, Shayla. 2016. "The WHO Says Being Transgender Is a Mental Illness. But That's About to Change." *Washington Post*, July 28. https://www.washingtonpost.com/news/morning-mix/wp/2016/07/28/the-w-h-o-says-being-transgender-is-a-mental-illness-but-thats-about-to-change/

Parry, Wynne. 2013. "Gender Dysphoria: DSM-5 Reflects Shift in Perspective on Gender Identity." *HuffPost*, June 4. https://www.huffpost.com/entry/gender-dysphoria-dsm-5_n_3385287

Russo, Francine. 2017. "Where Transgender Is No Longer a Diagnosis." *Scientific American*, January 6. https://www.scientificamerican.com/article/where-transgender-is-no-longer-a-diagnosis/

Schreiber, Katherine. 2016. "Why Transgender People Experience More Mental Health Issues." *Psychology Today*, December 6. https://www.psychologytoday.com/us/blog/the-truth-about-exercise-addiction/201612/why-transgender-people-experience-more-mental-health

World Health Organization (WHO). 2018. "WHO Releases New International Classification of Diseases (ICD 11)." World Health Organization, June 18. https://www.who.int/news/item/18-06-2018-who-releases-new-international-classification-of-diseases-(icd-11)

Q30: CAN CHILDREN REALLY KNOW THAT THEY ARE TRANSGENDER FROM AN EARLY AGE?

Answer: Yes. While some transgender people are not aware of their true gender identity until later in life, other people can know from an early age that they do not feel that they have been assigned the correct gender.

The Facts: Children, even young children, can develop strong, persistent gender identities that do not conform with their sexes assigned at birth. Some of the questions about whether children can truly *know* they are transgender stem from misunderstandings about the difference between being transgender and being gender nonconforming or gender-expansive. It is common for children to play dress-up, including dressing in clothes usually worn by another gender; this is a way for them to express their creativity and imagination and helps them develop empathy toward other people. This dress-up play is not a sign that a child is transgender or nonbinary; it is considered normal play. At the same time, however, dress-up play can also help young children figure out their own gender identity. According to Jack Maypole, a pediatrician at Boston Medical Center, children younger than four years old may think that changing your clothing or hairstyle means changing genders. When they play dress-up, they learn that isn't true—that gender isn't about your clothes (*Parenting* 2020). This kind of behavior expands a child's thinking about what gender they are and the possibilities of genders they are not, a process known as gender-expansive thinking or behavior.

Most gender-expansive young children (ages 5 to 10) do not turn out to be transgender. Gender-expansive children are comfortable with the sex they were assigned at birth but do not conform to gender stereotypes—examples include a boy who likes to play with dolls or a girl who likes short hair and refuses to wear skirts. Only a small percentage of gender-expansive children consistently assert a gender identity inconsistent with the gender they were assigned at birth or express discomfort with their gender. The difference between gender-expansive children and transgender children, however, is not always obvious at first, as a child is figuring things out. This ambiguity can be frustrating for parents and other adults but it does not necessarily mean the child is transgender. Studies show that as many as 80 percent of gender-expansive children assigned male at birth and 90 percent of gender-expansive children assigned female at birth grow up to be non-transgender adults (Zucker 2008).

Gender-expansive behavior is widely thought to be a common aspect of how children make sense of sex and gender. Defying gender stereotypes is a perfectly healthy development for all kids. While some kids who defy gender stereotypes do grow up to be transgender or gender nonconforming, there are important ways they differ from most kids who are gender-expansive.

A large, long-term study of 85 gender-nonconforming children that began in 2013, led by psychologist Kristina Olson, has found that while many children defy gender stereotypes, transgender children are more likely to consistently use the gender pronouns of the gender they eventually identify with and are more extreme in their gender nonconformity—to a degree that makes them similar to children who identify with the gender they were assigned at birth. Regardless of whether a child is allowed to live as their preferred gender, an arrangement often called social transition, those who persistently identify as a gender other than the sex they were labeled at birth will persist in that identity. Some critics claim that "indulging" a child who wants to present as the other gender will cause them to adopt the gender of that presentation. According to Olson, however, children who eventually transition do so because of their persistent identities (Olson 2016).

There are two kinds of gender transitions that a person can undertake: social and medical. First, social transitioning includes taking on a new name and/or new pronouns and changing their clothing choices to more closely align with the expectations of their new gender. Studies have found that transgender youth who are allowed to socially transition have much better levels of mental health (in terms of feelings of anxiety and depression) compared to peers who are not allowed to socially transition. Allowing children to socially transition is seen by many experts as an important tool for reducing suicides. "Why would we deny for the vast majority of kids something that is basically suicide prevention?" asked Diane Ehrensaft, mental health director at the UCSF Child and Adolescent Gender Center Clinic (Brooks 2016).

Some parents are concerned that their child will change their mind about their gender identity and are reluctant to encourage them to transition. While some younger children change their minds, it is easy to socially transition back to their birth name and pronouns and their previous manner of clothing. According to Turban, "a social transition is, of course, completely reversible, and not inherently dangerous" (Turban 2018).

Medical transitioning involves hormone therapies that temporarily stop puberty from progressing. This intervention allows the child time to further explore and understand their gender identity before making further decisions. This decision can be reversed, so that once hormone therapies are stopped, puberty will continue naturally. "Puberty blockers put puberty on hold so that adolescents have more time to decide what they want to do next. This is important because, while pubertal blockade is reversible, puberty itself is not," says Stanford University psychiatrist Jack Turban (Knox 2019). Supporters of these blockers say that the additional time they give kids to reflect on their identity also reduces the odds that a young transgender person will consider suicide (Turban 2020).

Older adolescents, usually at age 16, can also be prescribed gender-affirming hormones including estrogen and testosterone. These therapies cause cosmetic body changes like body fat redistribution and changes in body hair that are less easily reversed; further medical transitions are not available for children.

Very few people who transition later change their minds. A 2015 survey of nearly 28,000 transgender adults found that only 0.4 percent of respondents de-transitioned after realizing that transition was not right for them (James et al. 2016). Rates of de-transitioning are also low among adolescents: of adolescents who persist in their desire to transition as they approach puberty and are allowed to medically transition, the survey found that 1.9 percent later change their minds and 0.5 percent express regrets about their decision to transition.

Not all children who say that they are transgender will persist in that gender identity; there is a small percentage of older children who later change their minds. Data for younger children are not available. Some children experience gender dysphoria at a very young age but then the condition disappears and they become comfortable with the gender they were assigned at birth. These experiences are why some medical experts recommend not moving ahead with any permanent gender-affirming therapies until after considerable counseling and clear understandings of the risks and benefits of various choices.

FURTHER READING

Brooks, Jon. 2019. "Is Three Too Young for Children to Know They're a Different Gender? Transgender Researchers Disagree." KQED, August 26. https://www.kqed.org/futureofyou/440851/can-you-really-know-that-a-3-year-old-is-transgender

James, Sandy E., et al. 2016. *The Report of the 2015 U.S. Transgender Survey.* Washington, DC: National Center for Transgender Equality, December 17. https://transequality.org/sites/default/files/docs/usts/USTS-Full-Report-Dec17.pdf

Knox, Liam. 2019. "Media's 'Detransition' Narrative Is Fueling Misconceptions, Trans Advocates Say." NBCNews.com, December 19. https://www.nbcnews.com/feature/nbc-out/media-s-detransition-narrative-fueling-misconceptions-trans-advocates-say-n1102686

Olson, Kristina R. 2016. "Prepubescent Transgender Children: What We Do and Do Not Know." *Clinical Perspectives* 55, 3: 155–156.

Parenting magazine. 2020. "Why Kids Love to Play Dress-Up." https://www.parenting.com/activities/kids/why-kids-love-to-play-dress-up/

Singal, Jesse. 2018. "When Children Say They're Trans." *Atlantic Magazine*, July/August. https://www.theatlantic.com/magazine/archive/2018/07/when-a-child-says-shes-trans/561749/

Turban, Jack. 2018. "It's Okay to Let Your Transgender Kid Transition—Even If They Might Change Their Mind in the Future." Vox.com, October 22. https://www.vox.com/2018/10/22/18009020/transgender-children-teens-transition-detransition-puberty-blocking-medication

Turban, Jack. 2020. "What South Dakota Doesn't Get about Transgender Children." *New York Times*, February 6. https://www.nytimes.com/2020/02/06/opinion/transgender-children-medical-bills.html

Yong, Ed. 2019. "Young Trans Children Know Who They Are." *Atlantic Magazine*, January 15. https://www.theatlantic.com/science/archive/2019/01/young-trans-children-know-who-they-are/580366/

Zucker, Kenneth J. 2008. "On the 'Natural History' of Gender Identity Disorder in Children." *Journal of the American Academy of Adolescent Psychiatry* 47, 12: 1361–1363.

Q31: DO ALL TRANSGENDER AND NONBINARY PEOPLE FEEL THE NEED TO CHANGE THE WAY THEIR BODY LOOKS THROUGH SURGERY?

Answer: No. Transgender and nonbinary people transition to their preferred gender identity in different ways; sometimes it involves medical intervention, including surgical procedures. Sometimes, transgender and nonbinary people do not want to change their bodies at all.

The Facts: As is true for every identity group, not every transgender and nonbinary person has the same transition to the gender with which they identify. Not all transgender people transition in a physical way; for those who do, not all transition in the same way. Some may transition socially and not medically, transitioning only in that they adopt a new name and/or gender pronouns, or change the way in which they dress. Some may transition medically by doing one or only a few of the procedures available to them. Some may take hormones and decide not to have any surgeries or just choose one kind of surgery and none of the others. Some transitions are stable, meaning that an individual transitions from the gender they were assigned at birth and then adopts a new permanent gender identity while other transitions are more fluid, meaning that an individual may identify as a different gender at different points in time.

There are many reasons for the differences in whether and how people transition. Gender-affirming medical procedures can be very expensive and not everyone can afford them. Some transgender people may have health insurance that covers transition-related procedures and some may not. In addition, not all transgender people want all of the available medical procedures. For some, being transgender or nonbinary is about their core identity, not their outward appearance. "Surgery doesn't change one's gender—it changes the body in which one experiences that gender," says author KC Clements (Clements 2018). For these people, it may relieve their gender dysphoria to socially transition (to present in public as their preferred gender, changing their name, pronouns, and/or clothing) or they may not have gender dysphoria at all and are comfortable with their bodies.

About 20 percent of individuals who identify as transgender report gender identities that are temporarily or permanently neither exclusively male or female or are situated outside the gender binary. These nonbinary, genderfluid, and genderqueer individuals may also choose not to medically transition from one gender to another (Nieder, Eyssel, and Köhler 2019).

The 2011 National Transgender Discrimination Survey found 61 percent of transgender and gender-nonconforming respondents reported having medically transitioned and 33 percent said they had surgically transitioned. About 14 percent of transgender women and 72 percent of transgender men said they do not ever want to undergo full genital construction surgery.

However, being transgender or nonbinary is more than being concerned about surgery. Psychologists and psychiatrists who work with transgender people identify some people as living with a condition known as gender dysphoria, a state of emotional distress caused by how someone's body or the gender they were assigned at birth conflicts with their gender identity (see Q25). This condition, according to a 2008 American Medical Association (AMA) resolution, can lead to "distress, dysfunction, debilitating depression and, for some people without access to appropriate medical care and treatment, suicidality and death." The AMA and American Psychiatric Association say it can be treated by letting someone transition without enduring significant barriers and social stigma (Lopez 2015). A diagnosis of gender dysphoria is often necessary for transgender people to get other interventions, including surgery and hormone therapy, covered by insurance carriers.

Some transgender and nonbinary people simply don't have gender dysphoria—their gender assigned at birth does not match their gender identity but they are comfortable with their bodies or only suffer mild dysphoria that does not rise to the level of feeling surgical transition is appropriate.

In addition to economic concerns, a significant amount of stigma and discrimination prevents many transgender people from seeking medical care when they need it. The National Transgender Discrimination Survey, a joint partnership of the National Gay and Lesbian Task Force and National Center for Transgender Equality, conducted a national survey of transgender people in the United States in 2010. Their findings document a profound crisis in terms of transgender health care. Among their findings: 19 percent of transgender and gender-nonconforming people said they were refused care because of their gender identity or expression, 28 percent of transgender and gender-nonconforming respondents said they were subjected to harassment in medical settings, and 2 percent said they experienced violence. These experiences often led to delays in care for many people: 28 percent said they postponed medical care when sick or injured due to discrimination in the American health-care system (Grant et al. 2011).

In 2016, the Obama administration's Department of Health and Human Services (HHS) clarified that Obamacare regulations explicitly prohibit anti-transgender discrimination from medical providers and insurers

(Baron 2020). However, in 2019, the Trump administration published a formal proposal to roll back numerous provisions of the 2016 regulation, drastically cutting back its interpretation of the law's protection. In June 2020, the Trump administration finalized this rollback, instructing HHS to not take any action to help people who have faced anti-transgender discrimination in health care or to investigate complaints of anti-transgender discrimination. The rule would have removed all recognition by HHS that the law prohibits anti-transgender or anti-LGBTQ bias but it was blocked by the courts (Schmidt 2020). These rights were then positively affirmed by the Biden administration: in May 2021, the Biden administration expanded protections against discrimination based on sexual orientation or gender identity in health care (Goldstein 2021). Overall, since entering office, President Biden has taken strong action to improve the lives of LGBTQ people in the United States, including addressing discrimination and disparities in employment, health care, housing, and education (Medina and Santos 2021).

FURTHER READING

American Medical Association. n.d. "Policies on Lesbian, Gay, Bisexual, Transgender & Queer (LGBTQ) issues." American Medical Association. https://www.ama-assn.org/delivering-care/population-care/policies-lesbian-gay-bisexual-transgender-queer-lgbtq-issues

Clements, K. C. 2018. "What to Expect from Gender Confirmation Surgery." Healthline, December 19. https://www.healthline.com/health/transgender/gender-confirmation-surgery

Goldstein, Amy. 2021. "Biden Administration Revises Anti-Bias Protections in Health Care for Transgender People." *Washington Post*, May 10. https://www.washingtonpost.com/health/transgender-protection-hhs/2021/05/10/0852ce88-b17d-11eb-a980-a60af976ed44_story.html

Grant, Jaime M., et al. 2011. *Injustice at Every Turn: A Report of the National Transgender Discrimination Survey*. Washington, DC: National Center for Transgender Equality and National Gay and Lesbian Task Force. https://www.thetaskforce.org/injustice-every-turn-report-national-transgender-discrimination-survey/

HHS.gov. 2020. "Section 1557 of the Patient Protection and Affordable Care Act." Office for Civil Rights, U.S. Department of Health and Human Services. HHS.gov, November 19. https://www.hhs.gov/civil-rights/for-individuals/section-1557/index.html

Lopez, German. 2015. "Military's Transgender Ban Based on Bad Medical Science, Say Medical Scientists." Vox, June 8. https://www.vox.com/2015/6/8/8748341/ama-transgender-soldiers

Lopez, German. 2018. "Myth #5: All Trans People Medically Transition."
    Vox, November 14. https://www.vox.com/identities/2016/5/13/17938114
    /transgender-people-transitioning-surgery-medical
Medina, Caroline and Theo Santos. 2021. "A Timeline of the Biden Admin-
    istration's Efforts to Support LGBTQ Equality in the First 100 Days."
    Center for American Progress, April 28. https://www.americanprogress
    .org/issues/lgbtq-rights/news/2021/04/28/498775/timeline-biden
    -administrations-efforts-support-lgbtq-equality-first-100-days/
Nieder, Timo O., Jana Eyssel, and Andreas Köhler. 2019. "Being Trans
    without Medical Transition: Exploring Characteristics of Trans
    Individuals from Germany Not Seeking Gender-Affirmative Medical
    Interventions." *Archives of Sexual Behavior* 49: 2661–2672.
Planned Parenthood. n.d. "What Do I Need to Know about Transition-
    ing?" Planned Parenthood. https://www.plannedparenthood.org/learn
    /gender-identity/transgender/what-do-i-need-know-about-transitioning
Schmidt, Samantha. 2020. "Federal Judge Blocks Trump Administration
    from Ending Transgender Health-Care Protections." *Washington
    Post*, August 17. https://www.washingtonpost.com/dc-md-va/2020/08
    /17/federal-judge-blocks-trump-administration-ending-transgender
    -healthcare-protections/

Q32: ARE MORE AMERICANS USING
NONBINARY PRONOUNS?

Answer: Yes. The use of nonbinary pronouns used to be rare but has
become more common in the last 15–20 years (Baron 2020). Today, one in
four American LGBTQ youth use pronouns other than he/him or she/her,
according to a survey released in July 2020 (Venkatraman 2020). One in
five American adults say they know someone who uses nonbinary
pronouns.

The Facts: The use of nonbinary pronouns to refer to people who do
not fit a gender binary or whose gender was unknown has been around
since the late 1300s and in the United States since 1841. The first recom-
mended set of gender-neutral pronouns, *E/Es/Em*, appeared in a book of
grammar published in Brooklyn, New York, in 1841; *Ve/Vim/Vir* was offered
in a popular magazine in 1864. These and other early attempts to coin an
acceptable set of nonbinary pronouns did not catch on, however, because
as English professor emeritus Dennis Baron notes in his 2020 book *What's
Your Pronoun? Beyond He and She*, "people use the pronouns they like, not
the ones they're told to use" (2020, 82).

Since 2010 or so, however, the use of nonbinary pronouns (also known as gender-neutral pronouns) has become much more prevalent in the United States (Baron 2020; Merriam-Webster 2019). The use of "they" as a single gender-neutral pronoun has become particularly widespread, including in marketing copy, on social media, and in app interfaces (Manjoo 2019). In March 2019, United Airlines allowed individuals creating flight reservations to choose the gender-neutral Mx. instead of Mr. or Ms. In 2015, the American Dialect Society chose the singular "they" as the Word of the Year, recognizing "its emerging use as a pronoun to refer to a known person, often as a conscious choice by a person rejecting the traditional gender binary of *he* and *she*" (American Dialect Society 2016). In 2019, Merriam-Webster chose "they" as their 2019 Word of the Year and added it to their dictionary. The International Writing Center Association in 2018 advocated the use of the singular "they" when that is an individual's correct pronoun, noting: "One way that academic spaces inflict violence is through linguistic marginalization or exclusion surrounding gender, particularly through pronoun usage" (IWCA 2018).

The increased use of nonbinary pronouns has been accompanied by an increased tendency for individuals to state their pronouns in their email signatures or when introducing themselves to others (Saguy and Williams 2019). These acknowledgments are meant to signal an increased awareness of gender identity diversity and allyship with LGBTQ people. "We cannot assume someone's pronouns by the way they look, dress, or act—even when we know their gender identity," notes clinical psychologist Katharine Thomson (McCarthy 2017). While many people refer to pronouns as "preferred pronouns," a more recent trend is to recognize that pronouns are correct or incorrect, not a preference, just as gender identity itself is not a preference (GLSEN 2020).

At the same time, observers have also pointed out that asking someone their pronouns can inadvertently hurt people. They may still be sorting out their gender identity or they may not feel comfortable opening up about their gender identity in that moment. Social psychologist Devon Price cautions that not everyone feels like sharing because "we've been burned before. A lot of people are disrespectful or invasive towards us, and it's hard to predict how shitty a new acquaintance is going to be" (Price 2018).

In a 2018 Pew Research Center survey, 60 percent of U.S. adults said they had heard about gender-neutral pronouns and 18 percent said they personally knew someone who prefers them. Responses varied by age; younger people (aged 18 to 29) were more likely to have heard about gender-neutral pronouns (73 percent) or to personally know someone who uses them (32 percent). Democrats were also more likely to know about gender-neutral pronouns and to know someone who uses them compared to Republicans (Geiger and Graf 2019).

A 2020 survey of LGBTQ youth ages 13–24 found that 25 percent of respondents use a nonbinary gender. While most use more common pronouns such as them/they or combinations of she, he, and they, 4 percent reported that they use neopronouns such as ze/zir/zirs (Trevor Project 2020).

FURTHER READING

American Dialect Society. 2016. "2015 Word of the Year Is Singular 'They.'" AmericanDialect.org, January 8. https://www.americandialect .org/2015-word-of-the-year-is-singular-they

Baron, Dennis. 2020. *What's Your Pronoun? Beyond He and She.* New York: Norton.

Geiger, A. W., and Nikki Graf. 2019. "About One-in-Five U.S. Adults Know Someone Who Goes by a Gender-Neutral Pronoun." Pew Research Center, September 5. https://www.pewresearch.org/fact -tank/2019/09/05/gender-neutral-pronouns/

GLSEN. 2020. "Pronoun Guide." GLSEN. https://www.glsen.org/activity /pronouns-guide-glsen

IWCA. 2018. "Position Statement on the Use of the Singular 'They.'" https://docs.google.com/document/d/1VfQXCY18sSCKX _KPk4HpyR9aJHORDfs883oQEeF7gAk/edit

Manjoo, Farhad. 2019. "It's Time for 'They.'" *New York Times*, July 10. https://www.nytimes.com/2019/07/10/opinion/pronoun-they-gender .html

McCarthy, Maureen. 2017. "Gender Identity and Pronoun Use: A Guide for Pediatric Health Care Professionals." *Boston Children's Hospital's Clinical Health* (blog), June 8. https://notes.childrenshospital.org /clinicians-guide-gender-identity-pronoun-use/

Merriam-Webster. 2019. "Words We're Watching: Singular 'They.'" Merriam-Webster.com, September. https://www.merriam-webster.com /words-at-play/singular-nonbinary-they

Price, Devon. 2018. "When (& How) to Ask About Pronouns: A Shy Enby's Guide for Cis & Trans People." Medium,com, April 29. https://devonprice .medium.com/when-how-to-ask-about-pronouns-b7fc24df6653

Saguy, Abigail C., and Juliet A. Williams. 2019. "Why We Should All Use They/Them Pronouns." *Scientific American*, April 11. https://blogs .scientificamerican.com/voices/why-we-should-all-use-they-them-pronouns/

Tobia, Jacob. 2016. "Everything You Ever Wanted to Know about Gender-Neutral Pronouns." *Time*, May 12. https://time.com/4327915/gender-neutral-pronouns/

Trevor Project. 2019. "Research Brief: Pronouns Usage among LGBTQ Youth." TrevorProject.org, July 29. https://www.thetrevorproject.org/2020/07/29/research-brief-pronouns-usage-among-lgbtq-youth/

Venkatraman, Sakshi. 2020. "Beyond 'He' and 'She': 1 in 4 LGBTQ Youths Use Nonbinary Pronouns, Survey Finds." NBCNews.com, July 30. https://www.nbcnews.com/feature/nbc-out/beyond-he-she-1-4-lgbtq-youths-use-nonbinary-pronouns-n1235204

Q33: IS TRANSGENDER IDENTITY RELATED TO SEXUAL ORIENTATION, IN THAT TRANSGENDER MEN ARE FORMER LESBIANS AND TRANSGENDER WOMEN ARE FORMER GAY MEN?

Answer: No. Gender identity and sexual orientation are separate constructs. The gender with which a person identifies is not necessarily related to the gender to which they are sexually attracted.

The Facts: People who are not transgender, also known as cisgender people, can have any sexual orientation and the same is true for transgender people. Gender identity is not related to sexual orientation, although the two identity groups (people who identify with a nonheterosexual sexual orientation and people who identify as a non-cisgender gender identity) are both part of the larger LGBTQ community.

Transgender people are more likely to identify as queer on the sexual orientation spectrum: among participants in the 2015 National Transgender Discrimination Survey, only 23 percent of respondents identified as straight. However, being gay or lesbian can be a challenge for transgender people thinking about embracing their gender identity. Transgender activist Charlie Kiss recalled that he struggled for 18 years to be "a true lesbian," and to align his attraction to women with his desire to have a man's body. "It was confusing because I, like most lesbians, considered men's bodies unattractive. . . . The notion of a trans man being 'really a lesbian' is not supported by the facts" (Kiss 2018).

Multiple studies have found that transitioning to another gender—whether socially (changing one's name, pronouns, and clothing) or medically (using puberty blockers or hormones or having gender-confirming surgery)—can alter one's sexual orientation. Most of these changes include shifts from exclusive attraction to one gender pre-transition toward some level of bisexuality. In a 2013 study of 605 transgender men from 19 different countries, 40 percent of those who had begun to transition (using testosterone) reported a shift in their sexual orientation. In a 2005 study of 232 transgender women, 54 percent of participants had been predominantly attracted to women and 9 percent had been predominantly attracted to men prior to their gender-confirmation surgery. After the surgery, only 25 percent reported being predominantly attracted to women, and 34 percent said that they were predominantly attracted to men. Similar results have been documented in additional research studies.

The cause of these changes in sexuality is unclear. It may be that changes in sexual orientation are due to the suppression or addition of hormones (androgens and estrogens). It may also be that when a transgender person is able to align their physical body with their gender identity, they feel more comfortable exploring their true sexual attractions. Or it may be that prior to transitioning they suppressed their true sexual orientation to better fit in with the heterosexual norms given their gender assigned at birth (Vrangalova 2018).

Some of the confusion is also due to the time it can take a transgender person to realize their true gender identity. Author Jacob Anderson-Minshall, cofounder with his partner of the national lesbian magazine *Girlfriends*, identified as a lesbian until he was in his early 30s:

> When a girl wears "boy's clothes" and wants to hang out with the boys, she gets called a tomboy and her exploration of masculinity is seen as perfectly normal, maybe even laudable. If she continues this behavior into her teens, she starts being labeled a lesbian, which makes sense if she's attracted to women. I was, so I just assumed I was a lesbian. (Anderson-Minshall 2015)

Anderson-Minshall's story illustrates why many people believe that all transgender people are formerly gay and lesbian people and also why LGBTQ people are all included in the same acronym: people with these identities tend to violate gender norms. Because society associates the violation of gender norms with gay and lesbian sexual orientations, young people who violate gender norms are then told that they are gay or lesbian regardless of their true sexual orientation or gender identity. This can sometimes mean that they will eventually identify as gay or lesbian but it may also be because they will eventually identify as transgender or nonbinary. However, the two concepts are distinct. Not all transgender men previously identified as lesbians and not all transgender women previously identified as gay.

FURTHER READING

Anderson-Minshall, Jacob. 2015. "I Used to Be a Lesbian. Now I'm a Happily Married Man." *Glamour*, May 29. https://www.glamour.com/story /lesbian-transgender-married-couple-jacob-anderson-minshall-of-queerly -beloved

Kiss, Charlie. 2018. "The Idea That Trans Men Are 'Lesbians in Denial' Is Demeaning and Wrong." *The Economist*, July 3. https://www.economist .com/open-future/2018/07/03/the-idea-that-trans-men-are-lesbians-in -denial-is-demeaning-and-wrong

Lawrence, Anne A. 2005. "Sexuality Before and After Male-to-Female Sex Reassignment Surgery." *Archives of Sexual Behavior* 34, 2: 147–166.

Meier, S. Colton, Seth T. Pardo, Christine Labuski, and Julia Babcock. 2013. "Measures of Clinical Health among Female-to-Male Transgender Persons as a Function of Sexual Orientation." *Archives of Sexual Behavior* 42, 3: 463–474.

Vrangalova, Zhana. 2018. "Research Shows Many Trans Folks' Sexual Attractions Change After Transition." Them.us, June 25. https://www .them.us/story/sexual-attraction-after-transition

Q34: IS THERE TENSION BETWEEN THE FEMINIST MOVEMENT AND PEOPLE WHO IDENTIFY AS TRANSGENDER AND/OR NONBINARY?

Answer: Sometimes, yes. While some feminists support the inclusion of transgender and nonbinary people in the movement's common cause, others feel such inclusion is radical and unnecessarily blurs lines between biology and ideology in a way that hinders the feminist movement's overall goals.

The Facts: Feminism in general seeks social, economic, and political equality of men and women but the specific goals and scope of the feminist movement have shifted over time. The first wave pushed for votes for women, which culminated in the Nineteenth Amendment's ratification in 1920. The second wave, in the 1960s and 1970s, sought broader equal rights for women. The third wave, which emerged in the 1990s, sought to expand on the victories of the second wave but also to challenge dominant beliefs about gender norms and gender expression, including the performance of masculinity and femininity. Trans feminism—defined either as transgender perspectives on feminism or as feminist perspectives on transgender issues—is one of many classifications of third-wave feminisms (Serano 2012).

While trans feminism is fairly new, debates about the place of transgender people within the feminist movement have been around for decades. In 1979, women's studies professor and lesbian feminist Janice Raymond wrote that gender is an expression of biological sex, which is chromosomally dependent and cannot be changed. Raymond argued that transgender women are not, nor can they ever become, women, because the characteristics of womanhood are fixed at birth through chromosomes and strengthened by life experience (through gender socialization and experiences of gender discrimination) (Raymond 1979; Hines 2019). While Raymond did not invent anti-transgender prejudice, sociologist Carol Riddell writes that Raymond's book "did more to justify and perpetuate it than perhaps any other book ever written" (Riddell 1996, 131).

Transgender women challenge traditional definitions of what it means to be a woman and challenge gender as a biological fact, asserting that their unique experience as women should be recognized as a valid aspect of the feminist cause. Trans feminism extends existing feminist approaches challenging oppression and sexism to transgender issues, ones that have been overlooked and misinterpreted in the past (Serano 2012). According to transgender activist and author Julie Serano, anyone who does not conform to the gender binary—an intersex child, a tomboyish girl, a gay man, a transgender person—tends to be marginalized in different ways. Serano writes:

> Trans feminists have also focused on how trans people are impacted by institutionalized cissexism—forms of sexism that construe trans people's gender identities and expressions as less legitimate than those of cis people (those who are not trans). Cissexism—or as some describe it, transphobia—can be seen in how individuals, organizations and governments often refuse to respect trans people's lived experiences in our identified genders/sexes; in the discrimination we may face in employment or medical settings; and in how trans people are often targeted for harassment and violence. (Serano 2012)

In short, LGBTQ advocates suggest that anyone who holds views denying transgender people their full humanity go against what feminists and the medical community know to be true and deserve to be called out for their transphobic views (Miller and Yasharoff 2020).

On the other hand, some feminists continue to believe that because transgender women (and nonbinary people assigned male at birth) were raised as men and did not grow up experiencing sexism as children in the same ways in which cisgender women experience sexism throughout their lives, they cannot fully know what it means to be a woman. Contemporary feminism continues to include a strong strain of anti-transgender sentiment, according to professor of sociology and gender Sally Hines. While many feminist communities in the second wave were inclusive of transgender women, feminists continue to debate the "realness" of the gender identities and expressions of trans women and men (Hines 2019). "Trans scholars and activists . . . have written on the ways in which Raymond's book impacted on feminist communities in the 1970s and 1980s, creating divisions that have been hard to heal" (Hines 2019, 146). Throughout the 1990s, feminist scholars and transgender activists continued to debate the place of trans people within feminist communities.

These debates have at times spilled out into the public sphere. In the 1970s, transgender woman Allucquére Rosanne "Sandy" Stone was part of the famous radical feminist music collective Olivia Records. After Raymond mentioned her and the collective in her book, however, Stone received a wave of threatening mail. She eventually left Olivia after a highly publicized series of boycott threats and death threats from radical lesbian separatists (Drucker 2018; Male 2020). Another well-known battleground of trans feminism was at the Michigan Womyn's Music Festival, where a transsexual woman was ejected in the early 1990s. From then until its closing in 2015, the organizers enforced a strict "womyn-born-womyn only" policy (Merlan 2015).

The Kimberly Nixon case in Canada is another example of a high-profile clash. Kimberly is a transgender woman (who previously identified herself as a transsexual woman) who applied to train as a volunteer rape crisis counselor at Vancouver Rape Relief in Vancouver, British Columbia, in 1995. When her gender identity was revealed, she was forced to leave the training program because the staff felt her identity made it impossible for her to truly understand assigned-female-at-birth women who had experienced sexual assault and domestic violence. Nixon sued for discrimination and a multiyear court battle ensued. Vancouver Rape Relief eventually won the case in 2007 when the Canadian Supreme Court refused to hear Nixon's appeal (Rupp 2007).

Feminists who oppose the inclusion of transgender women and nonbinary people assigned male at birth are sometimes referred to as trans-exclusionary radical feminists (TERFs). The term was first published by feminist blogger Viv Smythe in 2008 as a descriptive term to distinguish them from other radical feminists who were transgender positive or neutral, although Smythe notes that while her blog popularized the term, she did not invent it (Hines 2019; Miller and Yasharoff 2020). TERF made headlines in 2020 when it was used to criticize *Harry Potter* author J. K. Rowling for tweets about gender and sex that many observers deemed transphobic. Rowling was widely criticized for her remarks. Daniel Radcliffe, who starred as Harry Potter in the movies based on Rowling's books, was one of her most high-profile critics; he wrote in an essay responding to Rowling that "transgender women are women." Overall, most feminists reject TERF views (Miller and Yasharoff 2020; Radcliffe 2020).

The discussion of how and whether to allow transgender women to be treated as valid women and the place of trans feminism within the wider world of feminism will likely continue as the feminist movement itself evolves and changes over time.

FURTHER READING

Ananda, Katchie. 2019. "Transfeminism and TERFs: A Clash between Biology and Ideology." Medium, January 18. https://medium.com/the-wvoice/transfeminism-and-terfs-a-clash-between-biology-and-ideology-eccd9853aa5f

Bains, Camille. 2019. "Trans Woman Says She Hopes Funding Cut to Vancouver Rape Crisis Group Will Result in Policy Changes." *Globe and Mail*, March 21. https://www.theglobeandmail.com/canada/british-columbia/article-trans-woman-says-she-hopes-funding-cut-to-vancouver-rape-crisis-group/

Drucker, Zackary. 2018. "Sandy Stone on Living Among Lesbian Separatists as a Trans Woman in the 70s." Vice, December 19. https://www.vice.com/en/article/zmd5k5/sandy-stone-biography-transgender-history

Hines, Sally. 2019. "The Feminist Frontier: On Trans and Feminism." *Journal of Gender Studies* 28, 2: 145–157.

Male, Andrew. 2020. "'Our Sound Engineer Got a Death Threat': How Lesbian Label Olivia Shook Up Music." *The Guardian*, July 19. https://www.theguardian.com/music/2020/jul/19/lesbian-record-label-olivia-linda-tillery-californian-feminists-death-threat-music

Merlan, Anna. 2015. "Trans-Excluding Michigan Womyn's Music Festival to End This Year." Jezebel, April 22. https://jezebel.com/trans-excluding-michigan-womyns-music-festival-to-end-t-1699412910

Miller, Ryan W., and Hannah Yasharoff. 2020. "What's a TERF and Why Is 'Harry Potter' Author J. K. Rowling Being Called One?" *USA TODAY*, June 9. https://www.usatoday.com/story/news/nation/2020/06/09/what-terf-definition-trans-activists-includes-j-k-rowling/5326071002/

Radcliffe, Daniel. 2020. "Daniel Radcliffe Responds to J. K. Rowling's Tweets on Gender Identity." The Trevor Project, June 8. https://www.thetrevorproject.org/2020/06/08/daniel-radcliffe-responds-to-j-k-rowlings-tweets-on-gender-identity/

Raymond, Janice. 1979. *The Transsexual Empire: The Making of the She-Male*. London: The Women's Press.

Riddell, Carol. 1996. "Divided Sisterhood: A Critical Review of Janice Raymond's *The Transsexual Empire*." In Richard Ekins and Dave King, eds., *Blending Genders: Social Aspects of Cross-Dressing and Sex-Changing*. New York: Routledge, pp. 171–189.

Rupp, Shannon 2007. "Transsexual Loses Fight with Women's Shelter." The Tyee, February 3. https://thetyee.ca/News/2007/02/03/Nixon/

Serano, Julia. 2012. "Trans Feminism: There's No Conundrum about It." *Ms. Magazine*, April 18. https://msmagazine.com/2012/04/18/trans-feminism-theres-no-conundrum-about-it/

6

Behaviors and Outcomes Associated with LGBTQ People

This chapter addresses behaviors and outcomes that are often equated with LGBTQ people including their relative vulnerability to HIV/AIDS, mental illness, drug and alcohol abuse, shortened life expectancy, homelessness, and bullying. Some of these behaviors and outcomes are, in fact, more common among LGBTQ people than straight people in the United States but not for the reasons that many may think.

Q35 discusses the relationship between LGBTQ people and HIV/AIDS, making the point that while there is a connection between HIV/AIDS and LGBTQ identity, identity doesn't cause infection. Q36 identifies patterns between LGBTQ identity and mental illness, clarifying that these patterns arise not because LGBTQ identity is, or causes, mental illness but because societal and cultural stigma and discrimination often contribute to the development of mental illness among LGBTQ people. Q37 discusses the controversial practice of "conversion therapy," the idea that someone can put aside their sexual orientation or gender identity. Q38 discusses the link between drug and alcohol abuse and LGBTQ identity, finding that one notable cause of substance abuse in the LGBTQ community is the bigotry that many members face. Q39 debunks the myth that LGBTQ people have significantly shorter life expectancies than straight people, a stereotype perpetuated in the 1980s and 1990s that persists today. Q40 and Q41 address homelessness and bullying among LGBTQ youth, significant problems that again are often rooted in bigotry and discrimination against

LGBTQ people. Finally, Q42 tackles the claims that children of LGBTQ people are worse off than kids of straight parents.

Q35: DO LGBTQ PEOPLE CONTRACT HIV/AIDS AT DIFFERENT RATES THAN STRAIGHT PEOPLE?

Answer: Yes. Men who have sexual contact with other men are far more susceptible to the spread of the Human Immunodeficiency Virus (HIV), the virus that causes Acquired Immunodeficiency Syndrome (AIDS), even with the same numbers of unprotected sexual partners. According to the Centers for Disease Control and Prevention (CDC), approximately 492,000 sexually active gay and bisexual men are at high risk for HIV (CDC 2020).

The Facts: As of the end of 2018 (the most recent year for which data are available), an estimated 1.2 million Americans had HIV, including 740,400 gay and bisexual men. An estimated 38,000 new HIV infections still occur in the United States each year (CDC 2020).

- In 2018, 37,968 people received an HIV diagnosis in the United States and six dependent areas (American Samoa, Guam, Northern Mariana Islands, Puerto Rico, Republic of Palau, and U.S. Virgin Islands).
- Most diagnoses of HIV infections (over 65 percent) are attributed to male-to-male sexual contact. Diagnoses are most common among young men (age 25–34), particularly among Black and Latino men.
- HIV diagnoses are not evenly distributed across states and regions. Diagnoses are most common in the South (about 50 percent) and least common in the Midwest (about 13 percent).

Transmission is not evenly distributed throughout the American population either. HIV continues to have a disproportionate impact on certain populations, particularly Black and Latino Americans and gay and bisexual men. According to the CDC, gay and bisexual men accounted for 69 percent of all HIV diagnoses in the United States and 86 percent of diagnoses among males in 2018 (CDC 2020).

It is important to remember that identity and behavior are not the same constructs. Many surveys, including the CDC surveillance systems, use the term *male-to-male sexual contact* to indicate *behavior* that is more likely to transmit HIV infection, not how individuals self-identify in terms of their sexual orientation (HIV.gov). Other sources use the term *men who have sex with men* or MSM. The figures in the CDC reports thus refer to diagnoses among men who have male-to-male sexual contact, which includes "gay, bisexual, and other men who have sex with men" (CDC 2020).

While HIV diagnoses are most common among gay and bisexual men, rates of infection are not evenly distributed by ethnorace. Non-Hispanic whites were 62 percent of the U.S. population in 2018 but they account for only 25 percent of HIV infections. Black Americans, in contrast, were 12 percent of the population but 42 percent of infections and Latino Americans were 17 percent of the population and 28 percent of infections. Dividing the data further to look at sexual orientation, in 2018, Black gay and bisexual men accounted for 37 percent of HIV diagnoses, Latino gay and bisexual men accounted for 30 percent, and white non-Hispanic gay and bisexual men accounted for 27 percent. Rates of infection in 2018 were highest among young gay and bisexual men aged 25 to 34 (39 percent of new HIV diagnoses), a rate that has been increasing in recent years (CDC 2020).

In part, these discrepancies are attributed to decreased use of condoms or other pre-exposure prophylaxis. Rates are also higher among people with limited access to quality health care, lower income and educational levels, and higher rates of unemployment and incarceration (CDC 2020). According to the CDC, most gay and bisexual men get HIV from having anal sex without protection (like using a condom or taking medicine to prevent or treat HIV). Anal sex is the riskiest type of sex for getting or transmitting HIV: receptive anal sex is 13 times as risky for getting HIV as insertive anal sex. As the rectal mucosa (the mucus membranes of the inner rectum and colon) is more fragile than the vaginal or oral mucosa, anal sex increases the risk for transmitting HIV and other sexually transmitted infections (STIs).

A community's relationship with sex plays a significant role as well. Many people in the gay community have a relatively liberal attitude toward sex and partnership. While no community is monolithic in its attitudes toward sex and relationships, "sexual contact [among MSM] is more instantaneous and spontaneous, and sexual intercourse may take place early in a relationship. Relationships between some MSM may be more flexible, and concurrent sex with casual partners during a relationship is generally more tolerable. . . . Early sexual debut is another reason for greater exposure to HIV, as MSM would have more partners during their lifetime" (Mor and Dan 2012). Sexuality and sexual behavior are, of course, not the same for every member of a community. Men who have sex with men are more likely to engage in riskier sexual behaviors, however, triggered by wider social and cultural changes and greater social acceptance for gay men (Mayer et al. 2010; Sullivan et al. 2009).

Public health experts also point to the increased use of the internet to find sexual partners as a factor in the spread of HIV/AIDS and other sexually transmitted diseases (Rosser et al. 2011). The internet is relatively affordable, discreet, and immediate, offering free and anonymous access to a pool of sexual partners. The anonymity also allows MSM to search explicitly for unprotected anal sex (McDaid and Hart 2010). Numerous studies have found that gay men who seek and meet sexual partners through the internet are more likely to engage in high-risk sexual behavior. However, this does not necessarily contribute to the spread of HIV, as many gay men who meet partners on the internet use online screening to find men of the same HIV status, a practice known as serosorting (Elford 2006).

A phenomenon called "AIDS optimism" also contributes to riskier sexual behavior among MSM. With the rise of highly active antiretroviral therapies (HAART), pre-exposure prophylaxis therapies (PrEP), and post-exposure prophylaxis (PeP), studies show that sexual behavior has changed. A HAART regimen can improve the quality of life of individuals with HIV and prevent transmission to others and PrEP and PeP therapies help people at high risk avoid getting HIV if they are exposed (Eggleton and Nagalli 2020; HIV.gov 2020). MSM may wrongly consider their sexual partners to be HIV-negative and engage in riskier, unprotected sex without considering that post-exposure treatment is not a cure or effective treatment in all cases (Poynten et al. 2009). Finally, many young MSM, not having witnessed the earlier devastation of AIDS, do not feel threatened by the disease and thus may be more likely to engage in unprotected sex. The advanced manageability of HIV, as portrayed in the media and advertisements sponsored by the pharmaceutical industry, may further disinhibit their sexual behavior (Mor and Dan 2012). HAART and PrEP in particular contribute to risky behavior because they have normalized unprotected anal sex (Kippax and Holt 2016).

Finally, lingering stigma and discrimination associated with being gay or bisexual affect the health and well-being of gay and bisexual men and may prevent them from seeking and receiving high-quality health services, including HIV testing, treatment, and other prevention services. According to the Medical Monitoring Project, roughly two-thirds of HIV+ people say it is difficult to tell others about their HIV infection; one-third report feeling guilty or shamed about their status and one in four say that being HIV-positive makes them feel dirty or worthless. These issues place gay and bisexual men at higher risk for HIV and make testing and disclosure more difficult. In addition, socioeconomic factors such as limited access to quality health care, lower income and educational levels, and higher rates of unemployment and incarceration place some gay and bisexual men at higher risk for HIV (CDC 2020).

FURTHER READING

Baugher, Amy R., et al. 2017. "Prevalence of Internalized HIV-Related Stigma among HIV-Infected Adults in Care, United States, 2011–2013." *AIDS and Behavior* 21, 9: 2600–2608.

BMJ Specialty Journals. 2007. "Different HIV Rates among Gay Men and Straight People Not Fully Explained by Sexual Behavior." *Science-Daily*, September 14. https://www.sciencedaily.com/releases/2007/09 /070913132930.htm

Centers for Disease Control and Prevention (CDC). 2020. *HIV Surveillance Reports, 2018 (Updated)*; vol. 31. http://www.cdc.gov/hiv/library /reports/hiv-surveillance.html

Cohen, Stacy M., et al. 2014. "The Status of the National HIV Surveillance System, United States, 2013." *Public Health Reports* 129, 4: 335–341.

Eggleton, Julie S., and Shivaraj Nagalli. 2020. "Highly Active Antiretroviral Therapy (HAART)." *National Center for Biotechnology Information*, July 5. https://www.ncbi.nlm.nih.gov/books/NBK554533/

Elford, Jonathan. 2006. "Changing Patterns of Sexual Behaviour in the Era of Highly Active Antiretroviral Therapy." *Current Opinion in Infectious Diseases* 19, 1: 26–32.

Fenton, Kevin A. 2010. "Prevention with HIV-Positive Men Who Have Sex with Men: Regaining Lost Ground." *Sexually Transmitted Infections* 86, 1: 2–4.

Hall, H. Irene, et al. 2008. "Estimation of HIV Incidence in the United States." *JAMA* 300, 5: 520–529.

HIV.gov. 2020. "Pre-Exposure Prophylaxis." Last updated Sept. 22, 2020. https://www.hiv.gov/hiv-basics/hiv-prevention/using-hiv-medication-to -reduce-risk/pre-exposure-prophylaxis

Kippax, Susan, and Martin Holt. 2016. "Diversification of Risk Reduction Strategies and Reduced Threat of HIV May Explain Increases in Condomless Sex." *AIDS* 30, 18: 2898–2899.

Mayer, Kenneth H., et al. 2010. "Which HIV-Infected Men Who Have Sex with Men in Care Are Engaging in Risky Sex and Acquiring Sexually Transmitted Infections: Findings from a Boston Community Health Centre." *Sexually Transmitted Infections* 86: 66–70.

McDaid, Lisa M., and Graham J. Hart. 2010. "Sexual Risk Behaviour for Transmission of HIV in Men Who Have Sex with Men: Recent

Findings and Potential Interventions." *Current Opinion in HIV and AIDS* 5, 4: 311–315.

Medical Monitoring Project. 2018. "Internalized HIV-Related Stigma." https://www.cdc.gov/hiv/pdf/statistics/mmp/cdc-hiv-internalized-stigma .pdf

Mor, Zohar, and Michael Dan. 2012. "The HIV Epidemic among Men Who Have Sex with Men—Behaviour Beats Science." *EMBO Reports* 13, 11: 948–953.

Poynten, I. Mary, et al. 2009. "Nonoccupational Postexposure Prophylaxis, Subsequent Risk Behaviour and HIV Incidence in a Cohort of Australian Homosexual Men." *AIDS* 23, 9: 1119–1126.

Rosser, B. R. Simon, et al. 2011. "The Future of Internet-Based HIV Prevention: A Report on Key Findings from the Men's INTernet (MINTS-I, II) Sex Studies." *AIDS and Behavior* 15: 91–100.

Sullivan, Patrick S., et al. 2009. "Reemergence of the HIV Epidemic among Men Who Have Sex with Men in North America, Western Europe, and Australia, 1996–2005." *Annals of Epidemiology* 19, 6: 423–431.

Q36: ARE LGBTQ PEOPLE MORE PRONE TO MENTAL ILLNESS THAN STRAIGHT PEOPLE?

Answer: Yes. LGBTQ people are more likely to face homophobia/ transphobia, harassment, and violence, leading to added stress, feelings of uncertainty, anxiety, and depression. Being LGBTQ doesn't *cause* mental illness but these experiences and trauma make mental illness more likely.

The Facts: Researchers have documented strong correlations between sexual and gender identity and mental health challenges. For example, gay and bisexual men and lesbians and bisexual women report higher levels of mental distress and depression than heterosexuals (Gonzales, Przedworski, and Henning-Smith 2016; Gonzales and Henning-Smith 2017). Transgender children and adolescents have higher levels of depression, suicidality, self-harm, and eating disorders than their non-transgender counterparts (Connolly et al. 2016).

LGBTQ people report symptoms of mental illness including anxiety, depression, substance abuse, and suicidal ideation far more than heterosexual people (NAMI, "LGBTQI"). These health disparities are attributed to the discrimination, societal stigma, and denial of civil and human rights that are frequently experienced by LGBTQ individuals. Coming out as gay, for example, can elicit traumatic rejection from family members, close friends, coworkers, or one's faith community.

Some members of the LGBTQ community also face homophobia, biphobia, transphobia, and general bullying, although their vulnerability varies tremendously depending on the region or community in which they live. In the worst cases, hostility toward LGBTQ members can erupt into hate crimes and violence, refusal of services, and various forms of verbal and emotional abuse. These traumatic experiences contribute both to mental health issues and to substance abuse among LGBTQ Americans. These challenges are often exacerbated among LGBTQ people who are also people of color or who are of lower socioeconomic status; these racial and class differences intersect with their sexual and gender identities to generate even greater vulnerabilities to stigma, discrimination, and violence and thus greater negative impacts on mental health. Moreover, these pressures often begin for LGBTQ people at a very young age. "It is a shame with which we were saddled as children, to which we continue to be culturally subjected," wrote journalist, author, and gay rights activist Matthew Todd. This internalized shame can cause long-term damage to the mental health of LGBTQ people (Todd 2012; Jones 2016).

The discrimination that LGBTQ people face is exacerbated when they lack adequate family support, according to psychiatrist James Lehman. "There's a unique feature of sexual and gender minorities that doesn't apply to other populations, and that's that you can be part of these minority groups while your family isn't," he explained. "Usually, people from disadvantaged groups find support from other community members or their own family, but that's not always the case with LGBTQ people, whose families may be unsupportive" (UW Health 2017). Conversely, emotional support from family and friends can help reduce these mental health issues—or keep them from ever appearing. For example, transgender adults are much more likely to have attempted suicide (40 percent) compared to cisgender adults (5 percent) and are four times as likely to have a mental health condition. They are also four times more likely to experience a substance use disorder (NAMI, "LGBTQI").

Young people who identify as LGBTQ are also more likely to suffer from mental health issues than those who do not. Clinical psychologists point to the overlap between the age of coming out and "the developmental period characterized by potentially intense interpersonal and social regulation of gender and sexuality" (Russell and Fish 2016). Because early adolescents tend to have their gender and sexuality highly regulated by their peers and because this stage in their development tends to be just when they are determining their own LGBTQ identities, they are particularly susceptible to mental health challenges: elevated rates of depression and anxiety disorders, self-harm, suicidal ideation, and suicidal behavior. In particular, transgender and gender-nonconforming youth are more likely to have mental health issues than their cisgender peers, including significantly higher rates of anxiety, attention deficit disorders, suicidal ideation, and self-inflicted injuries (Jenco 2018).

Individuals who suffer from chronic mental illness are at greater risk of dying of suicide; however, not all suicides are a result of mental illness, nor does mental illness necessarily lead to suicidal ideation or behavior (NAMI, "Risk of Suicide"). LGB youth are four times more likely to die of suicide than are straight youth. A study from the Centers for Disease Control (CDC) released in 2016 found that nearly one-third of gay and bisexual high schoolers had recently attempted suicide while 43 percent had seriously considered it. These rates are far higher than those reported by straight students, of whom 6 percent reported attempting suicide and 15 percent reported seriously considering it (Kann 2016). In the same survey, 60 percent of LGB youth and 47 percent of questioning youth reported being so sad or hopeless that they had stopped doing some of their usual activities compared to only 26 percent of heterosexual students.

LGB students are also more likely to have been raped (18 percent compared to 5 percent of straight students), twice as likely to have experienced physical and sexual dating violence, and twice as likely to have been bullied (Chen 2016). Sexual minority adolescents are more likely to experience multiple adverse childhood experiences and psychological and physical abuse than their straight peers and are more likely to report depression and bullying (Jenco 2018).

Overall, rates of mental health concerns are significantly higher among members of the LGBTQ community, particularly among youth, transgender people, and people of color. These mental health challenges are rooted in the stigma, discrimination, and violence that some LGBTQ Americans face in their everyday lives. Advocates for LGBTQ people thus regularly publicize resources like the National Suicide Prevention Lifeline (800-273-TALK) and the Trevor Project's 24-hour confidential suicide hotline for LGBTQ youth (866-488-7386 or text "Trevor" to 202-304-1200).

FURTHER READING

Chen, Angela. 2016. "Queer Teens Are Four Times More Likely to Commit Suicide, CDC Reports." TheVerge.com, August 11. https://www.theverge.com/2016/8/11/12438678/cdc-report-queer-teens-health-risk-suicide

Connolly, Maureen D., et al. 2016. "The Mental Health of Transgender Youth: Advances in Understanding." *Journal of Adolescent Health* 59, 5: 489–495.

Gonzales, Gilbert, and Carrie Henning-Smith. 2017. "Health Disparities by Sexual Orientation: Results and Implications from the Behavioral Risk Factor Surveillance System." *Journal of Community Health* 42, 6: 1163–1172.

Gonzales, Gilbert, Julia Przedworski, and Carrie Henning-Smith. 2016. "Comparison of Health and Health Risk Factors between Lesbian, Gay, and Bisexual Adults and Heterosexual Adults in the United States: Results from the National Health Interview Survey." *JAMA Internal Medicine* 176, 9: 1344–1351.

Jenco, Melissa. 2018. "Studies: LGBTQ Youths Have Higher Rates of Mental Health Issues, Abuse." AAP News, April 16. https://www.aappublications.org/news/2018/04/16/lgbtq041618

Jones, Owen. 2016. "Gay Men Are Battling a Demon More Powerful than HIV—and It's Hidden." *The Guardian*, October 20. https://www.theguardian.com/commentisfree/2016/oct/20/gay-men-hiv-homophobia-lgbt-drink-drugs

Kann, Laura, et al. 2016. "Sexual Identity, Sex of Sexual Contacts, and Health-Related Behaviors among Students in Grades 9–12—United States and Selected Sites, 2015." Morbidity and Mortality Weekly Report. Centers for Disease Control and Prevention *Surveillance Summaries* 65, 9: 1–202. https://www.cdc.gov/mmwr/volumes/65/ss/ss6509a1.htm

Leon, Alexander. 2017. "LGBT People Are Prone to Mental Illness. It's a Truth We Shouldn't Shy Away From." *The Guardian*, May 12. https://www.theguardian.com/commentisfree/2017/may/12/lgbt-mental-health-sexuality-gender-identity

National Alliance on Mental Illness (NAMI). "LGBTQI." Nami.org. https://www.nami.org/Your-Journey/Identity-and-Cultural-Dimensions/LGBTQI

National Alliance on Mental Illness (NAMI). "Risk of Suicide." Nami.org. https://www.nami.org/About-Mental-Illness/Common-with-Mental-Illness/Risk-of-Suicide

Russell, Stephen T., and Jessica N. Fish. 2016. "Mental Health in Lesbian, Gay, Bisexual, and Transgender (LGBT) Youth." *Annual Review of Clinical Psychology* 12: 465–487.

Todd, Matthew. 2012. *Straight Jacket: How to Be Gay and Happy*. London: Bantam Press.

UW Health. 2017. "Mental Health Risks Higher for LGBTQ People." UWHealth.org, May 8. https://www.uwhealth.org/health-wellness/mental-health-risks-higher-for-lgbtq-people/50847

Q37: CAN CONVERSION THERAPY CHANGE SOMEONE'S SEXUAL ORIENTATION OR GENDER IDENTITY?

Answer: No. Sexual orientation is a complex identity, including physical attraction but also romantic, emotional, mental, and/or spiritual attraction to other people. While proponents of conversion therapy insist that it is possible to change someone's sexual orientation or gender identity, medical experts agree this practice causes significant harm and does not do anything to change an individual's sexual or gender identity. In addition, all forms of conversion therapy are based on the scientifically discredited premise that being LGBTQ is a deviance, defect, or disorder.

The Facts: In 1899, German psychologist Albert von Schrenck-Notzing claimed he successfully turned a gay man straight through hypnosis and trips to a nearby brothel, manipulating the man's sexual impulses and diverting him from sexual attraction to men to a lasting desire for women (Blakemore 2019). Schrenck-Notzing's announcement was the beginning of a phenomenon that would later be termed *conversion therapy*, a set of pseudoscientific techniques to suppress a person's sexuality and to force LGBTQ people to conform to societal expectations of how they should behave.

Sigmund Freud, the founder of the field of psychiatry, did not believe that homosexuality was a mental illness but simply a variation in sexual function. As Freud wrote in a 1920 case report, "In general, to undertake to convert a fully developed homosexual does not offer much more prospect of success than the reverse" (Freud 1920, 151). Yet the profession disagreed and in the early twentieth century, many psychoanalysts promoted conversion therapies. However, these therapies were unsuccessful:

> In a rare, controlled analytic study, Bieber et al. (1962) treated 106 homosexual men. They claimed a 27% "cure" rate with psychoanalysis, but when challenged a decade later to produce a "cured" patient, they were unable to do so. Although practitioners of aversion therapy in the 1960s also claimed "cures," by the 1970s behavioral therapists admitted that few of their patients managed to stay "converted" for very long. (Drescher 2010, 433)

Today, conversion therapy is widely dismissed by medical and psychological experts (Dickinson 2016). In fact, it has been condemned by nearly every major health association, including the American Psychological

Association, the American Academy of Pediatrics, and the American Medical Association (Sopelsa 2020).

Conversion therapy has been called several things, including "reparative therapy" or more generally, sexual orientation change efforts (SOCE). SOCE has been controversial largely because of the tension between the values of some faith-based organizations and those held by the LGBTQ community and various professional and scientific organizations (Drescher 2003; Drescher and Zucker 2006). Those who promote the false idea that homosexuality is symptomatic of developmental defects, spiritual defects, or moral failings argue that SOCE, including psychotherapy and religious interventions, can permanently alter same-sex feelings and behaviors (Morrow and Beckstead 2004). Many of the individuals and groups in favor of SOCE have been embedded within the larger context of conservative religious political movements that have supported the stigmatization of homosexuality on political or religious grounds (Anton 2010).

While the conventional understanding is that it is not psychologically or medically possible to change a person's sexuality, there are still many who encourage repressing or denying homosexual desires from a religious standpoint. These beliefs stem from an ideology that homosexuality is a sin, not an identity (Eadens 2020), and that homosexuality is symptomatic of developmental defects or spiritual and moral failings. Its proponents have argued that SOCE, including psychotherapy and religious efforts, could eliminate homosexual feelings and behaviors (Drescher and Zucker 2006). Activists and survivors of the practice argue that attempts to use religious faith to change their sexual orientation often led to shame and guilt associated with their sexuality and faith but ultimately had no effect on their identity or behavior.

Nevertheless, conversion therapy is widespread, particularly among LGBTQ minors, according to the Trevor Project, the largest LGBTQ suicide prevention organization in the United States (Trevor Project n.d.). It is estimated that more than 700,000 LGBTQ people have been subjected to some form of conversion therapy (Mallory, Brown, and Conron 2019). The practice is still legal in most states in the United States, even for minors; as of December 2020, only 20 states as well as the District of Columbia, the Commonwealth of Puerto Rico, and dozens of municipalities have banned conversion therapy for minors. The District of Columbia is the only U.S. jurisdiction with a conversion therapy ban that also applies to adults (Movement Advancement Project n.d.).

Between 2017 and 2020, the number of state and local governments with bans on conversion therapy for minors increased from 9 states and D.C. in 2017 to 20 states and D.C. by 2020. However, there have also been reversals: in November 2020, a federal appeals court ruling in Florida struck down bans that had been in place since 2016, including bans in two dozen cities and counties including Miami Beach, Palm Beach County, and Boca Raton; the ruling also affects the states of Georgia and Alabama because they are part of the same federal judicial district (Vassolo 2020).

A 2009 report from the American Psychological Association (APA) concluded that conversion therapy practices are not supported by any reliable evidence and are harmful in many cases (APA 2009a). The report outlined the risks of SOCE, including depression, anxiety, suicidal ideation, substance abuse, struggle with emotional intimacy, sexual dysfunction, and high-risk sexual behaviors. The APA concluded that psychological studies that seek to explore and to understand human nature must rely on proven methods of scientific inquiry based on empirical data and on hypotheses and propositions that can be confirmed or disconfirmed; legislation legalizing non-scientific practices should be stopped. Further, the report concludes that there are no studies of "adequate scientific rigor" to conclude that SOCE efforts change a person's sexual orientation. The scientifically rigorous work that does exist in this area was largely performed in the 1970s and those studies found that sexual orientation was unlikely to truly change due to efforts designed for that purpose (APA 2009b). Those studies did find that some people appeared to learn how to ignore or to limit their attractions but their sexual orientation did not change.

There are significant risks and harms associated with SOCE, particularly for youth. A 2019 national survey conducted by the Trevor Project found that 42 percent of LGBTQ youth who underwent conversion therapy reported a suicide attempt in the past year, more than twice the rate of their LGBTQ peers who did not go through the practice. That number increased to 57 percent for transgender youth (Trevor Project 2019). A survey of cisgender lesbian, gay, and bisexual (LGB) adults found that 7 percent had experienced SOCE; of respondents who had undergone SOCE, 80.8 percent reported that the conversion therapy had been directed by a religious leader. LGB people exposed to SOCE had nearly twice the odds of lifetime suicidal ideation, 75 percent increased odds of planning to attempt suicide, and 88 percent increased odds of a suicide attempt with a minor injury compared to LGB people who had not been exposed to SOCE (Blosnich et al. 2020). "Rather than being therapy, so-called 'conversion therapy' is a minority stressor that reinforces stigma and conveys that being LGB is abnormal, sinful, and should be rejected," wrote Ilan H. Meyer, Distinguished Senior Scholar of Public Policy at the UCLA

School of Law's Williams Institute. "We found that people who undergo conversion therapy are at increased risk of suicide ideation and attempts. This is a devastating outcome that goes counter to the purpose of therapy" (Williams Institute 2020).

The 2009 APA Task Force advises families to avoid sexual orientation change efforts that "portray homosexuality as a mental illness or developmental disorder" and to instead seek therapy, social services, or support that provide accurate information on sexual orientation, sexuality, and gender identity. The APA encourages mental health professionals to utilize client-centered, affirmative, multiculturally competent approaches that acknowledge the negative impact of social stigma on sexual minorities. They also urge practitioners to "balance ethical principles of beneficence and nonmaleficence, justice, and respect for people's rights and dignity" (APA 2009b).

FURTHER READING

American Psychological Association (APA), Task Force on Appropriate Therapeutic Responses to Sexual Orientation. 2009a. "Report of the APA Task Force on Appropriate Therapeutic Responses to Sexual Orientation." APA, August. https://www.apa.org/pi/lgbt/resources/sexual-orientation

American Psychological Association (APA). 2009b. "Resolution on Appropriate Affirmative Responses to Sexual Orientation Distress and Change Efforts." APA, August 5. https://www.apa.org/about/policy/sexual-orientation

Anton, Barry S. 2010. "Proceedings of the American Psychological Association for the Legislative Year 2009: Minutes of the Annual Meeting of the Council of Representatives and Minutes of the Meetings of the Board of Directors." *American Psychologist* 65, 5: 385–475.

Blakemore, Erin. 2019. "Gay Conversion Therapy's Disturbing 19th-Century Origins." History Channel, June 28. https://www.history.com/news/gay-conversion-therapy-origins-19th-century

Blosnich, John R., et al. 2020. "Sexual Orientation Change Efforts, Adverse Childhood Experiences, and Suicide Ideation and Attempt among Sexual Minority Adults, United States, 2016–2018." *American Journal of Public Health* 110, 7: 1024–1030.

Dickinson, Tommy. 2016. *"Curing Queers": Mental Nurses and Their Patients, 1935–74*. Manchester, UK: Manchester University Press.

Drescher, Jack. 2003. "The Spitzer Study and the Culture Wars." *Archives of Sexual Behavior* 32, 5: 431–432.

Drescher, Jack. 2010. "Queer Diagnoses: Parallels and Contrasts in the History of Homosexuality, Gender Variance, and the *Diagnostic and Statistical Manual*." *Archives of Sexual Behavior* 39, 2: 427–460.

Drescher, Jack, and Kenneth J. Zucker, eds. 2006. *Ex-Gay Research: Analyzing the Spitzer Study and Its Relation to Science, Religion, Politics, and Culture*. Binghamton, NY: Harrington Park Press.

Eadens, Savannah. 2020. "What Is 'Conversion Therapy' and Why Is It Controversial? Everything You Need to Know." *Courier Journal*, February 17. https://www.courier-journal.com/story/life/wellness/health /2020/02/17/conversion-therapy-kentucky-what-is-it-why-controversial /4645356002/

Freud, Sigmund. 1920. "The Psychogenesis of a Case of Female Homosexuality." *International Journal of Psycho-Analysis* 1: 125–149.

Mallory, Christy, Taylor N. T. Brown, and Kerith J. Conron. 2019. "Conversion Therapy and LGBT Youth." Williams Institute, UCLA School of Law, June. https://williamsinstitute.law.ucla.edu/publications/conversion -therapy-and-lgbt-youth/

Moreau, Julie. 2018. "Thousands of Teens Will Undergo 'Conversion Therapy' in Near Future, Study Estimates." *NBC News*, January 26. https:// www.nbcnews.com/feature/nbc-out/80-000-teens-will-undergo-conversion -therapy-near-future-study-n841356

Morrow, Susan L., and A. Lee Beckstead. 2004. "Conversion Therapies for Same-Sex Attracted Clients in Religious Conflict: Context, Predisposing Factors, Experiences, and Implications for Therapy." *Counseling Psychologist* 32, 5: 641–650.

Movement Advancement Project. n.d. "Equality Maps: Conversion Therapy Laws." https://www.lgbtmap.org/equality-maps/conversion_therapy

Sopelsa, Brooke. 2020. "Virginia Becomes 20th State to Ban Conversion Therapy for Minors." *NBC News*, March 3. https://www.nbcnews.com /feature/nbc-out/virginia-becomes-20th-state-ban-conversion-therapy -minors-n1148421

Trevor Project. 2019. "National Survey on LGBTQ Youth Mental Health." https://www.thetrevorproject.org/wp-content/uploads/2019/06/The -Trevor-Project-National-Survey-Results-2019.pdf

Trevor Project. n.d. "About Conversion Therapy." https://www.thetrevorproject .org/get-involved/trevor-advocacy/50-bills-50-states/about-conversion -therapy/

Vassolo, Martin. 2020. "Appellate Ruling Scraps Conversion Therapy Bans in Miami Beach, Cities across Florida." *Miami Herald*, November. https://www.miamiherald.com/news/local/community/gay-south-florida /article247422645.html

Williams Institute. 2020. "LGB People Who Have Undergone Conversion Therapy Almost Twice as Likely to Attempt Suicide." Williams Institute, UCLA School of Law, June 15. https://williamsinstitute.law.ucla.edu/press/lgb-suicide-ct-press-release/

Q38: DO LGBTQ PEOPLE ABUSE DRUGS AND ALCOHOL AT DIFFERENT RATES THAN STRAIGHT PEOPLE?

Answer: Yes, people who identify as LGBTQ are at a greater risk for substance abuse compared to those who identify as heterosexual. It is important to note, however, that identifying as LGBTQ doesn't *cause* people to be more likely to abuse drugs and alcohol; rather, research suggests that mistreatment of LGBTQ people by others is a leading driver of substance abuse problems.

The Facts: Substance use and addiction is a significant problem in all sectors of the LGBTQ community. Historically, many federally funded surveys have not asked about sexual orientation or gender identity, making it difficult to draw long-term inferences about substance abuse in LGBTQ populations. However, within the last 10 years, several surveys have provided evidence that LGBTQ adults and heterosexual adults in the United States have different rates of substance use and abuse.

Rates of substance abuse reported in the 2018 National Survey on Drug Use and Health (NSDUH) were higher among lesbian, gay, and bisexual (LGB) adults than non-LGB adults and also higher among LGB adults with mental illness than among LGB adults with no mental illness. Adults who describe themselves as LGB had higher rates of use of marijuana and opioids (including prescription opioids and heroin) and higher rates of alcohol use disorders. More than twice as many LGB adults reported using drugs in the past year compared to heterosexual adults; those who identified as LGB were also more likely to smoke cigarettes, drink alcohol, and binge drink, and were nearly twice as likely to report having an alcohol or drug problem in the past year (NSDUH 2020). Overall illicit drug use among non-LGB adults was 15.7 percent compared to 37.8 percent of LGB adults with no mental illness, 53.9 percent of LGB adults with any mental illness (AMI), and 59.3 percent among LGB adults with serious mental illness (SMI).

Rates of marijuana use were the lowest for non-LGB adults at 13.2 percent, increasing to 31.2 percent for LGB adults with no mental illness, 45.6 percent for LGB adults with AMI, and 50.6 percent among LGB adults with SMI. Opioid misuse was 2.6 percent among non-LGB adults, 5.1 percent among LGB adults with no mental illness, 14.1 percent among LGB adults with AMI, and 16.6 percent among LGB adults with SMI. These results are similar to those from the first NSDUH in 2015 and are consistent across four years of data collection (NSDUH 2020; Medley 2016).

A 2013 survey conducted by the U.S. Census Bureau, meanwhile, found that a higher percentage of LGBTQ adults age 18 to 64 reported past-year binge drinking (five or more drinks on a single occasion) than heterosexual adults. LGBTQ people in treatment for substance use disorders began alcohol consumption earlier than their heterosexual counterparts as well (McCabe et al. 2013). Another study found that transgender, nonbinary, and gender-diverse (TGD) people are three times more likely to use illicit drugs compared to cisgender people (James et al. 2016). TGD youth have higher rates of mental health problems (including high rates of depression and suicidal ideation) and substance abuse, including higher rates of alcohol and drug use disorders (Newcomb et al. 2020). Transgender and sexual minority youth are also more likely than their straight, cisgender peers to use tobacco products (Johnson et al. 2019). Lesbian, gay, and bisexual older adults (aged 50 or older) are also more likely to use alcohol and drugs compared to their straight counterparts (Han, Miyoshi, and Palamar 2020).

It is important to remember, however, that identifying as LGBTQ does not *cause* substance use or misuse; these behaviors are simply more common among LGBTQ people for a variety of reasons. On a broad level, there are a number of socially imposed obstacles faced by the LGBTQ community, often on a daily basis, with which heterosexual people do not have to grapple. Those include antigay discrimination and stigmatization, hate crimes, emotional abuse, expressions of rejection or shame from family and friends after coming out, loss of employment, and internalized homophobia or self-hatred. (For more information on rates of mental illness among LGBTQ people, see Q36).

LGBTQ people who regularly encounter these negative forces are more likely to turn to substance use and abuse to cope with the unique struggles the community faces. Substances can temporarily numb the pain from these kinds of experiences and mask other concerns like depression, anxiety, anger, or fear. Transgender people are particularly vulnerable to turning to addictive substances. One study found that transgender students are more than two times more likely to use cocaine or methamphetamines, prescription opioids, and benzodiazepines compared to non-transgender students (De Pedro et al. 2017). While substance use and abuse may help temporarily, they almost always have long-term negative consequences.

Substance abuse treatment programs offer opportunities to reduce use, misuse, and dependency on substances in various ways. Research suggests that programs that offer specific solutions tailored to LGBTQ people have the best outcomes compared to nonspecialized programs. However, most facilities do not offer such programs: a 2016 survey of services available found that only 12.6 percent of mental health facilities and 17.6 percent of substance abuse facilities maintained LGBTQ-specific programs (Williams and Fish 2020).

In general, data on rates of substance abuse disorder among transgender populations are limited, though some research suggests that transgender people are more likely to seek treatment than the non-transgender population. Best practices suggest that treatment should address unique factors in these patients' lives that may include homophobia/transphobia, family problems, violence, and social isolation (Lombardi and van Servellen 2000; Keuroghlian et al. 2015).

In summary, the incidence of substance use and abuse is indeed higher among LGBTQ people, with more recent data allowing researchers to study these trends (earlier surveys on substance abuse issues typically did not ask about sexual orientation or gender identity). While sexual orientation and gender identity do not cause substance use or addiction, common life experiences for many LGBTQ people, including discrimination, alienation from family and friends, and violence and abuse, can lead to conditions and situations that make substances a coping mechanism. Treatment programs that target the unique causes of substance abuse among LGBTQ people are likely to have the most success.

FURTHER READING

De Pedro, Kris Tunac, Tamika D. Gilreath, Christopher Jackson, and Monica Christina Esqueda. 2017. "Substance Use among Transgender Students in California Public Middle and High Schools." *Journal of School Health* 87, 5: 303–309.

Green, Kelly E., and Brian A. Feinstein. 2012. "Substance Use in Lesbian, Gay, and Bisexual Populations: An Update on Empirical Research and Implications for Treatment." *Psychology of Addictive Behaviors* 26, 2: 265–278.

Han, Benjamin H., Mari Miyoshi, and Joseph J. Palamar. 2020. "Substance Use among Middle-Aged and Older Lesbian, Gay, and Bisexual Adults in the United States, 2015 to 2017." *Journal of General Internal Medicine* 35: 3740–3741. https://doi.org/10.1007/s11606-020-05635-2

James, Sandy E., et al. 2016. *The Report of the 2015 U.S. Transgender Survey.* Washington DC: National Center for Transgender Equality.

Johnson, Sarah E., et al. 2019. "Sexual and Gender Minority U.S. Tobacco Use: Population Assessment of Tobacco and Health (PATH) Study Wave 3, 2015–2016." *American Journal of Preventive Medicine* 57, 2: 256–261.

Keuroghlian, Alex S., Sari L. Reisner, Jaclyn M. White, and Roger D. Weiss. 2015. "Substance Use and Treatment of Substance Use Disorders in a Community Sample of Transgender Adults." *Drug and Alcohol Dependence* 152: 139–46.

Lombardi Emilia L., and Gwen van Servellen. 2000. "Building culturally Sensitive Substance Use Prevention and Treatment Programs for Trans-gendered Populations." *Journal of Substance Abuse Treatment* 19, 3: 291–296.

McCabe Sean Esteban, Brady T. West, Tonda L. Hughes, and Carol J. Boyd. 2013. "Sexual Orientation and Substance Abuse Treatment Uti-lization in the United States: Results from a National Survey." *Journal of Substance Abuse Treatment* 44, 1: 4–12.

Medley, Grace, et al. 2016. "Sexual Orientation and Estimates of Adult Substance Use and Mental Health: Results from the 2015 National Sur-vey on Drug Use and Health." *NSDUH Data Review*, October. https://www.samhsa.gov/data/sites/default/files/NSDUH-SexualOrientation-2015/NSDUH-SexualOrientation-2015/NSDUH-SexualOrientation-2015.htm

National Institute on Drug Abuse. n.d. "Substance Use and SUDs in LGBTQ Populations." NIDA. https://www.drugabuse.gov/drug-topics/substance-use-suds-in-lgbtq-populations

Newcomb, Michael E., et al. 2020. "High Burden of Mental Health Prob-lems, Substance Use, Violence, and Related Psychosocial Factors in Transgender, Non-Binary, and Gender Diverse Youth and Young Adults." *Archives of Sexual Behavior* 49: 645–659.

NSDUH. 2020. "2018 National Survey on Drug Use and Health: Lesbian, Gay, & Bisexual (LGB) Adults." U.S. Department of Health and Human Services, Substance Abuse and Mental Health Services Administra-tion, January 14. https://www.samhsa.gov/data/report/2018-nsduh-lesbian-gay-bisexual-lgb-adults

Williams, Natasha D., and Jessica N. Fish. 2020. "The Availability of LGBT-Specific Mental Health and Substance Abuse Treatment in the United States." *Health Services Research*, September. https://doi.org/10.1111/1475-6773.13559

Q39: DO STRAIGHT PEOPLE AND LGBTQ PEOPLE HAVE DIFFERENT LIFE EXPECTANCIES?

Answer: There is limited evidence that LGBTQ people currently have shorter life expectancies than straight people. Larger differences are only found in older studies conducted during the height of the HIV/AIDS epidemic in the 1980s and 1990s. Limited differences in life expectancy found in more recent studies can be traced to different rates of mental health between straight and LGBTQ populations (see Q36). Absent mental health challenges, there is no evidence that being LGBTQ means your life will be shorter than if you were straight.

The Facts: The origin of the idea that being LGBTQ shortens your life can be traced back to the 1990s, when anti-LGBTQ organizations sought to disparage the LGBTQ community in the eyes of the American public. These organizations promoted heterosexuality as a healthier "choice" and asserted that LGBTQ people had shorter lifespans and poorer physical and mental health. They also thought these arguments could be used as tools in their campaigns to keep LGBTQ people from being able to adopt or foster children. There is no valid evidence for these claims.

These false claims can often be traced directly to the discredited research of Paul Cameron and his Family Research Institute, a socially conservative organization fiercely opposed to LGBTQ rights that was active (and somewhat influential) in the 1990s. To be clear, Cameron's conclusions were not based on valid data. Even Nicholas Eberstadt, a demographer at the conservative American Enterprise Institute, called Cameron's methodology "just ridiculous" (Olson 1997). Nonetheless, the study and its statistics made their way into mainstream outlets. For example, conservative pundit William Bennett cited Cameron's research in an interview he gave to ABC News' *This Week* television show in 1997. There were other historical attempts by anti-LGBTQ organizations to distort data to try to push the narrative of shorter life expectancies in the gay community. For example, a 1997 study conducted by a team of Canadian researchers found their results being manipulated by anti-LGBTQ groups and issued a statement criticizing their faulty logic and their misrepresentation of their statistics (Hogg et al. 2001).

Relatedly, a well-publicized 2014 study (since retracted) incorrectly concluded that antigay prejudice was causing premature death among sexual minorities. Errors in that analysis led the authors to formally retract the piece in 2018 (Hatzenbuehler et al. 2018). However, some people may still falsely believe that LGBTQ people live significantly shorter lives due to the degree of publicity the initial study received.

When many people think about the life expectancy of LGBTQ people, their first thought is often about HIV/AIDS. That is because in the 1980s and 1990s, gay and bisexual men in particular were likely to have shorter life expectancies than straight men due to their increased chances of dying from HIV/AIDS. Peaking in 1995 at more than 40,000 annual deaths, the HIV/AIDS epidemic led to a significant rise in deaths among adults aged 25–44, especially among men who have sex with men, injection drug users, and African Americans. It was responsible for 15 percent of all deaths in San Francisco—and one in four deaths among men in that city—in 1992.

Following the introduction of combination anti-retroviral therapy and the proliferation of needle exchange programs, deaths from HIV/AIDS declined rapidly, falling by more than 70 percent in just five years and by 90 percent by 2015 (Fenelon and Boudreaux 2019). A study published in 2017 found that people with HIV were able to live almost as long as people without it: to age 73 for men and to age 76 for women (if they began treatment between 2008 and 2010) compared to average U.S. life expectancies of 77 for men and 81 for women (Foley 2017).

In stark contrast to earlier and retracted studies that found significant differences in life expectancy, more recent data suggest the current differences between straight and LGBTQ Americans are slight and tend to be based on increased health risks related to discrimination and prejudice that generate stress and other negative health impacts. LGBTQ people are much more likely to die from suicide compared to their straight peers (see Q36).

Social determinants of health also tend to have negative impacts on the health and life expectancy of LGBTQ people. LGBTQ people are more likely to live below the poverty line, to report food insecurity and reliance on federal food stamps, and to be homeless. This is particularly true for LGBTQ people of color. All of these factors have negative impacts on life expectancy. Additional negative impacts on health result from experiences of discrimination, harassment, and violence, which increases engagement in risky behaviors including smoking, alcohol use, and risky sexual behaviors. Chronic stress can lead to chronic diseases including cancer while discrimination within the health care system can lead to further negative impacts on LGBTQ health and longevity. Sexual minority status tends to be associated with higher rates of development of certain types of cancers, including breast cancer, anal cancer, lung cancer, and cancers associated with HIV/AIDS (Matthews, Breen, and Kittiteerasack 2018). In 2015, the

Inter-American Commission on Human Rights reported that the average life expectancy of trans women in Latin America was 30 to 35 years old. This statistic was picked up by numerous publications and falsely claimed to apply to transgender women in the United States. However, while violence against transgender women is a serious problem, there is no evidence that the statistic applies to the United States (Herzog 2019).

Overall, the life expectancy of LGBTQ people tends to be about the same as for straight people. There is nothing inherent in being LGBTQ that shortens life. However, LGBTQ people may live shorter lives if they suffer from mental illness stemming from discrimination and stigma based on their sexual orientation, or if they suffer from poverty, disease, substance abuse issues, or other problems that have been found to shorten life expectancy in LGBTQ people and straight people alike.

FURTHER READING

Fenelon, Andrew, and Michel Boudreaux M. 2019. "Life and Death in the American City: Men's Life Expectancy in 25 Major American Cities from 1990 to 2015." *Demography* 56, 6: 2349–2375.

Foley, Katherine Ellen. 2017. "Some People with HIV Are Starting to Live as Long as People without It." QZ.com, May 11. https://qz.com/980598 /the-life-expectancy-for-people-treated-for-hiv-has-increased-to-73-for -men-and-76-for-women-in-europe-and-north-america/

Hatzenbuehler, Mark L., Anna Bellatorre, Yeonjin Lee, Brian K. Finch, Peter Muennig, and Kevin Fiscella. 2018. RETRACTED: Corrigendum to "Structural Stigma and All-Cause Mortality in Sexual Minority Populations" [*Social Science & Medicine* 103 (2014), 33–41], *Social Science & Medicine* 200: 271.

Herzog, Katie. 2019. "Is the Life Expectancy of Trans Women in the U.S. Just 35? No." TheStranger.com, September 23. https://www.thestranger .com/slog/2019/09/23/41471629/is-the-life-expectancy-of-trans-women -in-the-us-just-35-no

Hogg, Robert S., et al. 2001. "Gay Life Expectancy Revisited." *International Journal of Epidemiology* 30, 6: 1499.

Matthews, Alicia K., Elizabeth Breen, and Priyoth Kittiteerasack. 2018. "Social Determinants of LGBT Cancer Health Inequities." *Seminars in Oncology Nursing* 34, 1: 12–20.

Olson, Walter. 1997. "William Bennett, Gays, and the Truth." *Slate*, December 19. https://slate.com/news-and-politics/1997/12/william-bennett -gays-and-the-truth.html

Q40: ARE LGBTQ YOUTH MORE LIKELY
TO BE HOMELESS?

Answer: Yes. Multiple studies confirm that LGBTQ youth in the United States are far more likely to experience homelessness than non-LGBTQ youth.

The Facts: Youth homelessness is a widespread social problem in the United States but efforts to estimate the scope of the problem have produced widely varying results due to imprecision as to how to define "homeless" or "youth." In addition, homeless youth are difficult to count because they are highly mobile; because they often experience more hidden forms of homelessness such as couch surfing instead of sleeping on the streets or in a shelter; and because they fear being counted will result in being forced to return home to an abusive family situation or being placed in foster care. Homeless youth who engage in illicit activities such as drug use or prostitution to survive also keep a notoriously low profile. Finally, youth may also be reluctant to identify themselves as homeless due to the associated stigma (Dworsky 2020).

These challenges notwithstanding, there is considerable evidence that youth who identify as LGBTQ are more likely to be homeless compared to their non-LGBTQ peers. In 2016 and 2017, Voices of Youth Count, a research initiative led by Chapin Hall, a nonpartisan policy research center at the University of Chicago, sought a robust estimate of homelessness among youth aged 13–25 using a large, nationally representative survey of youth and adults from households with youth as well as hundreds of in-depth interviews with youth who had experienced homelessness. Overall, they estimated homelessness among LGBTQ adolescent minors (ages 13–17) at 9.7 percent. They broke the numbers down further, classifying 5.2 percent of LGBTQ minors as truly homeless with another 4.5 percent unstably housed (e.g., couch surfing). Focusing on explicitly homeless young adults, they found LGBTQ respondents were 120 percent more likely to report homelessness than their straight counterparts (Morton et al. 2017).

Additional evidence comes from the annual report on youth homelessness by True Colors United and the National Law Center on Homelessness & Poverty. In 2019, these organizations estimated that LGBTQ youth comprise 40 percent of all youth experiencing homelessness. This finding means LGBTQ youth are significantly overrepresented in the homeless population since only 5–10 percent of youth identify as LGBTQ. The highest rates of youth homelessness are experienced by African American young men aged 18 to 25 who identify as LGBTQ, with nearly one in four reporting homelessness in the last 12 months and additional respondents reporting resorting to couch surfing (Waguespack and Ryan 2019). This finding confirms earlier research that African American and Native American youth are disproportionately represented among LGBTQ homeless youth (Centrone, Kenney, and Shapiro 2009; Choi et al. 2015). Another 2016 report found that 6.8 percent of homeless youth identified as transgender (Administration for Children and Families 2016); overall, transgender youth represent only about 1 percent of all youth. Not only are LGBTQ youth at higher risk of homelessness, they also face a greater risk of "high levels of hardship" compared to all young people experiencing homelessness (Morton et al. 2018a). Hardship includes higher rates of assault, trauma, exchanging sex for basic needs, and early death. The report also notes that Black youth who identify as LGBTQ, particularly young men, have the highest rates of homelessness.

These high rates of homelessness have significant negative consequences. Jordan Dashow, former Federal Policy Manager for Human Rights Campaign, an LGBTQ advocacy organization, noted those long-term negative consequences in a blog post responding to the Chapin Hill report:

> The consequences of homelessness, particularly for LGBTQ youth, are far reaching and can last a lifetime. Homelessness is harmful to mental and physical health, and youth who are homeless are at an increased risk for sexual abuse and exploitation, chemical and alcohol dependency, social stigma and discrimination. These youth also experience lower levels of long-term educational attainment—placing them at an even greater disadvantage when they enter the job market. Growing up without the critical family and social safety nets so many young people rely on results in catastrophic consequences for economic stability, educational attainment and life expectancy. (Dashow 2017)

More than half of homeless youth become homeless because they are asked to leave home by a parent or caregiver (Administration for Children and Families 2016). That LGBTQ youth are overrepresented among homeless youth is a reflection of the fact that some LGBTQ youth who come out to their families will be asked to leave. One analysis of homelessness among LGBTQ youth, in fact, identified the leading causes as: (1) family rejection resulting from sexual orientation or gender identity; (2) physical, emotional, or sexual abuse; (3) aging out of the foster care system; and (4) financial and emotional neglect (Durso and Gates 2012).

As of 2019, most states (34) have programs in place to address youth homelessness but only five states have programs or policies in place to explicitly serve homeless LGBTQ youth. One of these states, California, requires training about sexual orientation, gender identity and expression, and other issues specific to LGBTQ youth for staff working in runaway and homeless youth systems. Elsewhere, both Massachusetts and New York have state plans to end homelessness that contain components explicitly aimed at addressing the needs of LGBTQ youth (Waguespack and Ryan 2019).

While estimating the true scope of homelessness is challenging, it is clear from numerous studies that LGBTQ youth are disproportionately likely to be homeless or to suffer from housing insecurity compared to their non-LGBTQ peers, especially if they are Black and/or transgender. Despite these findings, most states do not have policies in place meant to explicitly serve LGBTQ homeless youth or address the root causes of their lack of stable housing.

FURTHER READING

Administration for Children and Families. 2016. "Administration for Children and Families, Family and Youth Services Bureau Street Outreach Program, Data Collection Study Final Report." https://www.acf.hhs.gov /archive/fysb/resource/street-outreach-program-data-collection-study

Centrone, W., R. R. Kenney, and L. Shapiro. 2009. *PATH Technical Assistance Resource Page: Transition Age Youth* (2nd ed.). Rockville, MD: Center for Mental Health Services, Substance Abuse and Mental Health Services Administration. http://homelesshub.ca/sites/default/files/youth _v%201%208_508.pdf

Choi, Soon Kyu, Bianca D. M. Wilson, Jama Shelton, and Gary J. Gates. 2015. "Serving Our Youth 2015: The Needs and Experiences of Lesbian, Gay, Bisexual, Transgender, and Questioning Youth Experiencing Homelessness." Los Angeles: The Williams Institute with True Colors Fund. https://escholarship.org/uc/item/1pd9886n

Dashow, Jordan. 2017. "New Report on Youth Homeless Affirms That LGBTQ Youth Disproportionately Experience Homelessness." HRC .org, November 15. https://www.hrc.org/news/new-report-on-youth -homeless-affirms-that-lgbtq-youth-disproportionately-ex

Durso, Laura E., and Gary J. Gates. 2012. "Serving Our Youth: Findings from a National Survey of Services Providers Working with Lesbian, Gay, Bisexual and Transgender Youth Who Are Homeless or At Risk of Becoming Homeless." Williams Institute, University of California. https://escholarship.org/uc/item/80x75033

Dworsky, Amy. 2020. "The Prevalence of Youth Homelessness in the United States." In Curren Warf and Grant Charles, eds., *Clinical Care* for Homeless, Runaway, and Refugee Youth: Intervention Approaches, Education and Research Directions. New York: Springer, pp. 1–10.

Morton, Matthew H., Amy Dworsky, and Gina M. Samuels. 2017. *Missed Opportunities: Youth Homelessness in America. National Estimates.* Chicago, IL: Chapin Hall at the University of Chicago. http://voicesofyouthcount.org/brief/national-estimates-of-youth-homelessness/

Morton, Matthew H., Gina M. Samuels, Amy Dworsky, and Sonali Patel. 2018a. *Missed Opportunities: LGBTQ Youth Homelessness in America.* Chicago, IL: Chapin Hall at the University of Chicago. https://voicesofyouthcount.org/brief/lgbtq-youth-homelessness/

Morton, Matthew H., Amy Dworsky, Jennifer L. Matjasko, Susanna R. Curry, David Schlueter, Raúl Chávez, and Anne F. Farrell. 2018b. "Prevalence and Correlates of Youth Homelessness in the United States." *Journal of Adolescent Health* 62, 1: 14–21.

Waguespack, Dylan, and Brandy Ryan. 2019. *State Index on Youth Homelessness.* True Colors United and the National Law Center on Homelessness and Poverty. https://truecolorsunited.org/index/

Q41: IS BULLYING OF LGBTQ KIDS FOR THEIR SEXUAL ORIENTATION BECOMING LESS COMMON?

Answer: It depends. While LGBTQ youth and those perceived as LGBTQ are more likely to be bullied than non-LGBTQ youth, overall rates of victimization are declining. While rates of victimization are decreasing for some youth, they are increasing for others.

The Facts: Multiple large national studies have found that youth who identify as LGBTQ or who are perceived by their peers to be LGBTQ are more likely to be victims of bullying, with serious, lifelong impacts on their physical and behavioral health (Kahle 2020; Heiden-Rootes et al. 2020; McKay, Misra, and Lindquist 2017). While bullying victimization rates are improving in general, lesbian, gay, and bisexual (LGB) youth still experience bullying at higher rates than their straight peers and some groups have not benefited from decreases at all. Due to the lack of gender identity questions included on most large surveillance surveys, trend data are not yet available for transgender and gender-nonconforming (TGN) youth (Gower et al. 2018).

A 2011 survey of 8,500 LGBTQ youth aged 13–20 found that a majority had experienced some form of bullying, including 92.3 percent reporting verbal bullying, 44.7 percent reporting physical bullying (hitting, kicking, tripping, and spitting), and 21.2 percent reporting assault (being punched, kicked, or injured with a weapon). More than half (55.2 percent) reported being cyberbullied (bullying via technology). Another 2011 study of youth aged 13–18 found that LGB youth reported more than twice as much online and in-person bullying as heterosexual youth (Earnshaw et al. 2016).

Six years later, a 2017 national survey of 23,001 students aged 13–21 found that in the prior year, 70.1 percent of LGBTQ students reported being verbally bullied, 28.9 percent reported being physically bullied, 12.4 percent reported being physically assaulted, and 48.7 percent reported being cyberbullied. Because of these experiences, 35 percent of students reported missing at least one entire school day in the past month because of concerns for safety and comfort. In total, nearly 60 percent of LGBTQ students reported feeling generally unsafe at school (Kosciw et al. 2018). All of these rates of reported bullying by LGBTQ youth are somewhat lower than that reported in 2011 but still higher than that reported by non-LGBTQ youth.

The Youth Risk Behavior Survey (YRBS), a project of the Centers for Disease Control, includes 15,624 youth surveyed in 2015, 14,765 youth in 2017, and 13,677 youth in 2019, including students in grades 9–12. The YRBS has been collected biennially since 1991 but only began to collect information about sexual orientation in 2015. These data indicate that while rates of bullying are decreasing for lesbian and bisexual young women, the opposite is true for gay and bisexual young men. In 2019, 32 percent of LGB youth reported being bullied at school in the past year, a slight change from the 33.0 percent reported in 2017 and the 34.2 percent reported in 2015. However, among gay and bisexual young men, rates of reported bullying at school increased from 26.3 percent in 2015 to 31.7 percent in 2019; lesbian and bisexual young women reported bullying at school decreased from 37.2 percent in 2015 to 32.0 percent in 2019. Among heterosexual youth, in contrast, rates of bullying were much lower, at 18.8 percent in 2015 and 17.1 percent in 2017 and 2019 (Johns et al. 2020).

The Cyberbullying Research Center has collected survey data from youth since 2010. In their original survey of 4,400 students aged 11–18 from a single public school district, they found that 36.1 percent of LGBTQ students reported being cyberbullied compared to only 20.1 percent of non-LGBTQ students. In 2016, the center conducted a national survey of 5,500 middle and high school students aged 12–17, finding that 56 percent of LGBTQ students had been cyberbullied compared to 32 percent of non-LGBTQ students. In 2019, researchers at the center again conducted a national survey of 4,500 students, finding 52 percent of LGBTQ students and 35 percent of non-LGBTQ students had been cyberbullied.

The effects of these experiences are well documented. Studies show that students who experience bullying are at an increased likelihood of anxiety, sleep difficulties, depression, lower academic achievement, headaches and stomachaches, deteriorating relationships with friends and family, and dropping out of school (Gower et al. 2018; Johns et al. 2020). A study of death by suicide among youth aged 10–19 from 2013 through 2017 found that bullying is often a deadly antecedent to suicide. Youth who had identified as LGBTQ were five times more likely to have reported being bullied before their deaths compared to non-LGBTQ youth (Clark et al. 2020).

FURTHER READING

Clark, Kirsty A., Susan D. Cochran, and Anthony J. Maiolatesi. 2020. "Prevalence of Bullying among Youth Classified as LGBTQ Who Died by Suicide as Reported in the National Violent Death Reporting System, 2003–2017." *JAMA Pediatrics*, May 26. https://jamanetwork.com /journals/jamapediatrics/article-abstract/2766457

Earnshaw, Valerie A., et al. 2016. "Bullying among Lesbian, Gay, Bisexual, and Transgender Youth." *Pediatric Clinics of North America* 63, 6: 999–1010.

Gower, Amy L., et al. 2018. "Bullying Victimization among LGBTQ Youth: Critical Issues and Future Directions." *Current Sexual Health Reports* 10, 4: 246–254.

Heiden-Rootes, Katie, et al. 2020. "Peer Victimization and Mental Health Outcomes for Lesbian, Gay, Bisexual, and Heterosexual Youth: A Latent Class Analysis." *Journal of School Health* 90, 10: 771–778.

Hinduja, Sameer, and Justin W. Patchin. 2020. "Bullying, Cyberbullying, and LGBTQ Students." https://cyberbullying.org/bullying-cyberbullying -sexual-orientation-lgbtq.pdf

Johns, Michelle M., et al. 2020. "Trends in Violence Victimization and Suicide Risk by Sexual Identity among High School Students—Youth Risk Behavior Survey, United States, 2015–2019." Centers for Disease Control and Prevention, *Morbidity and Mortality Weekly Report Supplements* 69, 1, August 21. https://www.cdc.gov/mmwr/ind2020_su.html

Kahle, Lindsay. 2020. "Are Sexual Minorities More at Risk? Bullying Victimization among Lesbian, Gay, Bisexual, and Questioning Youth." *Journal of Interpersonal Violence* 35, 21–22: 4960–4978.

Kosciw, Joseph G., et al. 2018. *The 2017 National School Climate Survey: The Experiences of Lesbian, Gay, Bisexual, Transgender, and Queer Youth in Our Nation's Schools.* New York: GLSEN. https://www.glsen.org/sites

/default/files/2019-10/GLSEN-2017-National-School-Climate-Survey
-NSCS-Full-Report.pdf
McKay, Tasseli, Shilpi Misra, and Christine Lindquist. 2017. "Violence and
LGBTQ+ Communities: What Do We Know, and What Do We Need
to Know?" RTI International Report. https://www.rti.org/sites/default
/files/rti_violence_and_lgbtq_communities.pdf

Q42: ARE CHILDREN OF LGBTQ PARENTS WORSE OFF THAN CHILDREN OF STRAIGHT PARENTS?

Answer: No. With few exceptions, research studies find that children of same-sex parents do just as well or perhaps even better in terms of their emotional health and educational outcomes compared to children with straight parents.

The Facts: In a meta-analysis of 79 scholarly studies compiled by Cornell University in December 2017, researchers report that 75 studies found that children with gay or lesbian parents fare no worse than other children. Only four studies found that children of same-sex parents face added disadvantages and those studies were later determined to be unreliable. "Taken together, this research forms an overwhelming scholarly consensus, based on over three decades of peer-reviewed research, that having a gay or lesbian parent does not harm children" (Cornell University 2017).

Some studies have found that children do better than their peers when raised by same-sex parents. For example, adolescents with same-sex parents reported feeling more connected at school (Mazrekaj, De Witte, and Cabus 2020). Children raised by same-sex parents may do better in elementary and secondary school (Long 2019; Mazrekaj, De Witte, and Cabus 2020). Another study found that children in gay and lesbian households are more likely to talk about emotionally difficult topics and they are often more resilient, compassionate, and tolerant (Goldberg, Gartrell, and Gates 2014; Lamb 2012). In a study of 17-year-olds raised by lesbian mothers from birth, adolescents were found to be significantly more socially competent and exhibited lower likelihood of social problems, rule breaking, and aggressive behavior compared to age and gender-matched groups of adolescents with different-sex parents (Gartrell and Bos 2010).

There are three main concerns that have been raised about the influence of same-sex parents raising children (Falk 1989; Patterson, Fulcher, and Wainright 2002). First, some have suggested that children raised by lesbian, gay, or bisexual (LGB) parents would exhibit confusion or disturbances with their own sexual identity and with their understanding of gender roles. The second set of concerns has to do with children's development in ways other than sexual identity or gender roles. For example, some people have expressed fears that children in the custody of gay or lesbian parents would be more vulnerable to mental breakdown, would exhibit more adjustment difficulties and behavior problems, or would be less psychologically healthy than other children. Finally, opponents of LGB parents often cite difficulty in social relationships as a negative outcome. Specifically, they suggest that increased levels of stigmatization, bullying and teasing, or other forms of victimization of peers can negatively affect children with same-sex parents. Researchers have failed to find evidence that any of these concerns are valid (Goldberg, Gartrell, and Gates 2014; Gartrell and Bos 2010; Lamb 2012).

There *is* evidence to suggest that there are differences in understanding of gender in different kinds of families. According to the Williams Institute, a think tank at UCLA focused on LGBTQ issues, LGB parents held fewer gender-stereotyped attitudes and were more accepting of gender-atypical behavior in their children compared to heterosexual parents (Goldberg, Gartrell, and Gates 2014). Researchers at the Williams Institute also note that some studies show that play behavior between boys and girls in same-sex parent families tends to be less reflective of traditional gender roles compared to the play behavior of children in different-sex-parent families.

While studies of gay male parents are more limited, robust research suggests that children of lesbian mothers develop their sexual identities (e.g., gender identity, gender-role behavior, and sexual orientation) in the same ways as children of heterosexual parents. Scholars also find no significant differences for personal development markers such as personality, self-concept, and behavior. Children of gay and lesbian parents have been shown to have normal social relationships with both peers and adults. Finally, researchers also find no differences in terms of self-esteem, quality of life, internalizing problems (e.g., depression), externalizing problems (e.g., behavioral problems), or social functioning (Patterson, Fulcher, and Wainright 2002; Patterson 2009).

There is also not enough evidence to support the idea that LGB parents are more likely to have LGBTQ children. Some empirical evidence does suggest a possible relationship between the sexual orientation of parents and children, particularly among lesbian parents, but it is far from conclusive. Even if there were such a connection, the nature of it is unclear: on the one hand, geneticists and other scientists continue to uncover more about the biological basis of homosexuality. On the other hand, LGBTQ parents are often more open-minded and supportive of their children's sexual and gender identities. While there may not be a causal effect, LGB parents may encourage their children to express those innate identities more openly than their heterosexual counterparts. Thus, the data about children of lesbian parents being more likely to identify as LGBTQ may be a result of increased willingness to identify themselves that way while children in other families who hold those same identities may be less likely to share that information with their families or others. In other words, they are more likely to remain "in the closet," a term for LGBTQ individuals who keep their sexual orientation or behavior a secret from those they know.

Some critics of these parenting studies suggest the science behind them is flawed. Specifically, they claim that small sample sizes make the studies unreliable. However, some of the research does use large and representative data. For example, a 2010 report by Michael Rosenfeld at Stanford University that used U.S. Census data to study the academic advancement of 3,500 kids with same-sex parents found no differences between kids with same-sex and opposite-sex parents.

In sum, research has documented few differences in the psychological and social outcomes of children and adolescents as a function of family structure. Scientific studies show no evidence to substantiate fears about children of lesbian or gay parents and suggest the development, adjustment, and well-being of children with lesbian and gay parents do not differ markedly from that of children with heterosexual parents. The picture that emerges from social and psychological research is one of normal and healthy engagement in social life with peers, parents, family members, and friends regardless of the sexual orientation of parents.

FURTHER READING

Armesto, Jorge. C. 2002. "Developmental and Contextual Factors That Influence Gay Fathers' Parental Competence: A Review of the Literature." *Psychology of Men & Masculinity* 3, 2: 67–78.
Cornell University. 2017. "What We Know: What Does the Scholarly Research Say about the Well-Being of Children with Gay or Lesbian Parents?" https://whatweknow.inequality.cornell.edu/topics/lgbt-equality /what-does-the-scholarly-research-say-about-the-wellbeing-of-children -with-gay-or-lesbian-parents/
Crouch, Simon R., et al. 2014. "Parent-Reported Measures of Child Health and Wellbeing in Same-Sex Parent Families: A Cross-Sectional Survey." *BMC Public Health* 14: 635.

Falk, Patricia J. 1989. "Lesbian Mothers: Psychosocial Assumptions in Family Law." *American Psychologist* 44, 6: 941–947.

Farr, Rachel H. 2016. "Does Parental Sexual Orientation Matter? A Longitudinal Follow-up of Adoptive Families with School-Age Children." *Developmental Psychology* 53, 2: 252–264.

Gartrell, Nanette, and Henny Bos. 2010. "US National Longitudinal Lesbian Family Study: Psychological Adjustment of 17-year-old Adolescents." *Pediatrics* 126, 1: 28-36.

Goldberg, Abbie E., Nanette Gartrell, and Gary J. Gates. 2014. "Research Report on LGB-Parent Families." The Williams Institute, UCLA School of Law, July. https://williamsinstitute.law.ucla.edu/publications/report-lgb-parent-families/

Goldberg, Shoshana K., and Kerith J. Conron. 2018. "How Many Same-Sex Couples in the U.S. Are Raising Children?" The Williams Institute, UCLA School of Law, July. https://williamsinstitute.law.ucla.edu/publications/same-sex-parents-us/

Lamb, Michael E. 2012. "Mothers, Fathers, Families, and Circumstances: Factors Affecting Children's Adjustment." *Applied Developmental Science* 16, 2: 98–111.

Linville, Deanna, and Maya O'Neil. n.d. "Same Sex Parents and Their Children." American Association for Marriage and Family Therapy. https://www.aamft.org/Consumer_Updates/Same-sex_Parents_and_Their_Children.aspx

Long, Heather. 2019. "Children Raised by Same-Sex Couples Do Better in School, New Study Finds." *Washington Post*, February 6. https://www.washingtonpost.com/business/2019/02/06/children-raised-by-same-sex-couples-do-better-school-new-study-finds/

Mazrekaj, Deni, Kristof De Witte, and Sofie Cabus. 2020. "School Outcomes of Children Raised by Same-Sex Couples: Evidence from Administrative Panel Data." *American Sociological Review* 85, 5: 830–856.

Ngun, Tuck C., and Eric Vilain. 2014. "The Biological Basis of Human Sexual Orientation: Is There a Role for Epigenetics?" *Advances in Genetics* 86: 167–184.

Patterson, Charlotte J. 2009. "Lesbian and Gay Parents and Their Children: A Social Science Perspective." In Debra A. Hope, ed., *Nebraska Symposium on Motivation: Vol. 54. Contemporary Perspectives on Lesbian, Gay, and Bisexual Identities.* New York, NY: Springer, pp. 141–182.

Patterson, Charlotte J., Megan Fulcher, and Jennifer Wainright. 2002. "Children of Lesbian and Gay Parents: Research, Law, and Policy." In Bette L. Bottoms, Margaret Bull Kovera, and Bradley D. McAuliff, eds., *Children, Social Science and the Law.* New York: Cambridge University Press, pp. 176–199.

Stacey, Judith, and Timothy J. Biblarz. 2001. "(How) Does the Sexual Orientation of Parents Matter?" *American Sociological Review* 66, 2: 159–183.

"What We Know" Project. n.d. "What Does the Scholarly Research Say about the Well-Being of Children with Gay or Lesbian Parents?" Cornell University. https://whatweknow.inequality.cornell.edu/topics /lgbt-equality/what-does-the-scholarly-research-say-about-the-wellbeing -of-children-with-gay-or-lesbian-parents/

7

❖

Diversity within the LGBTQ Community

Chapter 7 highlights the incredible diversity within the LGBTQ community, making the point that there is no one *correct* way to be LGBTQ. While there is much that holds the LGBTQ community together, not every LGBTQ person is the same; they differ based on characteristics like race, geographic region, age, physical appearance, and behavior just like members of every other identity group.

The first questions in this chapter focus on the diversity of LGBTQ people. Q43 addresses racial and age diversity, noting that younger Americans and people of color are more likely to identify as LGBTQ; Q44 discusses geographic diversity and the misconception that LGBTQ people all live in cities; and finally, Q45 focuses on socioeconomic diversity, including variations in wealth and education. Q46 confronts the myth that LGBTQ people are all sexually promiscuous, underscoring that sexual behavior is not monolithic among any one identity group. Q47 tackles the common stereotype that LGBTQ people live a "gay lifestyle," explaining how that phrase can narrow people's attitudes and perpetuate a variety of myths and misconceptions, even unintentionally. Q48 discusses the common idea that LGBTQ people have unique, distinct differences in appearance, behavior, and speech, explaining that while differences are present, they, too, represent the range and diversity of LGBTQ people in the community. Finally, Q49 outlines the depth and breadth of contributions LGBTQ people have made in American life, from art and fashion to medicine, business, and literature.

Q43: DO LGBTQ PEOPLE TEND TO BE OF A CERTAIN RACE, GENDER, OR AGE?

Answer: The LGBTQ community includes people of a variety of races and from all different age groups, although people of color and younger people are more likely to identify as LGBTQ than are white people or older people. The LGBTQ community is younger and more racially diverse than the general U.S. adult population but both the general population and the LGBTQ community are majority white.

The Facts: LGBTQ people are most commonly stereotyped as white men and, in fact, most LGBTQ people in the United States do identify as white and non-Hispanic. At the same time, however, survey evidence indicates that Latinos, Black Americans, and Asian Americans are more likely to identify as LGBTQ compared to white non-Hispanic Americans. Women are also more likely to identify as LGBTQ compared to men (Gates 2017; Newport 2018).

Gallup surveys have tracked LGBTQ identification by race and gender (defined as men and women) since 2012. Overall, these data indicate that the number of American adults who identify as LGBTQ has increased over time (from 3.5 percent in 2012 to 4.5 percent in 2017). That increase has been driven by the nation's youngest adults (millennials, defined as those born between 1980 and 1999), who are more likely to identify as LGBTQ and have been increasingly likely to do so over time. In 2012, 5.8 percent of millennials identified as LGBTQ; by 2017, that proportion had risen to 8.2 percent. In contrast, only 1.8 percent of traditionalists (defined as those born between 1913 and 1945), 2.7 percent of baby boomers (born between 1946 and 1964), and 3.2 percent of Generation X (born between 1965 and 1979) identified as LGBTQ in 2012; by 2017, those proportions had changed only slightly, to 1.4 percent, 2.4 percent, and 3.5 percent, respectively (Newport 2018). A 2019 Williams Institute report found that overall, most LGBTQ people (58 percent) are white (non-Hispanic), while 21 percent are Latino, 12 percent are Black, 5 percent identify with more than one race, and 2 percent are Asian American (Williams Institute 2019).

People who identify as belonging to all four major racial groups have also become more likely to identify as LGBTQ since 2012, with the largest increases found among Latino and Asian Americans. In 2012, 3.2 percent of white (non-Hispanic) Americans, 3.5 percent of Asian Americans, 4.3 percent of Latino Americans, and 4.4 percent of Black Americans identified as LGBTQ. By 2017, those proportions had increased to 4.0 percent of white Americans, 4.9 percent of Asian Americans, 6.1 percent of Latino Americans, and 5.0 percent of Black Americans (Newport 2018).

Women are consistently more likely than men to identify as LGBTQ. In 2012, 3.4 percent of men and 3.5 percent of women identified as LGBTQ. By 2017, these proportions had increased to 3.9 percent of men and 5.1 percent of women (Newport 2018). While there is no definitive reason for this gender gap, researchers know that female sexuality is different than male sexuality and some of their findings suggest that female sexuality is more malleable over time (Diamond 2008).

UCLA demographer Gary Gates notes that some of these differences by racial group are due to the fact there are more young people within non-white populations in the United States. "According to the Gallup data, the average age of Asian adults in the U.S. is 35, the youngest among the race/ethnicity groupings. Average age is 39 among Hispanics, 44 among blacks, 51 among white adults, and 44 among 'other' racial and ethnic groups. Given the big changes in LGBT identification among millennials, the youngest generation, it's not surprising that younger racial and ethnic groups report larger LGBT identification increases" (Gates 2017). Overall, LGBTQ individuals in the United States have an average age of 37.3 years while non-LGBTQ people have an average age of 47.9 years. These differences in age can also be seen in the distribution of LGBTQ and non-LGBTQ people by age group: among people who identify as LGBTQ, 30 percent are age 18–24, 26 percent are age 25–34, 20 percent are age 35–49, 16 percent are age 50–64, and only 7 percent are age 65 or older. In contrast, among people who do not identify as LGBTQ, 12 percent are age 18–24, 16 percent are age 25–34, 25 percent are age 35–49, 26 percent are age 50–64, and 21 percent are age 65 or older (Williams Institute 2019).

Differences in rates of LGBTQ identification among younger and older Americans could be due to a number of factors, according to Gates. "Gallup research shows that data security and confidentiality are not major concerns of millennials. . . . They are more comfortable than their older counterparts with the idea of sharing what some might consider private information" (Gates 2017). In other words, younger LGBTQ people are more comfortable coming out and are less likely to view their sexuality as something to be kept from other people as a secret. Another possible explanation is the greater societal support for LGBTQ people (see Q14 and Q15). Gates notes, "It's likely that millennials are the first generation in the U.S. to grow up in an environment where social acceptance of the

LGBT community markedly increased. This may be an important factor in explaining their greater willingness to identify as LGBT" (Gates 2017).

A 2018 GenForward survey of millennials found that 14 percent identified as LGBTQ but rates of identification varied by racial group. Latino millennials were the most likely to identify as LGBTQ, at 22 percent, compared to 14 percent of Black millennials, 13 percent of white millennials, and 9 percent of Asian American millennials. The most common LGBTQ identity among millennials was bisexual, including 8 percent of both Latinos and African Americans as well as 7 percent of whites and 3 percent of Asian Americans. The next most common identity was gay or lesbian, including 6 percent of millennial Latinos, 4 percent of African Americans, 5 percent of whites, and 2 percent of Asian Americans (Cohen et al. 2018; Duran 2018). The GenForward survey also found that LGBTQ millennials do not think the issues being promoted by mainstream LGBTQ organizations are sufficiently attentive to how LGBTQ identity intersects with racial identity (Cohen et al. 2018).

FURTHER READING

Cohen, Cathy J., et al. 2018. "Millennial Attitudes on LGBT Issues: Race, Identity, and Experience." *GenForward*, June. https://genforwardsurvey.com/download/?did=135

Diamond, Lisa. 2008. "The Evolution of Plasticity in Female-Female Desire." *Journal of Psychology and Human Sexuality* 18, 4: 245–274.

Duran, Eric. 2018. "Latino Millennials Least Likely to Identify as Heterosexual, Survey Finds." NBCNews.com, July 23. https://www.nbcnews.com/feature/nbc-out/latino-millennials-least-likely-identify-heterosexual-survey-finds-n893701

Gates, Gary J. 2017. "In U.S., More Adults Identifying as LGBT." Gallup.com, January 11. https://news.gallup.com/poll/201731/lgbt-identification-rises.aspx

Mirza, Shabab Ahmed. 2019. "A Closer Look at Bisexual People of Color." September 27. https://www.americanprogress.org/issues/lgbtq-rights/reports/2019/09/27/475134/closer-look-bisexual-people-color/

Newport, Frank. 2018. "In U.S., Estimate of LGBT Population Rises to 4.5%." Gallup, May 22. https://news.gallup.com/poll/234863/estimate-lgbt-population-rises.aspx

Williams Institute. 2019. "LGBT Demographic Data Interactive." Williams Institute, UCLA School of Law. January. https://williamsinstitute.law.ucla.edu/visualization/lgbt-stats/?topic=LGBT#economic

Q44: DO LGBTQ PEOPLE TEND TO LIVE IN
PARTICULAR GEOGRAPHIC REGIONS?

Answer: No. LGBTQ people live all over the United States, including urban, suburban, and rural communities.

The Facts: LGBTQ people live throughout the United States in areas that are rural, suburban, and urban. A 2019 report published by the Movement Advancement Project (MAP) found that about one-third (35 percent) of LGBTQ people in America live in the South, 20 percent in the Midwest, 19 percent in the Northeast, and 25 percent in the West (Miller 2019). According to UCLA demographer Gary Gates, the largest concentrations are in metropolitan areas including the San Francisco Bay Area; Los Angeles; Austin, Texas; Portland, Oregon; and New Orleans, Louisiana. Comparing these data to similar data collected in 1990 shows that the LGBTQ community is less concentrated in major metropolitan areas and more evenly distributed across the United States than in previous years, according to Gates. "In 1990, San Francisco had a concentration of same sex couples that was ten times higher than the lowest metro area on my list. In the recent Gallup data, the relative difference between San Francisco and the lowest city is only about two times higher" (Florida 2015).

Gallup survey data analyzed by the UCLA Law School's Williams Institute finds that rates of LGBTQ identification vary among the 50 states from a low of 2.7 percent of adults in North Dakota to a high of 5.6 percent of adults in Oregon. LGBTQ identification is much higher, at 9.8 percent, in the District of Columbia (Williams Institute 2019). This variation may reflect local norms and levels of comfort with disclosing LGBTQ identity in a survey—states with lower proportions of adults identifying as LGBTQ tend to be in more conservative states such as North Dakota, Idaho, Montana, South Dakota, and Alabama while states with higher proportions of adults identifying as LGBTQ tend to be in more progressive states such as Oregon, Nevada, Massachusetts, and California (Movement Advancement Project 2020).

The MAP report found that LGBTQ people are just as likely to live in rural parts of the country compared to non-rural areas, in contrast to the stereotype that they live overwhelmingly in urban settings. Surveys find that 3 to 5 percent of adults who live in rural areas identify as LGBTQ, similar to the 4.5 percent of the overall adult U.S. population. In addition, about 10 percent of youth in both rural and urban areas identify as LGBTQ. Overall, this means that 15–20 percent of all LGBTQ people in the United

States, an estimated 2.9 to 3.8 million LGBTQ people, live in rural areas. The report notes: "In reality, not only do LGBT people live in rural America, but many of them want to and enjoy living in rural America" (Movement Advancement Project 2020, iii).

Again, these findings conflict with stereotypes about LGBTQ people only living in (or trying to move to) urban areas or coastal cities. "LGBT people live in rural areas for the same reasons as other people, such as love of family, the strength of tight-knit rural communities, and connection to the land," according to Ineke Mushovic, executive director of MAP (Snyder 2019). The MAP report found that LGBTQ people living in rural areas reported similar levels of subjective well-being, health, and satisfaction with their lives as did LGBTQ people in urban areas (Movement Advancement Project 2020).

> In discussions with LGBT people living in rural communities, researchers find that many LGBT people living in rural areas not only enjoy rural ways of life, but also that living in a rural community directly shapes their own LGBT identity and their broader understanding of what it means to be an LGBT person. In fact, a key finding of this research is that, for many LGBT people in rural areas, living in a rural area may be just as important to who they are as being LGBT. (Movement Advancement Project 2020, 8)

At the same time, living in rural America can create additional challenges for LGBTQ people, including increased risk of anti-LGBTQ discrimination. In part, these effects stem from the tight-knit nature of rural communities; once an LGBTQ person is out in one area of life (e.g., at work), it is likely that other community members outside of that area will soon know about it. What happens in one community (e.g., work or church) can ripple outward to other areas of an individual's life. This may be why LGBTQ youth living in rural areas are more likely to look online for support communities and guidance on how to come out to their families. If an LGBTQ person in a rural area experiences discrimination at work or when seeking health care, they may have fewer other options available due to the lower density of healthcare providers and employers in rural areas (Movement Advancement Project 2020).

In addition, rural areas tend to have fewer support structures in place and fewer other LGBTQ people in terms of raw numbers which can make it difficult for LGBTQ individuals, especially youth who are just figuring out their sexual orientation or gender identity and their families. Rural areas are less likely to have supportive laws and policies in place and more likely to have discriminatory policies; LGBTQ people in rural areas are also more likely to have less political power and are less likely to have LGBTQ-identified elected officials to whom they can go for support (Movement Advancement Project 2020).

FURTHER READING

Florida, Richard. 2015. "Where LGBTQ Americans Live: New Polling from Gallup Tells a Tale of Growing Tolerance." Bloomberg CityLab, March 23. https://www.bloomberg.com/news/articles/2015-03-23/a-new -gallup-poll-shows-where-lgbtq-americans-live

Gates, Gary J. 2015. "Comparing LGBT Rankings by Metro Area: 1990 to 2014." Williams Institute, UCLA School of Law, March. https:// williamsinstitute.law.ucla.edu/publications/lgbt-rankings-metro-areas/

Miller, Susan. 2019. "Nearly 4 Million LGBTQ People Live in Rural America, and 'Everything Is Not Bias and Awful.'" *USA Today*, April 3. https://www.usatoday.com/story/news/nation/2019/04/03/lgbtq-lesbian -gay-transgender-rural-america/3282217002/

Movement Advancement Project. 2020. "Where We Call Home: LGBT People in Rural America." LGBTMAP, November 27. https://www .lgbtmap.org/rural-lgbt

Scher, Avichai. 2019. "Gay in Rural America: Up to 5 Percent of Rural Residents Are LGBTQ, Report Finds." NBCNews.com, April 12. https:// www.nbcnews.com/feature/nbc-out/gay-rural-america-5-percent-rural -residents-are-lgbtq-report-n993936

Snyder, Mark. 2019. "The 3 Million+ LGBTQ People in Rural America . . ." Equality Federation, April 3. https://www.equalityfederation.org/2019/04 /the-3-million-lgbtq-people-in-rural-america/

Williams Institute. 2019. "LGBT Demographic Data Interactive." Williams Institute, UCLA School of Law. January. https://williamsinstitute.law .ucla.edu/visualization/lgbt-stats/?topic=LGBT#economic

Q45: DO LGBTQ PEOPLE TEND TO BE FROM A PARTICULAR SOCIOECONOMIC BACKGROUND?

Answer: Yes. While LGBTQ people have a variety of socioeconomic backgrounds, they are more likely to live in poverty compared to non-LGBTQ people. This reality is a stark contrast to the stereotype of LGBTQ people as wealthy.

The Facts: LGBTQ people tend to have lower levels of income and higher levels of poverty and unemployment compared to non-LGBTQ people. Gallup survey data from 2017 analyzed by the UCLA School of Law's Williams Institute found that 9 percent of LGBTQ people were unemployed compared to 5 percent of non-LGBTQ people; 25 percent of LGBTQ people had incomes of less than $24,000 compared to 18 percent of non-LGBTQ people. More than a quarter (27 percent) of LGBTQ people reported food insecurity compared to 15 percent of non-LGBTQ people (Williams Institute 2019). Multiple other studies have also found that LGBTQ people are more likely to live in poverty compared to non-LGBTQ people (Badgett et al. 2013; Grant et al. 2011).

Economics professor M. V. Lee Badgett has documented significant differences in socioeconomic status both between the LGBTQ and the non-LGBTQ community and within the LGBTQ community. Overall, 21.6 percent of LGBTQ people live in poverty compared to 15.7 percent of cisgender straight people. Breaking down the numbers by identity group, transgender people and bisexual women have the highest rates of poverty (29.4 percent) compared to cisgender bisexual men (19.5 percent), cisgender lesbians (17.9 percent), cisgender straight women (17.8 percent), cisgender straight men (13.4 percent), and cisgender gay men (12.1 percent) (Badgett et al. 2019).

Food insecurity is a significant problem as well. A 2018 report from the City University of New York's Social Justice Sexuality Project found that 25 percent of LGBTQ people did not have enough money to feed themselves or their families at some point during the previous year compared to 18 percent of non-LGBTQ people. For Black LGBTQ individuals, that rate of food insecurity increased to 37 percent; the average Black transgender person reported earning less than $10,000 a year (Hunter, McGovern, and Sutherland 2018).

The tendency for LGBTQ people to have lower incomes than non-LGBTQ people has been true for some time. Self-reported survey data from 2017 finds that people who self-reported their annual household income as less than $36,000 a year were more likely to identify as LGBTQ (6.2 percent) compared to those reporting the highest-income category of $90,000 a year or more (3.9 percent). These differences have persisted in Gallup polling since 2012, when Gallup first began tracking these data. In 2012, 4.7 percent of people reporting the lowest incomes identified as LGBTQ compared to 3.0 percent of people reporting the highest incomes (Newport 2018).

These differences are all the more striking because they are not mirrored in levels of educational attainment. In 2017, 4.5 percent of people who reported the lowest level of educational attainment (high school or less) identified as LGBTQ, compared to 4.7 percent of those with some college education, 4.4 percent of those who graduated from college, and 4.3 percent of those with postgraduate education (Newport 2018). Overall, among people who are LGBTQ, 41 percent have a high school education or less, 30 have some college education, 17 percent graduated from college, and 13 percent have some postgraduate education. In contrast, among people who are not LGBTQ, 39 percent have a high school education or less, 29 percent have some college education, 18 percent graduated from college, and 14 percent have some postgraduate education (Williams Institute 2019).

The reality of the demographics of the LGBTQ community in the United States stands in stark contrast to popular stereotypes which tend to bring to mind wealthy, white, male individuals. However, the truth is that many LGBTQ people are people of color and many live in poverty: LGBTQ people of color are even more likely to live in poverty and experience food insecurity, housing instability, and unemployment (Hunter, McGovern, and Sutherland 2018).

FURTHER READING

Badgett, M. V. Lee, Laura E. Durso, and Alyssa Schneebaum. 2013. "New Patterns of Poverty in the Lesbian, Gay, and Bisexual Community." Williams Institute, UCLA School of Law, June. https://williamsinstitute.law.ucla.edu/publications/lgb-patterns-of-poverty/

Badgett, M. V. Lee, Soon Kyu Choi, and Bianca D. M. Wilson. 2019. "LGBT Poverty in the United States: A Study of Differences between Sexual Orientation and Gender Identity Groups." Williams Institute, UCLA School of Law, https://williamsinstitute.law.ucla.edu/wp-content/uploads/National-LGBT-Poverty-Oct-2019.pdf

Grant, Jaime M., et al. 2011. *Injustice at Every Turn: A Report of the National Transgender Discrimination Survey*. Washington, DC: National Center for Transgender Equality and National Gay and Lesbian Task Force.

Hunter, Lourdes Ashley, Ashe McGovern, and Carla Sutherland, eds. 2018. *Intersecting Injustice: A National Call to Action. Addressing LGBTQ Poverty and Economic Justice for All*. New York: Social Justice Sexuality Project, Graduate Center, City University of New York. https://socialjusticesexuality.com/intersecting_injustice/

Newport, Frank. 2018. "In U.S., Estimate of LGBT Population Rises to 4.5%." Gallup, May 22. https://news.gallup.com/poll/234863/estimate-lgbt-population-rises.aspx

Williams Institute. 2019. "LGBT Demographic Data Interactive." Williams Institute, UCLA School of Law. January. https://williamsinstitute.law .ucla.edu/visualization/lgbt-stats/?topic=LGBT#economic

Q46: ARE LGBTQ PEOPLE MORE SEXUALLY ACTIVE THAN STRAIGHT PEOPLE?

Answer: Sexual behavior is strongly related to cultural norms, religion, and many other environmental factors, and there just aren't enough data to say for certain that LGBTQ people are more or less sexually active than heterosexual people.

The Facts: Movies and television often portray LGBTQ people—and gay men in particular—as having more sex with more people compared to heterosexual people. Even further, when it comes to sexual activity, many gay men are depicted in popular culture as promiscuous, predatory, and generally obsessed with sex—and often indiscriminately so. This trope is deeply ingrained, contributing not only to fear and hate of LGBTQ people but also to discriminatory laws and policies. Part of President Bill Clinton's "Don't Ask, Don't Tell" policy, which prevented LGBTQ people from serving openly in the military from 1993 to 2011, was fueled by the belief that it would help straight colleagues feel safer from unwanted sexual advances from LGBTQ people, particularly gay men. As suggested in other chapters of this book (see Q6, Q11, Q39), LGBTQ people are no more likely to be aggressive or predatory when it comes to sex than non-LGBTQ people are. People of all sexual orientations and gender identities can be perpetrators and victims of sexual assault so these blanket stereotypes about members of LGBTQ communities are incorrect and hurtful.

Skewed narratives and irrational fears about LGBTQ sexual activities and practices are not rooted in reality but are remnants of stereotypes that emerged during the sexual liberation movement of the 1970s. However, there is an incredible amount of variation in sexual behavior among both LGBTQ and straight people and mixed evidence suggests that *some* of these stereotypes have a factual basis. Psychologist Barbara Leigh (1989) surveyed households in the San Francisco Bay Area on reasons for having (or avoiding) sex and the frequency of individuals' sexual behavior. She found no significant differences in reported rates of sexual activity among gay and straight people but did find significant differences between men and women regardless of sexual orientation. Multiple studies have confirmed that men have higher levels of sexual thoughts and desires compared to women and that they desire and have more sexual partners compared to women. Some research has also found that gay and bisexual men have a greater desire to engage in sexual activity compared to straight men (Peixoto 2019).

The stereotype of LGBTQ promiscuity is rooted in the liberationist sexual ethos of the 1970s, particularly in regard to gay men. Gay urban masculinity in the 1970s was depicted through "hypermasculine sexuality" that included "celebrations of erotic prowess, and participation in the sexual 'marketplace' of gay bars and bathhouses" (Hindman 2019, 56). Barred by law from marriage, stereotypes of gay men as unable to sustain relationships led to images of them as "promiscuous deviates incapable of love" (Hindman 2019, 56). The era also saw the rise of Turkish baths as a cruising spot for gay men to have anonymous sex. While most gay men did not frequent them, the existence of the baths further reinforced stereotypes.

In the 1980s and 1990s, as fear of AIDS spread and gay rights advocates sought to improve public attitudes, gay men were urged to confront the "promiscuity of the past" and conform to heteronormative standards of sexual behavior (Hindman 2019, 61). LGBTQ activists sought to downplay reports of promiscuity of gay men to project a positive public image and advance gay rights; many encouraged gay men to change their sexual behavior and even abstain from sex to stop the spread of HIV/AIDS and to improve public perceptions. To cultivate an image as a group "worthy" of inclusion, most gay rights advocates asked the community to constrain its sexual behavior. The onset of the AIDS crisis in the 1980s intensified calls by many gay leaders for individuals to curtail the community's alleged promiscuity (Hindman 2019). (An important outlier in this regard is the grassroots HIV/AIDS political and activist group AIDS Coalition to Unleash Power, commonly known as ACT UP.) At the same time, perceptions of gay men as promiscuous were encouraged in the fundraising efforts of the Religious Right, a network of antigay Christian organizations.

To be sure, sex has been an important and often overlooked part of the history of the LGBTQ movement. For example, until recently and still in many places around the world, LGBTQ people couldn't express themselves openly in public due to legitimate safety concerns that hand-holding and kissing in public might trigger hostile reactions from others. The reality for many years was that one of the few ways for LGBTQ people in many parts of the country to safely express their sexual identity was through private sexual behavior.

With increased acceptance and safety of LGBTQ identity comes the freedom to express one's sexual identity in other ways. Without denigrating or criticizing those who experience and express their identity through sexual behavior, the stereotypes around promiscuity and the LGBTQ community can perpetuate unhealthy biases. Many observers believe that Americans feel too much shame about enjoying sex and embracing their sexuality and they urge society to adopt more sex-positive attitudes. In addition, scholars assert that Americans need to be more informed and mindful about important differences between sexual identity and sexual behavior.

FURTHER READING

Gremore, Graham. 2016. "Just How Many Gay Men Are in Open Relationships? These New Stats May Surprise You (Or Not)." Queerty, February 4. https://www.queerty.com/just-how-many-gay-men-are-in-open -relationships-these-new-stats-may-surprise-you-or-not-20160204

Haupert, Mara L., et al. 2017. "Prevalence of Experiences with Consensual Nonmonogamous Relationships: Findings from Two National Samples of Single Americans." *Journal of Sex & Marital Therapy* 43, 5: 424–440.

Hindman, Matthew Dean. 2019. "Promiscuity of the Past: Neoliberalism and Gay Sexuality Pre- and Post-AIDS." *Politics, Groups, and Identities* 7, 1: 52–70.

Jones, Benji. 2019. "From 'Sex Means Penetration' to 'All Effeminate Guys Are Bottoms,' These Are the Most Common Myths about Gay Sex between Men." Insider, June 25. https://www.insider.com/the-most -common-myths-about-gay-sex-between-men-2019-6

Kheraj, Alim. 2018. Not Every Gay Man Is DTF." GQ, April 5. https:// www.gq.com/story/not-every-gay-man-is-dtf

Lang, Nico. 2017. "I'm Proud to Be a Gay 'Slut.'" Daily Beast, April 13. https://www.thedailybeast.com/im-proud-to-be-a-gay-slut

Leigh, Barbara C. 1989. "Reasons for Having and Avoiding Sex: Gender, Sexual Orientation, and Relationship to Sexual Behavior." *Journal of Sex Research* 26, 2: 199–209.

OKCupid Blog. 2016. "A Digital Decade: Sex." OKCupid, February 5. https://theblog.okcupid.com/a-digital-decade-sex-c95e6fb6296b

Peixoto, Maria Manuela. 2019. "Sexual Satisfaction, Solitary, and Dyadic Sexual Desire in Men According to Sexual Orientation." *Journal of Homosexuality* 66, 6: 769–779.

Strudwick, Patrick. 2010. "So You Think Gay Men Are Promiscuous?" *The Guardian*, October 19. https://www.theguardian.com/commentisfree /2010/oct/19/gay-men-promiscuous-myth

Q47: IS THERE SUCH A THING AS A "GAY LIFESTYLE"?

Answer: No. The LGBTQ community is incredibly diverse in the same way that America's straight community is diverse. Despite stereotypes to the contrary, members of the LGBTQ community do not conform to any one way of living their lives, whether it be about style, attitudes, possessions, or beliefs.

The Facts: Merriam-Webster Dictionary defines the word *lifestyle* as "the typical way of life of an individual, group, or culture." In context, lifestyle is usually used to make a broad, general statement about a group of people and how they live, their consumer choices, how they think, and how they behave. This book has provided many examples of how the LGBTQ community is not a monolithic group of people: it varies in so many ways, from race and ethnicity, political partisanship and ideology, socioeconomic status, region, expressions of masculinity and femininity, and gender identity, just to name a few. In short, there is no "right way" to be a member of the LGBTQ community and as such, there is no one "typical way of life" as it relates to the community either.

Some religious leaders have asserted that homosexuality (and being a part of the LGBTQ community more generally) goes against the tenets of their religion. One way for a person who is told that biased piece of information might make themselves feel better about it is to believe the myth that LGBTQ people don't believe in God and can't be religious themselves. In a 2018 poll from BuzzFeed News and Whitman Insight Strategies, 39 percent of LGBTQ respondents claimed to have no religious affiliation at all. At the same time, 23 percent identified as Protestant or Christian, 18 percent identified as Catholic, and smaller percentages reported identifying as Jewish or Buddhist. In total, nearly 60 percent of LGBTQ people reported feeling connected to religion (Holden 2018), indicating that the stereotype that the "LGBTQ lifestyle" does not accommodate religious faith is false. In contrast, only 26 percent of the overall U.S. adult population describe their religious identity as atheist, agnostic, or "nothing in particular" while 74 percent report a particular religious affiliation, including 65 percent who identify as Protestant or Christian and another 20 percent who identify as Catholic (Pew Research 2019).

Another way that people can fall into the trap of believing that all LGBTQ people are the same has to do with gender norms. American culture is rife with stereotypes of masculine lesbians and feminine gay men. While it is true that many LGBTQ people do not conform to gender norms or stereotypes, behavior and appearance run the gamut. Every lesbian is different: while some are more masculine in appearance and disposition, others are not. While some gay men behave in a more flamboyant and stereotypically feminine manner, a large number do not. The way someone acts or lives is not the same for every LGBTQ person and as a result, asserting that a "lifestyle" of rejecting gender norms is typical for every LGBTQ person is inaccurate (see Q20, Q24, and Q25).

Finally, persistent stereotypes exist about how LGBTQ people spend their time. For example, the word "gay" itself had been used to describe someone overly loud, happy, and cheerful; over the years, the etymology of the word has had a strong effect on how gay men are perceived or stereotyped—specifically, that all gay men like to drink and to do illegal drugs, have many sexual partners, and spend much of their free time at bars or clubs. Similarly, many assume that all transgender women are drag queens, men who take on a female persona while in costume or in performance (see Q27). While many people do in fact do those things and behave in those ways, it does not typify the entire community; there is significant variation in sexual behavior and a multitude of other ways in which LGBTQ people spend their time and structure their families. For example, in the same 2018 poll mentioned above, 56 percent of the LGBTQ people surveyed either definitely wanted to have/raise children, would like to have them, or weren't sure, while 44 percent reported they did not want to have a family. Sixty-one percent were married or wanted to get married, 14 percent did not, and another 25 percent were not sure about whether they would ever marry. Only 4 percent of those in the LGBTQ community who were surveyed reported having sex daily; 23 percent reported not having sex in the last year, with 44 percent responding they had sex once or twice a month or once or twice a week (Holden 2018). By comparison, a 2017 study found that the average American adult has sex 54 times a year, an average of about once a week; the study does not ask about sexual orientation and thus is a measure of sexual activity of all Americans (Twenge, Sherman, and Wells 2017).

That is not to say, however, that there is no such thing as LGBTQ culture. On the contrary, LGBTQ people have contributed to literature, art, music, business, medicine, politics, and history in meaningful and robust ways (see Q49). In some cities, particularly in North America, some LGBTQ people live in neighborhoods with a high proportion of LGBTQ residents. Examples include places like the Castro and West Hollywood in California, Boystown in Chicago, and the Gay Village in Montreal. These communities organize events and facilitate the creation of cultural events such as Pride, the Gay Games, and Southern Decadence that celebrate and affirm the LGBTQ experience. What has been known as "ball culture" or the ballroom scene has become better known thanks to the TV show *Pose*. Ball culture refers to a young African American and Latino underground LGBTQ subculture that originated in New York City (The Black Youth Project 2009). People "walk" (i.e., compete) for trophies, prizes, and glory at events known as balls where they mix performance, dance, lip-synching, and modeling. There is a rich history of the LGBTQ community creating culture of its own from all across the United States and around the world.

Even within the LGBTQ community, there are some who think that everyone needs to act and to behave a certain way. For example, many activists think that every single person should be open about their sexuality, regardless of circumstance. However, there are intolerant or pedantic elements in every community. There is simply no right way or wrong way to be LGBTQ. There is tremendous diversity in those who identify as LGBTQ and that diversity is an element of strength for the community. Attempts to limit what is seen as acceptable or to classify everyone who is LGBTQ as having to live or to behave in a certain way—as conforming to the idea of one "lifestyle"—fails to acknowledge the myriad ways members of the LGBTQ community live, love, worship, and behave differently from one another. Celebrating those differences help to humanize and to better understand people rather than to make them fit into a box that may not be appropriate.

FURTHER READING

The Black Youth Project. 2009. "The Ballroom Scene: A New Black Art." http://blackyouthproject.com/ballroom-scene-a-new-black-art/

Haslop, Craig, Helene Hill, and Ruth A. Schmidt. 1998. "The Gay Lifestyle—Spaces for a Subculture of Consumption." *Marketing Intelligence & Planning* 16, 5: 318–326.

Holden, Dominic. 2018. "Who Are LGBTQ Americans? Here's a Major Poll on Life, Sex, and Politics." Buzzfeed News, June 13. https://www.buzzfeednews.com/article/dominicholden/lgbtq-in-the-us-poll

Merriam-Webster. n.d. "Lifestyle." In Merriam-Webster, September 22, 2020. https://www.merriam-webster.com/dictionary/lifestyle

Pew Research. 2019. "In U.S., Decline of Christianity Continues at Rapid Pace." Pew Research Center, October 17. https://www.pewforum.org/2019/10/17/in-u-s-decline-of-christianity-continues-at-rapid-pace/

Schlatter, Evelyn, and Robert Steinback. 2011. "10 Anti-Gay Myths Debunked." *The Intelligence Report*, Southern Poverty Law Center,

February 27. https://www.splcenter.org/fighting-hate/intelligence-report
/2011/10-anti-gay-myths-debunked

Twenge, Jean M., Ryne A. Sherman, and Brooke E. Wells. 2017. "Declines
in Sexual Frequency among American Adults, 1989–2014." *Archives of
Sex Behavior* 46, 8: 2389–2401.

Q48: DO LGBTQ AND STRAIGHT PEOPLE DISPLAY DISTINCT DIFFERENCES IN THEIR PHYSICAL APPEARANCE, BEHAVIOR, OR SPEECH?

Answer: Yes. LGBTQ people do tend to have different physical appear-
ances and mannerisms than straight people in ways that people often refer
to as "acting gay" and differences in pitch and pronunciation between gay
men and other people that people often refer to as "sounding gay" (Swanson 2015). At the same time, there is no "one" way to be gay, lesbian, or any
other sexual orientation or gender identity, and there is wide and overlap-
ping variation in the appearance, behavior, and speech traits of both
LGBTQ and straight people.

The Facts: Multiple studies have shown that people are able to accurately guess male and female sexual orientation based simply on photos of
their faces, even if those photos are only shown for a brief moment. In a set
of five studies conducted by psychology professor Nicholas Rule and his
colleagues, men and women were able to accurately identify if a face was
that of a gay or straight man, even if certain parts of the face were removed
(hair, eyes, mouth), and that accuracy was similar to that for the full face
when participants were only shown hairstyles (Rule et al. 2008). Additional studies by Rule and his colleagues have found similar results for
predicting the sexual orientation of female faces or partial faces and that
these abilities to accurately perceive male and female sexual orientation
persist even when participants are only shown the photo for a fraction of a
second (Rule et al. 2009; Rule and Ambadi 2008). These initial studies
used photos of real people. Subsequent research by psychology professor
Jonathan Freeman and his colleagues using computer-generated faces confirmed that the ability to accurately judge the sexual orientation of an
individual based on their face is reliant on the degree to which their face
exhibits gender-inverted shapes and textures—male faces with more feminine features are more likely to belong to gay men and female faces with
more masculine faces are more likely to belong to lesbians. When faces do

not exhibit these stereotypical inverted features, people are less able to accurately identify them as belonging to gay or lesbian individuals (Freeman et al. 2010).

Other research has examined whether gay men and lesbians move their bodies in a particular way that differentiates them from their straight counterparts. Gay men move their hips differently than do straight men and lesbians have a different way of moving their shoulders compared to straight women: gay men are more likely to sway their hips and lesbians are more likely to swagger with their shoulders. However, while observers were better able to distinguish the sexuality of straight and gay men based on how they walked, they were not able to do so for women. The lead author of the study, communications professor Kerri Johnson, attributed this to the greater latitude that U.S. society gives to women. "Women in our society are permitted a greater latitude of behaviors. They're able to act in masculine ways, and adopt traditional masculine roles" while men are punished if they adopt feminine traits (Johnson et al. 2007; Dahl 2007).

Studies have also examined the degree to which gay men, in particular, "sound" gay—whether they have a stereotypical gay voice: higher pitched and more melodious. A 2015 documentary called *Do I Sound Gay?* shared stories of gay men and their discomfort with their voices and the degree to which this discomfort was due to internalized homophobia, which is what happens when a LGBTQ person takes the biases, prejudices, and hatred reinforced by society and turns these biases inward back on themselves (Lyons 2020). However, scientific tests have found that while stereotypically gay voices are more likely to be labeled gay by listeners, they are not able to accurately identify an individual's sexuality based only on listening to their voice. "Some men with 'gay voices' are straight, and some men with 'straight voices' are gay," according to linguist Ron Smyth (Smyth, Jacobs, and Rogers 2003; Swanson 2015).

In 2017, researchers at Stanford University claimed that they had developed facial recognition software that was able to distinguish between gay and straight people. Humans were able to correctly distinguish between gay and heterosexual men 61 percent of the time and lesbians and heterosexual women 54 percent of the time; in contrast, the artificial intelligence algorithm was able to accurately distinguish male faces 81 percent of the time and women 74 percent of the time. Leading LGBTQ advocacy organizations GLAAD and Human Rights Campaign denounced the "junk science" as potentially dangerous. "These reckless findings could serve as a weapon to harm both heterosexuals who are inaccurately outed, as well as gay and lesbian people who are in situations where coming out is dangerous," they wrote in a joint press release (BBC News, 2017). In response to this and other backlash, the authors noted in their published work: "given that companies and governments are increasingly using computer vision algorithms to detect people's intimate traits, our findings expose a threat to the privacy and safety of gay men and women" (Kosinski and Wang 2018).

A consistent finding across these studies is that individuals who are "correctly" identified as gay or lesbian by observers or AI are those who exhibit stereotypical attributes. At the same time, not all gay or lesbian (or other members of the LGBTQ community) exhibit those stereotypical attributes and many straight people can be perceived as "acting" or "sounding" gay when they exhibit these attributes. These evaluations are based on stereotypes, not on the reality of diversity of human appearance and behavior. Members of the LGBTQ community, cisgender, and straight people come in all shapes and sizes and exhibit a wide variety of ways of speaking, walking, dressing, and presenting themselves to the wider world.

FURTHER READING

BBC News. 2017. "Row over AI That 'Identifies Gay Faces.'" BBC.com, September 11. https://www.bbc.com/news/technology-41188560

Dahl, Melissa. 2007. "Gay or Straight? Watch His Walk." NBCNews.com, September 13. https://www.nbcnews.com/health/health-news/gay-or-straight-watch-his-walk-flna1c9465734

Freeman, Jonathan B., Kerri L. Johnson, Nalini Ambady, and Nicholas O. Rule. 2010. "Sexual Orientation Perception Involves Gendered Facial Cues." *Personality and Social Psychology Bulletin* 36, 10: 1318–1331.

Johnson, Kerri L., Simone Gill, Victoria Reichman, and Louis G. Tassinary. 2007. "Swagger, Sway, and Sexuality: Judging Sexual Orientation from Body Motion and Morphology." *Journal of Personality and Social Psychology* 93, 3: 321–334.

Kosinski, Michal W., and Yilun Wang. 2018. "Deep Neural Networks Are More Accurate Than Humans at Detecting Sexual Orientation from Facial Images." *Journal of Personality and Social Psychology* 114, 2: 246–257.

Lyons, Daniel. 2020. "What Is Internalized Homophobia?" *Psychology Today*, February 24. https://www.psychologytoday.com/us/blog/queering-psychology/202002/what-is-internalized-homophobia

Rule, Nicholas O., and Nalani Ambady. 2008. "Brief Exposures: Male Sexual Orientation Is Accurately Perceived at 50 Ms." *Journal of Experimental Social Psychology* 44, 4: 1100–1105.

Rule, Nicholas O., Nalani Ambady, and Katherine C. Hallett. 2009. "Female Sexual Orientation Is Perceived Accurately, Rapidly, and

Automatically from the Face and Its Features." *Journal of Experimental Social Psychology* 45, 6: 1245–1251.

Rule, Nicholas O., Nalini Ambady, Reginald B. Adams, Jr., and C. Neil Macrae. 2008. "Accuracy and Awareness in the Perception and Categorization of Male Sexual Orientation." *Journal of Personality and Social Psychology* 95, 5: 1019–1028.

Smyth, Ron, Greg Jacobs, and Henry Rogers. 2003. "Male Voices and Perceived Sexual Orientation: An Experimental and Theoretical Approach." *Language in Society* 32, 3: 329–350.

Swanson, Ana. 2015. "What It Means to 'Sound Gay.'" WashingtonPost .com, July 28. https://www.washingtonpost.com/news/wonk/wp/2015/07 /28/what-it-means-to-sound-gay/

Q49: HAVE LGBTQ PEOPLE MADE POSITIVE IMPACTS ON AMERICAN LIFE AND CULTURE?

Answer: Yes. LGBTQ people have made numerous important and positive contributions to American society in myriad ways, from music, art, and literature to science, technology, politics, and business.

The Facts: Throughout history, people who identified as LGBTQ, openly or otherwise, have been significant influences on American life and culture. For example, LGBTQ writers have made huge and enduring contributions to the world of literature. Oscar Wilde (1854–1900), Walt Whitman (1819–1892), Tennessee Williams (1911–1983), Virginia Woolf (1882–1941), James Baldwin (1924–1987), Truman Capote (1924–1984), Emily Dickinson (1830–1886), and Langston Hughes (1902–1967) are just some of the famous writers who identified as LGBTQ. Their work has endured for decades and many of their writings are included in the American canon of the best poetry, novels, plays, essays, and other literary works that the nation has produced.

Art is another area where LGBTQ people have made significant contributions. Openly LGBTQ photographer and artist Andy Warhol (1928–1987) put his stamp on the art world with works addressing complex and divergent sexualities, particularly in some of his lesser-known works in the 1980s. Annie Leibovitz (1949–) is one of the most famous modern portrait photographers in the world; she is perhaps most famous for the portrait of musician John Lennon she took on the day he was murdered (Lopatko 2018). Other famous American artists include Jasper Johns, Robert Mapplethorpe, and Grant Wood, among others.

LGBTQ people have made their mark in the music industry as well. Dusty Springfield came out as bisexual in an interview in 1970. Freddie Mercury, lead singer of the band Queen, had same-sex relationships and came out as bisexual in the early 1970s. George Michael was an openly gay singer who died in 2016. Elton John is one of the most well-known musicians of all time, coming out in 1988 and famously marrying his husband David Furnish in 2014. Other famous LGBTQ recording artists include Brandi Carlile, Ricky Martin, David Bowie, and Melissa Ethridge. More recent artists like Jason Mraz, Fergie, Frank Ocean, Miley Cyrus, Steve Grand, Troye Sivan, Janelle Monae, and Lil Nas X have been open about their LGBTQ identities in ways that have opened doors, hearts, and minds for a variety of audiences (Butler 2019).

Many LGBTQ people fought against bigotry on many fronts in addition to homophobia. For example, Audre Lorde (1934–1992) was an activist and writer who confronted and addressed injustices of racism, sexism, classism, and heterosexism (Poetry Foundation 2020). Bayard Rustin (1912–1987) worked alongside Dr. Martin Luther King in the civil rights movement, urging leaders of that movement to openly embrace the fight for civil rights for LGBTQ people as well (Morgan 2020). Not only did people like Lorde and Rustin make significant advances in stamping out homophobia but their intersectional work raised awareness of how people with multiple marginalized and disenfranchised identities were in need of attention and support too.

Though perhaps not as well-known as celebrities, LGBTQ people have made important strides in the fields of science as well. Sally Ride (1951–2012), the first American woman to fly in space, later became the director of the California Space Institute at the University of California, San Diego. Upon her death, it was revealed that she had been in a loving relationship with a woman for 27 years (Hamer 2019). More recently, Ben Barres (1954–2017), a neurobiologist at Stanford University, was a noted researcher in brain science. Barres transitioned in his late 40s and in 2013, he became the first openly transgender man to be offered membership into the National Academy of Science. Upon his death in 2017, his university said his research on the brain's glial cells "revolutionized the field of neuroscience" (Lotto Persio 2018). And there are many others who are not yet famous but nonetheless are trailblazers in their respective fields in science, technology, engineering, and math (STEM) and related fields (500QueerScientists.com n.d.).

American business and technology have seen their trajectories influenced by LGBTQ people as well. Arlan Hamilton, cofounder and CEO of Backstage Capital, is believed to be the "only black, queer woman to have ever built a venture capital firm from scratch" (Harris 2018). Megan Smith, former executive of several high-tech companies, was appointed in 2014 by President Obama as the first ever "chief technology officer" of the United States (Leskin 2019). Leanne Pittsford is the founder and CEO of Lesbians Who Tech, a company that offers programming, visibility, and opportunities to LGBTQ+ women and nonbinary people in the tech sector (Leskin 2019). Probably the most prominent LGBTQ person in business and technology is Tim Cook, the CEO of Apple, the first company to reach a valuation of $1 trillion. He came out in a 2014 personal essay as a way to help the gay community raise its profile in the business and tech sectors (Cook 2014).

Moving to politics, Harvey Milk (1930–1978) is perhaps the most famous LGBTQ elected official in U.S. history. He won a seat on the San Francisco Board of Supervisors in 1977 before being assassinated in 1978 (Kaufman and Kaufman 2013). The first openly gay person (male or female) to be elected to public office was Kathy Kozachenko, who won a seat on the Ann Arbor City Council in 1974 as an out lesbian (Barnes 2015). Joanne Conte was the first openly transgender person to win a city council race, serving on the Arvada City Council from 1991 to 1995 (Calhoun 2013). Since these firsts, there has been a significant increase in the number of LGBTQ people running for and winning higher political offices, including Kate Brown, the first openly bisexual governor (Oregon); Tammy Baldwin, the first openly lesbian U.S. Senator (Wisconsin); Lori Lightfoot, mayor of the city of Chicago; and Pete Buttigieg, the first openly gay person to win a U.S. presidential primary or caucus. In 2020, president-elect Joe Biden nominated Buttigieg to be Secretary of Transportation and on February 3, 2021, he became the first openly LGBTQ person to serve in a cabinet position.

According to the LGBTQ Victory Institute, there has been a significant rise in the number of openly LGBTQ people serving in elected office in the United States over time (see Q18). Prior to the November 2020 election, openly LGBTQ officeholders included two governors, nine members of Congress, seven statewide officials, 43 mayors, 156 state legislators, 474 other local officials, and 107 judicial members across the United States. In the 2020 election, at least 1,006 LGBTQ candidates ran for office in the United States, more than ever before. The 2020 numbers marked a 41 percent increase over the 2018 midterms, according to the LGBTQ Victory Fund (Bussey 2020). As of December 2020, 334 of the 782 known general election candidates won their November races. Overall, 43 percent of LGBTQ candidates who made it to the general election won their races (Moreau 2020). In total, the November 2020 election was the strongest showing for LGBTQ candidates in electoral history. Of particular note are pronounced increases in the number of LGBTQ mayors, the number of bisexual and queer-identified people, and the number of transgender women serving in elected office (Moreau 2020; Victory Institute 2020).

All of these people, in the past and in the present, demonstrate the significant contributions that LGBTQ people have made to American culture and society. While their accomplishments range widely in scope and in content, they underscore the importance of a diversity of voices in different industries and domains in facilitating positive change in this country. While history books may not yet fully acknowledge LGBTQ people in the development of the United States, the fact remains that those who identify as LGBTQ have played and continue to play significant and positive roles in a wide variety of areas in American life.

FURTHER READING

500QueerScientists.com. n.d. "500 Queer Scientists." https://500queer scientists.com

Barnes, Katie. 2015. "Elaine Noble & Kathy Kozachenko: The First Openly LGBT People to Be Elected." Feministing, May 27. http://feministing .com/2015/05/27/elaine-noble-kathy-kozachenko-the-first-openly-lgbt -people-to-be-elected/

Bussey, Timothy R. 2020. "'Rainbow Wave' of LGBTQ Candidates Run and Win in 2020 Election." *The Conversation*, November 4. https:// theconversation.com/rainbow-wave-of-lgbtq-candidates-run-and-win -in-2020-election-149066

Butler, Tijen. 2019. "30 Singers You May Not Know Are LGBT." PinkNews, April 18. https://www.pinknews.co.uk/2019/04/18/35-lgbt-singers-queer/

Calhoun, Patricia. 2013. "Joanne Conte Shook Up Arvada as a City Council Member—and a Transgendered Person." Westword, February 4. https://www.westword.com/news/joanne-conte-shook-up-arvada -as-a-city-council-member-and-a-transgendered-person-5838611

Cook, Tim. 2014. "Tim Cook Speaks Up." Bloomberg, October 30. https:// www.bloomberg.com/news/articles/2014-10-30/tim-cook-speaks-up

Hamer, Ashley. 2019. "5 LGBT Scientists Who Changed the World." *Discovery.com*, August 1. https://www.discovery.com/science/LGBT -Scientists-Who-Changed-World

Harris, Ainsley. 2018. "Memo to the Silicon Valley Boys' Club: Arlan Hamilton Has No Time for Your BS." Fast Company, September 13. https://www.fastcompany.com/90227793/backstage-capitals-arlan -hamilton-brings-diversity-to-venture-capital

Kaufman, Diane, and Scott Kaufman. 2013. *Historical Dictionary of the Carter Era*. Lanham, MD: Scarecrow Press, p. 180.

Leskin, Paige. 2019. "The 23 Most Powerful LGBTQ+ People in Tech." *Business Insider*, June 2. https://www.businessinsider.com/most-powerful -lgbtq-people-in-tech-2019-2

Lopatko, Katya. 2018. "Did You Know These 11 Famous Artists Were Queer?" TheArtGorgeous.com, December 6. https://theartgorgeous .com/know-10-famous-artists-queer/

Lotto Persio, Sofia. 2018. "10 LGBT Scientists Who Made History to Celebrate LGBTSTEM Day." PinkNews, July 5. https://www.pinknews .co.uk/2018/07/05/queer-scientists-history-first-lgbtstemday

Moreau, Julie. 2020. "Record Number of LGBTQ Candidates Won in November, New Data Reveals." NBCNews.com, December 10. https:// www.nbcnews.com/feature/nbc-out/record-number-lgbtq-candidates -won-november-new-data-reveals-n1250718

Morgan, Thad. 2020. "Why MLK's Right-Hand Man, Bayard Rustin, Was Nearly Written Out of History." History.com, January 15. https://www .history.com/news/bayard-rustin-march-on-washington-openly-gay-mlk

Poetry Foundation. 2020. "Audre Lorde," Poetry Foundation. https://www .poetryfoundation.org/poets/audre-lorde

Portwood, Jerry, et al. 2019. "Music's Unsung LGBTQ Heroes," *Rolling Stone*, June 1. https://www.rollingstone.com/music/music-lists/musics -unsung-lgbtq-heroes-629374/rob-halford-2-628916/

Victory Institute. 2020. "LGBTQ Victory Fund 2020 Election Results." https://victoryfund.org/lgbtq-victory-fund-2020-election-results/

Index

"Acting gay," 192
Activism. *See* LGBTQ activism
ACT UP, 77, 187
Addiction. *See* Substance abuse
Adolescents
    gender transitioning in, 130
    mental health of, 150, 151, 152
    risky behavior in, 28
    with same-sex parents, 172
    sexual abuse of, 27, 28
Advocate (magazine), 99
Affordable Care Act (2010), 45
Africa
    history of homosexual behavior
        in, 23
    homophobia in, 17
    LGBTQ activism in, 17
    LGBTQ people criminalized in, 16
    same-sex marriage in, 16
African American LGBTQ people.
    See Black LGBTQ people
Age, of LGBTQ people, 178, 179
Agender, definition of, 115, 120
Age of consent, 20
Ai (emperor), 22

AIDS. *See* HIV/AIDS
AIDS Coalition to Unleash Power
    (ACT UP), 77, 187
AIDS optimism, 148
Aikane, 23
Albatrosses, 7
Alcohol abuse, 160
Aldrich, Robert, 20–21
Altitude Express v. Zarda, 45
American Academy of Pediatrics,
    155
American Dialect Society, 136
American Enterprise Institute,
    163
American Family Association, 50
American Medical Association, 125,
    133, 155
American Psychiatric Association
    on gender dysphoria, 133
    on homosexuality as mental
        disorder, 50
    on homosexuality as normal variant
        of sexuality, 49, 50, 51
    on paraphilias, 49, 51, 52
    on transgender identity, 125

American Psychological Association
   (APA)
  on childhood sexual trauma, 27
  on conversion therapy, 154–155,
   156, 157
  on gender, 2
  on sex, 2
Anal sex, and HIV transmission, 147
Anderson-Minshall, Jacob, 139
Androgynous, definition of, 3
Androgynous lesbians, 92, 93, 109
Animals. *See* Same-sex behavior in
   animals
Antigay laws, 16–17, 45–46
Antigay slurs, reclaiming, 29–31
Antiretroviral therapies, 148, 164
Anxiety
  bullying and, 171
  conversion therapy and, 156
  in LGBTQ people, 150, 151
  in transgender people, 126–127
Arab Sappho, 24
Aravosis, John, 112–113
Argentina, LGBTQ activism in, 17
Argentine Homosexual Community
   (CHA), 17
Aristotle, 20
Armenia, same-sex marriage in, 16
Aromantic attraction, 4
Artificial intelligence (AI), 193
Artists, LGBTQ, 195
Asia
  homophobia in, 18
  LGBTQ people criminalized in, 16
  same-sex marriage in, 16
Asian American LGBTQ people,
   as percentage of LGBTQ
   community, 178, 179, 180
Assault, 170
Associated Press, 54
Athletes, inspection of, 122
Attraction
  capacity for, in bisexuals, 101
  expressing, 4

romantic orientation and, 4
young people in tune with capacity
   for, 103
Australia, same-sex marriage in, 16
Aversion therapy, 154

Baby boomers, 178
Backstage Capital, 196–197
Badgett, M. V. Lee, 184
Bagemihl, Bruce, 6, 7, 8
Baldwin, Tammy, 81, 197
Ball culture, 191
Barker, Meg-John, 14
Baron, Dennis, 135
Barres, Ben, 196
Barrett, Rusty, 116
Basic Instinct (film), 96
Basile, Vic, 80
Bathhouses, 187
Behavior, of LGBTQ people, 192–194
Benjamin, Rich, 99
Bennett, William, 163
Bestiality, definition of, 50
Biden, Joe
  Buttigieg nominated by, 79, 197
  on discrimination in health care,
   46, 134
  on gender, 123
  on same-sex marriage, 86
Bigender, definition of, 115, 120
Bill of Rights for homosexuals, 38
Binge drinking, 160
Biological Exuberance (Bagemihl), 6
Biopsychosocial approach, 14
Bio queens, 116
Bisexual, definition of, 4
Bisexuality
  gender transitioning and, 139
  homosexuality compared to, 101
  as valid identity, 101
Bisexual men, 102, 103
Bisexuals
  bullying experienced by, 170
  of color, 102

coming out, 77, 102–103
discrimination against, 57
as elected officials, 81, 82, 197
HIV/AIDS in, 146, 147
invisibility of, 102
in poverty, 103, 184
proportion in LGBTQ community,
 102, 180
sexual activity of, 187
stereotype of, as confused people,
 101–103
substance abuse in, 160
as TV/film characters, 85
Bisexual women, 102, 103
Bissu (holy people), 121
Black churches, on homosexuality, 71
"Black is Beautiful" (slogan), 38
Black leaders, on same-sex marriage, 65
Black LGBTQ people
in ball culture, 191
discrimination against, 57
HIV/AIDS in, 146, 147
homeless, 166–167
as percentage of LGBTQ
 community, 178, 179, 180
in poverty, 184
terms used by, 4
Black rights movement, and LGBTQ
 rights movement, 35, 37, 38
Blankley, Bethany, 51
Blue discharges, 34–35
Bonobos, 6, 9–10
Booker, Cory, 65
Bostock v. Clayton County, 44, 45, 46,
 59, 77–78
Boston Children's Hospital, 126
Boston Medical Center, 128
Botswana, LGBTQ activism in, 17
Bottlenose dolphins, 9
Bowers v. Hardwick, 63
Boys Don't Cry (film), 87
*Brain Storm: The Flaws in the Science
 of Sex Differences* (Jordan-Young),
 14

Brazil, LGBTQ activism in, 17–18
Brevard, Aleshia, 115
Brokeback Mountain (film), 86
Bronski, Michael, 99
Brown, Kate, 81, 197
Brown, Michael, 38–39
Brunei, 16
Buddhist LGBTQ people, 189
Bugis society (Indonesia), 121
Bullying
cyberbullying, 170
effects of, 171
of LGBTQ children, 169–171
and mental health, 151, 169, 171
physical, 170
rates of, 169–170
verbal, 170
Burns, Ken, 35
Bush, George H., 55
Businesses
discrimination against LGBTQ
 people by, 44–45, 47, 73
LGBTQ people influencing,
 196–197
Butch-identifying partner, 92, 110
Buttigieg, Pete, 79–80, 197
BuzzFeed News, 189
Byers, Stephanie, 82
Byrd, James, Jr., 55

Cairo 52, 18
Cameron, Paul, 163
Canadian geese, 8
Carothers, Bobbi, 109
Casey, Logan S., 57
Castor, Jane, 82
Catholic Church, 70–71, 72, 73
Catholic LGBTQ people, 189
Catholic Social Services, 46, 68
Celebrities
LGBTQ, 195–196
on same-sex marriage, 64, 65
Census Bureau, 54, 160
Center for American Progress, 58

Centers for Disease Control and
Prevention (CDC), 146–147,
152, 170
Central Europe, same-sex unions
in, 16
CHA. *See* Argentine Homosexual
Community
Chapin Hall, 166
Chen Weisong, 21–22
Chicago Society for Human Rights, 34
Child and Adolescent Gender Center
Clinic (UCSF), 130
Children
bullying experienced by, 169–171
conversion therapy for, 154–157
dress-up play by, 128–129
gender-expansive, 129
gender-nonconforming behavior in,
28, 106, 129
gender-typed behavior in, 105–106
in lesbian separatist collectives,
95–96
of LGBTQ parents, 172–174
mental health of, 150, 151, 152
pronouns used by, 129
same-sex couples adopting, 66–69
same-sex parents of, 66–69, 172–174
sexual trauma in, 25–28
survey on LGBTQ people
wanting, 190
transgender, 128–131, 150
See also Young people
Children, Youth, and Families
Program (Human Rights
Campaign Foundation), 102
The Chilling Adventures of Sabrina
(TV show), 88
China
history of homosexual behavior
in, 21–22
homophobia in, 18, 22
Christianity
on homosexuality, 21, 71
on LGBTQ people and rights, 71–73

Christian LGBTQ people, 189
Christopher Street Liberation Day,
38–39
Chromosomes, 121
Chromosome testing, for athletes, 122
Cisgender, definition of, 4, 138
Cissexism, 141
Civil Rights Act (1964), 44, 45, 46, 59,
77–78
Clements, KC, 132
Clinton, Bill, 34, 186
"Closet" culture, 105
Collins, Kathleen, 110
Colonialism, and suppression of
homosexual relationships, 23
Colorado Anti-Discrimination Act, 45
Coming out, 75–78
as bisexual, 77, 102–103
definition of, 75
hardship caused by, 76
and homelessness, 167
increase in, 75–78
and mental health, 150, 151
Milk, Harvey, on, 76
as process, 75–76
Compton's Cafeteria, 37
Condoms, decreased use of, 147
Consent
age of, 20
lack of, in paraphilias, 51–52
lack of, in sexual abuse, 28
Conservative political movement
and conversion therapy, 155
false claims by, 163
See also Republicans
Conte, Joanne, 197
Conversion therapy, 154–157
ban on, 155–156
medical experts dismissing,
154–155, 156, 157
and mental health, 156–157
number of participants in, 155
origins of, 154
other terms for, 155

Cook, Tim, 197
Cornell University, 172
Couch surfing, 166
Coworkers, coming out to, 75,
    77–78, 103
Cox, Laverne, 87, 115
Craig, Larry, 41
Crepidula, 8
Criminalizing LGBTQ people,
    15, 16–18
Crompton, Louis, 20, 21
Cross-dressing, 115–117
    definition of, 115, 116
    example of, 116
    prevalence of, 116
    research on, 117
Crouch, Simon, 67
The Crying Game (film), 87
Culture
    and gender, 2–3, 120
    and gender roles, 93–94
    LGBTQ, 190, 195–198
Cunningham, Philippe, 81
Curry, Tim, 87
Cut sleeve (story), 22
Cyberbullying, 170
Cyberbullying Research Center,
    170

The Dallas Buyers Club (film), 87
Darwin, Charles, 6
Dashow, Jordan, 167
Daughters of Bilitis (DOB), 35–36
Davids, Sharice, 81
Davidson, Jaye, 87
Dawood, Khytam, 13
DeGeneres, Ellen, 85
Democrats
    as LGBTQ elected officials, 80,
        81, 82
    on LGBTQ rights, 73
    on loss of religion, 44
    on marriage equality, 63
    on same-sex adoption, 68

Depression
    bullying and, 171
    conversion therapy and, 156
    in LGBTQ people, 150, 151
    in transgender people, 126–127, 133
De-transitioning, 130
*Diagnostic and Statistical Manual
    (DSM),* 50, 52, 125–126
Diethylstilbestrol (DES), 13
Discrimination against LGBTQ
    people, 57–59
    by adoption agencies, 69
    by businesses, 44–45, 47, 73
    childhood sexual trauma myth and,
        25–26
    forms of, 57, 58
    in foster care, 46, 68, 72
    in health care, 46, 133, 134, 148
    heterosexism and, 25–26
    HIV+ people, 148
    homeless youth, 167
    laws on, 44, 59, 77–78, 134
    and life expectancy, 164
    and mental health, 150–152
    in military, 34–35, 37
    people of color, 57
    pervasive, 58–59
    in politics, 80, 81
    public opinion on, 72, 73
    in rural areas, 182
    and substance abuse, 159–161
    during Trump administration, 45–46
    See also Employment
        discrimination; Prejudice against
        LGBTQ people
Discrimination against transgender
    people
    and coming out, 77
    extent of, 57–58
    in health care, 46, 133, 134
    and mental health issues, 127
    as shared experience with LGB
        people, 112
    at work, 77

DOB. *See* Daughters of Bilitis
Do I Sound Gay? (documentary), 193
Dolphins, 7–8, 9
Dong Xian, 22
"Don't Ask, Don't Tell" policy, 186
Drag kings, 116
Drag queens, 115–117, 190
Dreger, Alice, 2, 14
Drescher, Jack, 112
Dress-up play, 128–129
Drug use. *See* Substance abuse
Duke Ling of Wei, 22
Dunbar, Robin, 10
Dynamics. *See* Gender dynamics

East Coast Homophile Organizations
    (ECHO), 37
Eastern Europe, same-sex unions
    in, 16
Eberstadt, Nicholas, 163
Educational attainment
    homelessness and, 167
    of LGBTQ people, 184–185
Effeminate behavior, 98, 105,
    107, 109
Ego Dystonic Homosexuality
    (EDH), 50
Egypt
    ancient, homosexual behavior
        in, 20
    LGBTQ people punished in, 18
Ehrensaft, Diane, 130
Eichberg, Robert, 76
Eisenhower, Dwight, 36
Elected officials
    LGBTQ people as, 79–83, 197–198
    See also Politicians
Ellen (TV show), 85, 86
Emotional abuse, 151, 160
Employment discrimination
    against bisexuals, 103
    coming out and, 77
    forms of, 57
    by government, 36

laws protecting from, 44, 59,
    77–78, 113
against transgender people, 77
Employment division v. Smith, 68
Employment Non-Discrimination Act
    (ENDA), 113
Epprecht, Marc, 23
Equality Act, 113
Equal rights, for women, 140
Essig, Laurie, 24
Estrogen, 130
Europe, same-sex marriage in, 16
Evolution
    and advantages of homosexuality,
        14
    same-sex behavior in animals and,
        6, 7, 9
Executive Order 10450, 36

Facial recognition software,
    193–194
Faith-based conversion therapy, 155
Family
    coming out to, 75, 76, 77
    lack of support from, 151, 160, 167
Family Research Institute, 163
Featherstone, David, 9
Federal Bureau of Investigation (FBI),
    on hate crimes, 54, 55
Felmlee, Diane, 93
Female pronouns, used by drag
    performers, 116
Feminine-presenting lesbians, 109
Femininity
    of gay men, 104, 105, 107, 189–190
    of lesbians, 109–111
    in LGBTQ relationships, 92, 93
    research on, 107
    as social construct, 93
"Femininity certificates," 122
Feminism
    first wave of, 140
    goal of, 140
    second wave of, 140, 142

third wave of, 140–141
on transgender people, 140–143
Femme-identifying lesbians, 92, 109–110
Femme queer people, 110
Fertility, same-sex behavior in animals and, 9
50 Cent, 65
Films, LGBTQ characters in, 84–88, 96, 109
First Amendment, 43
Flatworms, 8
Flour beetles, 9
Foley, Mark, 41
Food insecurity, 164, 184, 185
Foster care, transgender youth in, 166, 167
Foster parents, LGBTQ couples as, 46, 68, 72
"Four Dimensions" (Ross and Rosser), 40
Francesco (documentary), 70
Francis (pope), 70
Frank, Barney, 113
Fraternal birth order effect, 13
Freedom to Marry, 64
Freeman, Jonathan, 192
Freud, Sigmund, 92, 154
Frogs, 8
Fruit flies, 9
Fulton v. City of Philadelphia, 46, 68

Ganna, Andrea, 12
Garrison, Althea, 81
Gartner, Richard, 26, 27
Gates, Gary, 179–180, 181
Gay
definition of, 3
etymology of, 190
history of word, 30
as white term, 4
Gay adoption rights, 66–69
"Gay gene," 12
"Gay is Good" (slogan), 38

Gay Liberation Front, 38
Gay Liberation March, 76
Gay lifestyle, 189–191
Gayly (magazine), 97
Gay men
attitude of, toward lesbians, 98–100
bullying experienced by, 170
coming out, 77
as cross-dressers, 115
as elected officials, 79, 80, 81, 82, 197
femininity of, 104, 105, 107, 189–190
historical overview of, 19–24
HIV/AIDS in, 146–149
masculinity of, 104–107
as misogynists, 98–100
physical appearance and behavior of, 192–194
in poverty, 184
sexual activity of, 186–188
substance abuse in, 160
as TV/film characters, 85–86
"Gay propaganda law" (Russia), 18
Gay urban masculinity, 187
Gay World Cup of soccer, 17
Geese, 8
Gender
as binary concept, 123
culture and, 2–3
definition of, 2
as nonbinary concept, 120, 123
vs. sex, 2
Gender-affirming hormones, 130
Gender confirmation surgery. *See* Surgeries, for transgender people
Gender dynamics, 91–117
of bisexuals, 101–103
of cross-dressers, 115–117
of gay men and lesbians, 98–100
of gay men and masculinity, 104–107
of lesbians and femininity, 109–111
of lesbians and men, 95–97

of relationships, 92–94
of transgender people, 112–114
Gender dysphoria
    in children, 131
    definition of, 125, 133
    diagnosis of, 133
    and mental health, 126, 133
    in nonbinary people, 126
    social transitioning relieving, 132
Gender-expansive children, 129
Gender expression
    definition of, 2–3
    feminism on, 141
    in gay men, 105
    in lesbians, 109–111
Genderfluid, definition of, 3, 115, 120
Gender identity
    of children of same-sex parents, 173
    conversion therapy and, 154–157
    definition of, 2, 102
    vs. sexual orientation, 102, 112,
        138–140
    suppression of, 39–42
    of transgender people, 132
Gender identity disorder, 125, 127
Gender incongruence, 127
Gender-neutral pronouns, 135–137
Gender nonconfirming, definition
    of, 3
Gender-nonconforming behavior, in
    children, 28, 106, 129
Gender pronouns. See Pronouns
Genderqueer, definition of, 3, 115, 120
Gender roles
    children of same-sex parents
        developing, 173
    culture and, 93–94
    flexibility in, 93
    in LGBTQ relationships, 92–94
Gender transitions, 129–130, 132–134
    de-transitioning, 130
    medical, 130, 132, 133
    and sexual orientation, 138–139
    social, 129–130, 132

survey on, 133
    See also Surgeries, for transgender
        people
Gender-typed behavior, in children,
    105–106
Generation X, 178
Genetic causes of sexual orientation,
    12–13
Genetics, of intersex people, 121–122
GenForward, 180
Geographic regions, 181–183
Gerber, Henry, 34
Gernreich, Rudi, 35
Ghana, homophobia in, 17
Ghulām, 24
GI Bill (1944), 35
Girlfriends (magazine), 139
GLAAD
    on bisexuals in LGBTQ
        community, 102
    on facial recognition software, 193
    on LGBTQ TV characters, 85
    on religious groups in media, 72–73
    on transgender TV characters,
        86–87
Gomorrah. See Sodom and Gomorrah
Gooren, Louis, 13
Gorsuch, Neil, 44, 77–78
Government, homosexuals dismissed
    from, 36
Greece, ancient, homosexual behavior
    in, 20–21, 24

Hadrian (Roman emperor), 21
Haggard, Ted, 41
Hale, Sadie, 99
Hamer, Dean, 12
Hamilton, Arlan, 196–197
Harassment of LGBTQ people
    and life expectancy, 164
    and mental health, 150–152
    survey on, 57
    transgender people, 57–58, 133
Harris, Torrey, 82

Hate crimes against LGBTQ people
  awareness of, 56
  blaming victims of, 55
  documenting, 54–55
  increase in, 53–56
  laws on, 55
  masculinity and, 106
  and mental health, 151
  number of incidents, 54
  reporting, 54
  and substance abuse, 160
  survey on, 54
  See also Violence against LGBTQ
    people
Hate Crimes Prevention Act (HCPA)
  (2009), 55
Hate Crimes Statistics Act (HCSA)
  (1990), 55
Hawaii, 23
Hay, Harry, 35
"He," 136
Healey, Dan, 23
Health care
  discrimination in, 46, 133, 134, 148
  for transgender people, 125–126,
    132
Health insurance, of transgender
  people, 125–126, 132
Hegemonic masculinity, 98
Herek, Gregory, 55
Hermaphrodite animals, 8
Heteronormativity, 25
Heteroromantic attraction, 4
Heterosexism, 25
Hijra (third gender), 121
Hines, Sally, 142
HIV/AIDS, 146–149
  advanced manageability of, 148
  and discrimination, 148
  and life expectancy, 164
  risky sexual behavior and, 147–148
  serosorting, 148
  statistics, 146, 147
  transmission of, 146–147

HIV/AIDS crisis
  and confronting promiscuity,
    187
  deaths in, 164
  masculine behavior during and
    after, 105
  and public opinion on LGBTQ
    people, 62–63
Homelessness, 166–168
Homophile groups, 36
Homophobia
  in Africa, 17
  among American voters, 80
  in Asia, 18
  in Brazil, 17–18
  by closeted gay people, 39–42
  confronting, 30
  fighting, 196
  internalized, 40, 160, 193
  Lavender Scare, 36, 37
  and mental health, 150–152
  research on, 40–41
"Homophobic? Maybe You're Gay"
  (Ryan and Ryan), 40
Homoromantic attraction, 4
Homosexual, definition of, 3
Homosexual Bill of Rights, 38
Homosexuality
  in animals (*see* Same-sex behavior
    in animals)
  APA on, 49, 50, 51, 52
  bisexuality compared to, 101
  causes of, 12–14
  conversion therapy for, 154–157
  evolutionary advantages of, 14
  Freud on, 154
  in history, 19–24
  medical understanding of, 50
  as mental disorder, 50
  myths on, 25–28
  as normal variant of human
    sexuality, 49, 50, 51
  religions on, 71
  as sexual deviation, 50

as sin, 155
society's perception of, 50
Hormones, and sexual orientation, 13
Hormone testing, for athletes, 121
Hormone therapies, 130, 132, 139
Hoskin, Rhea Ashley, 110
"How Did the T Get in LGBT?"
    (Aravosis), 112–113
Huerta, Dolores, 64
Hull, Bob, 35
Human Rights Campaign (HRC),
    113, 193
Human Rights Campaign Foundation,
    77, 102
Hypermasculinity, 99, 187
Hypothalamus, 9, 13

Al-Idrisi, Sharif, 24
Ignoring LGBTQ people, 15–16
India, nonbinary identity in, 121
Indonesia, nonbinary identity in, 121
Insects, 9
Insertive anal sex, 147
Inter-American Commission on
    Human Rights, 165
Internalized homophobia, 40, 160, 193
International Amateur Athletic
    Federation, 122
International Classification of
    Diseases (WHO), 127
International Gay Association, 17
International Lesbian, Gay, Bisexual,
    Trans and Intersex Association
    (ILGA), 17
International Olympics Committee
    (IOC), 122
Internet, finding sexual partners on, 148
Intersex
    definition of, 3, 115, 121
    vs. nonbinary, 121, 122
    overview of, 121–122
Iran, LGBTQ people punished in, 18
Islam, on homosexuality, 71
Israel, same-sex marriage in, 16

Jackson, Jesse, 65
Japan
    history of homosexual behavior
        in, 22
    homophobia in, 18
Jay-Z, 64, 65
Jenkins, Andrea, 81
Jennings, Dale, 35
Jewish LGBTQ people, 189
John, Elton, 196
Johnson, David, 36
Johnson, Kerri, 193
Johnson, Lyndon B., 45
Johnson Amendment, 45
Jones, Gina Ortiz, 81
Jones, Mondaire, 82
Jones, Shevrin, 81
Jordan-Young, Rebecca, 14
Judaism, on homosexuality, 71
Julius' (New York City bar), 37

Kahn, Ellen, 102
Kama Sutra, 23
Kameny, Frank, 38
Kea, Perry, 71
Kenyatta, Malcolm, 81
King, Martin Luther, 196
Kinsolving, Les, 51
Kiss, Charlie, 138
Kiss-ins, 76
Klein, Aaron, 47
Klein, Melissa, 47
Klein v. Oregon, 47
Klinefelter syndrome, 122
Klobukowska, Ewa, 122
Kozachenko, Kathy, 79,
    197
Kūkai, 22

The Ladder (magazine), 36
Lang, Nico, 99
Latin America
    LGBTQ activism in, 17–18
    same-sex marriage in, 16

Latino/Latina LGBTQ people
  in ball culture, 191
  HIV/AIDS in, 146, 147
  as percentage of LGBTQ
    community, 178, 179, 180
Laughton, Stacie, 81
Lavender Scare, 36, 37
The Lavender Scare (Johnson), 36
Lawrence v. Texas, 51, 62–63
Laws
  protecting LGBTQ people, 43–47,
    59, 77–78, 113, 134
  on religious freedom, 43–47
Laws (Plato), 20
Laysan albatross, 7
Lebow, Wendy, 93
Legal rights of LGBTQ people
  adoptive rights, 68–69
  countries granting, 15, 16
  in Homosexual Bill of Rights, 38
  laws on, 43–47, 59, 77–78, 113, 134
  and legalization of paraphilias, 49–52
  opponents of, 39–42, 49
  religions on, 70–74
  religious freedom and, 43–47, 68–69
  same-sex marriage, 16, 62–63
  See also LGBTQ activism; LGBTQ
    rights movement
Lehman, James, 151
Leibovitz, Annie, 195
Leigh, Barbara, 186–187
Leitsch, Dick, 37
Lesbian
  definition of, 3
  as white term, 4
Lesbianism, 24
Lesbians
  attitude of, toward men, 95–97
  bullying experienced by, 170
  of color, 95–96
  coming out, 77
  discrimination against, 57
  as elected officials, 79, 80, 81,
    82, 197

femininity of, 109–111
gay men's attitude toward, 98–100
gender roles in relationships of,
    92, 93
historical overview of, 24
masculinity of, 109–111, 189–190
in poverty, 184
sexualization of, 109
substance abuse in, 160
as TV/film characters, 85–86,
    96, 109
Lesbian separatist movement, 95–96
Lesbians Who Tech, 197
Leto, Jared, 87
LeVay, Simon, 9
Levitt, Heidi, 110
Lewis, Sonya Jaquez, 81
LGBTQ, as acronym, 3
LGBTQ activism
  for marriage equality, 64
  "queer" term reclaimed by, 29–31
  worldwide, 17–18
  See also LGBTQ rights movement
LGBTQ animals. *See* Same-sex
    behavior in animals
LGBTQ culture, 190, 195–198
LGBTQ identity
  concepts in, 2–5
  four dimensions of, 40
  origins of, 1–31
  outside Western societies, 15–18
LGBTQ people
  as adoptive parents, 66–69
  age of, 178, 179
  behaviors and outcomes associated
    with, 145–174
  coming out (*see* Coming out)
  conversion therapy for (*see*
    Conversion therapy)
  discrimination against (*see*
    Discrimination against LGBTQ
    people)
  diversity of, 177–198
  educational attainment of, 184–185

as elected officials, 79–83, 197–198
ethnicity of, 178–179
in geographic regions, 181–183
harassment of (*see* Harassment of LGBTQ people)
hate crimes against (*see* Hate crimes against LGBTQ people)
historical overview of, 19–24
legal rights of (*see* Legal rights of LGBTQ people)
life expectancy of, 163–165
lifestyle of, 189–191
mental health of, 150–152
millennials identifying as, 178, 179–180
number of people identifying as, 78
as parents, 66–69, 172–174
physical appearance and behavior of, 192–194
in poverty, 164, 183–185
public visibility of, 61–88
religions on, 70–74
religious, 73, 189
sexual activity of, 186–188
stereotypes of (*see* Stereotypes)
substance abuse in, 150, 151, 159–161
as TV and film characters, 84–88
violence against (*see* Violence against LGBTQ people)
See also Bisexuals; Gay men; Lesbians; Transgender people
LGBTQ people of color
bisexuals, 102
discrimination against, 57
as elected officials, 81, 82
lesbians, 95–96
life expectancy of, 164
mental health of, 151
survey on, 178–179, 180
transgender people, 58, 77, 88
See also Asian American LGBTQ people; Black LGBTQ people;

Latino/Latina LGBTQ people; Native American LGBTQ people
LGBTQQ2SIAA, 3
LGBTQ rights movement, 33–59
and Black rights movement, 35, 37, 38
on coming out, 76–77
early groups in, 34–36
love as focus of, 64
in 1960s, 36–38
sexism in, 98
on sexual behavior, 187
start of, 34–39
Life expectancy, 163–165
discrimination and prejudice and, 164
HIV/AIDS and, 164
homelessness and, 167
myth on, 163–164
Lifestyle
definition of, 189
gay, 189–191
Lightfoot, Lori, 82, 197
Ling of Wei. *See* Duke Ling of Wei
Lippa, Richard, 110
"Lipstick lesbians," 109
Lives (Plutarch), 24
Lorde, Audre, 196
Louÿs, Pierre, 36
Lyon, Phyllis, 35

MacFarlane, Geoff, 10
Magazines, 35, 36
Maines, Nicole, 88
Malawi, antigay laws in, 16–17
Malaysia, antigay laws in, 16
"Male gaze" preference, 109
Male-to-male sexual contact, 146–147
Man-haters (stereotype), 95–97
Mannis, Eddie, 82
MAP. *See* Movement Advancement Project
Marijuana use, 159–160
Marriage. *See* Same-sex marriage

Marriage equality, 64, 72
Marshall, Bob, 81
Martin, Del, 35
Masculine overcompensation thesis,
106–107
Masculine-presenting lesbians, 109
Masculinity
of gay men, 104–107
gay urban, 187
and hate crimes, 106
hegemonic, 98
hypermasculinity, 99, 187
of lesbians, 109–111, 189–190
in LGBTQ relationships, 92, 93
and misogyny, 98
performing, 98
research on, 106–107
as social construct, 93
toxic, 106
and transphobia, 107
Masterpiece Cakeshop, 44–45
*Masterpiece Cakeshop v. Colorado Civil
Rights Commission*, 45
Mattachine Foundation, 35
Mattachine Review (magazine), 35, 36
Mattachine Society, 36, 37, 38
Matthew Shepard and James Byrd Jr.
Hate Crimes Prevention Act
(2009), 55
Maypole, Jack, 128
McBride, Sarah, 82
McCain, John, 68
McCarthy, Joseph, 36
McClain, Linda, 71
McGowan, Rose, 98
Media
lesbians as man-haters in, 96
on religious leaders, 72–73
Medical care. *See* Health care
Medical Monitoring Project, 148
Medical transitioning, 130, 132, 133
See also Surgeries, for transgender
people
Memmott, Mark, 31

Men
bullying experienced by, 170
as cross-dressers, 115–117
female prejudice against, 95–97, 98
as misogynists, 98–100
sexual activity of, 186–187
See also Bisexual men; Gay men;
Transgender men
Mental disorders
homosexuality as, 50
paraphilias as, 49
transgender identity as, 125–127
Mental health
bullying and, 151, 169, 171
of children, 150, 151, 152
conversion therapy and, 156–157
homelessness and, 167
lack of family support and, 151
of LGBTQ people, 150–152
and substance abuse, 159, 160
of transgender people, 126–127, 133,
150, 151, 156
Men who have sex with men (MSM)
HIV infection in, 146
term, 4–5
Mercury, Freddie, 196
Me Too movement, 98
Metropolitan areas, LGBTQ people
living in, 181, 182
Meyer, Ilan H., 156–157
Michael, George, 196
Michigan Womyn's Music Festival, 142
Middle Ages, homosexuality during,
21
Middle East, LGBTQ people
criminalized in, 16
Middleton, Lisa, 81
Military
blue discharges from, 34–35
"Don't Ask, Don't Tell" policy
in, 186
homosexuals excluded from, 37
transgender people in, 72
Milk, Harvey, 76, 80, 197

Millennials, identifying as LGBTQ,
178, 179–180
Misandry, 95–97, 98
Misogyny, 98–100
Mizi Xia, 22
Mock, Janet, 88
Moonlight (film), 86
Mosaic genetics, 121
Movement Advancement Project
(MAP), 181–183
Movies, LGBTQ characters in, 84–88,
96, 109
Murphy, Glenn, Jr., 41
Murray, Stephen O., 23
Mushovic, Ineke, 182
Musicians, LGBTQ, 196
Muslim countries
history of homosexual behavior
in, 24
LGBTQ people criminalized
in, 16
Musto, Michael, 99–100
"Mutant male theory," 95
"Mx.," 136
Myths
childhood sexual trauma and sexual
orientation, 25–28
shorter lifespans of LGBTQ people,
163–164

National Center for Transgender
Equality, 57–58, 133
National Coming Out Day, 76
National Crime Victimization Survey
(NCVS), 54
National Gay and Lesbian Task Force,
57–58, 133
National Health Interview Survey, 68
National Law Center on Homelessness
& Poverty, 166
National Suicide Prevention
Lifeline, 152
National Survey on Drug Use and
Health (NSDUH), 159, 160

National Transgender Discrimination
Survey, 133, 138
Native American LGBTQ people
homeless, 167
relationships of, 23
two-spirit people, 3, 121
Necrophilia, definition of, 50
Needle exchange programs, 164
Neopronouns, 137
New York City
pride parades in, 38–39
protests in, 37, 38, 76
New Zealand, same-sex marriage
in, 16
Nigeria, LGBTQ people punished
in, 18
Nineteenth Amendment, 140
Nixon, Kimberly, 142
"No Gays Allowed" (sign), 45
Nonbinary
definition of, 3, 120
vs. intersex, 121, 122
Nonbinary identity, 119–143
in history, 120–121
as mental illness, 125–127
overview of, 120
and transitioning, 132
See also Transgender identity
Nonbinary pronouns, 135–137
North America, same-sex marriage in,
16
North American Conference of
Homophile Organizations
(NACHO), 37, 38

Obama, Barack
on anti-transgender discrimination
in health care, 133–134
on gender, 123
on marriage equality, 64, 65
Matthew Shepard Act signed by, 55
Stonewall Inn designated as
National Monument by, 34
Obamacare, 45, 133–134

Ojeda, Tomás, 99
O'Leary, Jean, 76
Olson, Kristina, 129
Olympic athletes, inspection of, 122
One (magazine), 36
One, Inc., 36
Opioid use, 160
Orange Is the New Black (TV show), 87
Orthodox Judaism, on homosexuality, 71
Out (magazine), 99–100
Outright International, 30

Paiderastia, 20
Pan Africa International Lesbian, Gay, Bisexual, Trans and Intersex Association (PAI), 17
Pangender, definition of, 115
Pansexual, definition of, 101
Paraphilias
  definition of, 49, 51, 52
  forms of, 52
  legalization of, 49–52
Parasocial contact, 84, 87
Parents
  controlling, 40
  foster, 46, 68, 72
  same-sex, 66–69, 172–174
Parker, Annise, 80
Patrick, Deval, 65
Pederasty, 20
Pedophilia, definition of, 50
Penguins, 7
"Penis fencing," 8
Performing masculinity, 98
Persia, homosexual behavior in, 24
Pervasive discrimination, 58–59
Pew Research, 44
Phenotypically male, 121
Phillips, Jack, 45
Physical appearance, of LGBTQ people, 192–194
Physical bullying, 170
Pittsford, Leanne, 197

Plato, 20
Plutarch, 24
Police, persecution and arrests by, 36, 37
Polis, Jared, 81
Politicians
  LGBTQ people as, 79–83, 197–198
  on same-sex marriage, 64–65
  scandals of, 41–42
Politics (Aristotle), 20
Pose (TV series), 88, 191
Poverty
  bisexuals living in, 103, 184
  LGBTQ people living in, 164, 183–185
Powell, Colin, 65
Pre-exposure prophylaxis therapies (PrEP), 147, 148
Preferred pronouns, 136
Prejudice against LGBTQ people
  bisexuals, 102
  controlling parents and, 40
  heterosexism and, 25–26
  and internalized homophobia, 193
  and life expectancies, 163, 164
  transgender people, 112, 141
  TV shows and movies eliminating, 84
  See also Discrimination against LGBTQ people
Prejudice against men, 95–97, 98
Prejudice against women, 98–100
Price, Devon, 136
Pride parades
  in Brazil, 17
  first, 38–39
Promiscuity, 186, 187
"Promoting Free Speech and Religious Liberty" (executive order), 45
Pronouns
  neopronouns, 137
  nonbinary, 135–137
  preferred, 136
  survey on, 136–137

used by children, 129
used by drag performers, 116
Protestants
    LGBTQ people identifying as, 189
    on same-sex marriage, 72
Protests
    early, 36
    in 1960s, 36–38
Prum, Richard, 6
Psychosexual disorder, 125
Puberty blockers, 130
Publication Manual (APA), 2
Public opinion, on same-sex
        relationships, 62–65
Public Religion Research Institute
    (PRRI), 72, 73
Purple Clouds, 21–22
Putin, Vladimir, 18
Pyramid Texts, 20

Queer, 29–31
    definition of, 4
    as derogatory term, 4, 29, 30
    history of word, 30
    reclaiming term, 4, 29–31
Queer: A Graphic History (Barker), 14
Queer Eye for the Straight Guy (TV
    series), 31
Queer Nation, 29–30, 76–77
"Questioning," 31

Racism, in lesbian separatist
        collectives, 95–96
Radcliffe, Daniel, 143
"Rainbow Wave," 79
Rape
    of LGB students, 152
    statutory, 20
Raymond, Janice, 141, 142
Rayner, Michele, 82
Receptive anal sex, 147
Redman, Anna, 97
Red Scare, 37
Reed, Geoffrey, 125, 127

Relationships. *See* Same-sex
    relationships
Religion(s)
    decline of, 44
    and LGBTQ lifestyle, 189
    of LGBTQ people, 73, 189
    on LGBTQ people and rights,
        70–74
    survey on, 44
Religious freedom
    as fundamental right, 43
    and rights of LGBTQ people,
        43–47, 68–69
Religious leaders
    conversion therapy directed by, 156
    on LGBTQ lifestyle, 189
    on LGBTQ people and rights, 71–73
    media on, 72–73
    on same-sex marriage, 64
    scandals of, 41
Religious organizations, conversion
        therapy offered by, 155
Reparative therapy. *See* Conversion
    therapy
Republicans
    as LGBTQ elected officials, 80
    on LGBTQ rights, 73
    on loss of religion, 44
    on marriage equality, 63
    on same-sex adoption, 68
    scandals of, 41–42
Rhodes-Conway, Satya, 82
Riddell, Carol, 141
Ride, Sally, 196
Rieger, Gerulf, 106, 110
Rights of LGBTQ people. *See* Legal
    rights of LGBTQ people
Rind, Bruce, 27–28
Roberts, Andrea, 27
Roberts, John, 77
The Rocky Horror Picture Show (film),
    87
Rodman, Monica, 99
Rodwell, Craig, 37

Roem, Danica, 81
Rogers, Mike, 41–42
Roman Empire, homosexual behavior in, 21
Romantic orientation, 4
Rosenberg, Robin, 126
Rosenfeld, Michael, 174
Rosenzweig, Julie, 93
Ross, Michael, 40
Rosser, Simon, 40
Rowland, Chuck, 35
Rowling, J. K., 143
Ruiz, Susan, 80–81
Rule, Nicholas, 192
RuPaul's Drag Race (TV show), 116
Rural areas, LGBTQ people living in, 181–183
Russia
    history of homosexual behavior in, 23–24
    homophobia in, 18
Rustin, Bayard, 196
Ryan, Richard M., 40
Ryan, William S., 40

Same-gender loving, 4
Same-sex adoption, 66–69
Same-sex behavior in animals, 5–10
    evolution and, 6, 7, 9
    examples of, 7–8
    explanations for, 8–10
    and fertility, 9
    research on, 6–7
    seen as anomaly, 5–6
Same-sex loving, 4
Same-sex marriage
    Catholic Church on, 71
    legality of, 16, 62–63
    opponents of, 50–51
    public opinion on, 61, 62–65, 72, 73, 86
    religions on, 71, 72, 73
    survey on, 190
Same-sex parenting, 66–69, 172–174

Same-sex relationships
    countries criminalizing, 16–17
    dynamics of, 92–94
    in history, 19–24
    legality of, 16, 62–63
    morality of, 63
    public opinion on, 61, 62–65, 72, 73
    religions supporting, 70–71
San Bushmen, 23
San Francisco
    lesbian group in, 35–36
    protests in, 37
San Francisco Human Rights Commission, 102
Sapphism, 24
Sappho, 24, 36
Savage, Dan, 31
"Say it loud, gay is proud" (slogan), 38
Scandals, 41–42
Schrag, Ariel, 96–97
Schrenck-Notzing, Albert von, 154
Schrock, Edward L., 41
Scientists, LGBTQ, 196
Self-hated, 160
Serano, Julie, 141
Serosorting, 148
Servicemen's Readjustment Act. *See* GI Bill (1944)
Sex
    animals changing, 8
    definition of, 2
    vs. gender, 2
    as nonbinary concept, 120
Sex chromosomes, 121
Sex-positive attitudes, 188
Sexual activity, 186–188
Sexual behavior
    activity, 186–188
    in animals, 5–10
    definition of, 4
    vs. sexual orientation, 2–5
    terms emphasizing, 4–5
Sexual dating violence, 152
Sexual deviation, 125

Sexual orientation
  Black terms for, 4
  causes of, 12–14
  childhood sexual trauma and,
    25–28
  of children of same-sex parents,
    173
  conversion therapy and, 154–157
  definition of, 3, 102
  gendered play and, 105–106
  vs. gender identity, 102, 112,
    138–140
  research on, 12–14, 105–106
  vs. sexual behavior, 2–5
  of transgender people, 138–140
Sexual orientation change efforts
    (SOCE). *See* Conversion therapy
Sexual Orientation Disturbance
    (SOD), 50
Sexual trauma, childhood, 25–28
Shared peach (story), 22
Sharpton, Al, 65
"She," 136
Sheep, 9
Shepard, Matthew, 55
"Sip-in," 37
Slipper snails, 8
Slogans, 30, 38, 76–77
Smalls, Taylor, 82
Smith, Megan, 197
Smith, Will, 65
Smyth, Ron, 193
Smythe, Viv, 143
Social bonding, in animals, 9–10
Social Justice Sexuality Project, 184
Social rejection
  and mental health, 150
  and substance abuse, 160
  of transgender people, 127
Social transitioning, 129–130, 132
Society
  and gender, 2–3
  homosexuality perceived by, 50
  responses to LGBTQ people, 15

Sociopathic personality disturbance,
    50
SOD. *See* Sexual Orientation
    Disturbance
Sodom and Gomorrah, 71
"Sodomites," 21
Solomon, Marc, 64
"Sounding gay," 192, 193
South Africa, same-sex marriage
    in, 16
Southern Poverty Law Center, 49
Spack, Norman, 126
Speech, of LGBTQ people, 192, 193
Springfield, Dusty, 196
Sprinkle, Stephen V., 55
Sri Lanka, antigay laws in, 16
Stanford University, 193
Statutory rape, 20
Stereotypes
  of bisexuals as confused people,
    101–103
  children defying, 129
  of gay lifestyle, 189–190
  of gay men as feminine, 104, 105,
    107, 189–190
  of gay men as promiscuous, 186, 187
  of gay men as sensitive, 99
  of lesbians as man-haters, 95–97
  of lesbians as masculine, 109,
    189–190
  of LGBTQ people as wealthy, 183,
    185
  of LGBTQ people as white men, 178
  of LGBTQ people living in urban
    areas, 181
  of masculine behavior, 105
  of transgender women as drag
    queens, 190
  TV shows and movies eliminating,
    84
Stern, Jessica, 30
Stone, Allucquére Rosanne "Sandy,"
    142
Stone, Sharon, 96

Stonewall Inn, 34, 38
Stonewall Riots (1969), 34, 38
Straight, definition of, 3
Substance abuse
    causes of, 160–161
    conversion therapy and, 156
    in LGBTQ people, 150, 151,
        159–161
    rates of, 159, 160
    surveys on, 159, 160
    treatment programs for, 161
Suicidal attempts
    conversion therapy and, 156–157
    in transgender people, 126, 151
Suicidal ideation
    conversion therapy and, 156–157
    in LGBTQ people, 150, 151
    in transgender people, 126
Suicide
    bullying and, 171
    in transgender people, 133
Suicide prevention
    resources for, 152
    in transgender youth, 130
Supergirl (TV show), 88
Surgeries, for transgender people, 120
    barriers to, 126
    economic concerns of, 132
    insurance and, 125–126, 132
    survey on, 133
Swaab, Dick, 13–14
Swank, Hilary, 87
The Symposium (Plato), 20

Taiwan, same-sex marriage in, 16
Tale of Genji (Murasaki), 22
Tambor, Jeffrey, 87
Tannehill, Brynn, 112
Technology, LGBTQ people in,
    196–197
Television shows
    drag queens on, 116
    LGBTQ characters on, 84–88, 96, 109
    queer on, 31

Testosterone, 130
The Kids Are All Right (film), 86
"They," 136
Thomson, Katharine, 136
Timmons, John, 37
Title VII of Civil Rights Act, 44
Titus, Tyler, 81
Todd, Matthew, 151
Torres, Ritchie, 82
Toxic masculinity, 106
Traditionalists, 178
Trans-exclusionary radical feminists
    (TERFs), 143
Trans feminism, 141–142
Transgender, definition of, 3, 4, 115
Transgender identity, 119–143
    as mental illness, 125–127
    and transitioning, 132
    See also Nonbinary identity
Transgender men
    definition of, 3
    medical transitioning for, 133
Transgender people
    children, 128–131, 150
    of color, 58, 77, 88
    coming out, 77
    discrimination against (*see*
        Discrimination against
        transgender people)
    as elected officials, 81, 82, 197
    feminism on, 140–143
    gender dynamics of, 112–114
    grouped together with LGB people,
        112–114
    harassment of, 57–58, 133
    hate crimes against, 54
    in history, 120–121
    homeless, 166–168
    masculine overcompensation and
        attitude toward, 107
    mental health of, 126–127, 133, 150,
        151, 156
    in military, 72
    in poverty, 184

sexual orientation of, 138–140
substance abuse in, 160–161
surgeries for (*see* Surgeries, for transgender people)
transitions for (*see* Gender transitions)
as TV/film characters, 85, 86–88
Transgender women
definition of, 3
vs. drag queens, 116
in feminism, 141–143
life expectancy of, 165
medical transitioning for, 133
stereotypes of, 190
Transparent (series), 87
Transphobia, 107, 141
Trevor Project, 152, 155, 156
True Colors United, 166
Trump, Donald, 45, 123, 134
Turban, Jack, 130
Turkish baths, 187
Two-spirit, 3, 121

Unemployment, of LGBTQ people, 184
Unfinished Lives (Sprinkle), 55
United Airlines, 136
University of California, San Francisco (UCSF), 130
Urban areas, LGBTQ people living in, 181, 182

Values Voter Summit, 113
Vancouver Rape Relief, 142
Vanguard (group), 37
Vargas, Jose Antonio, 42
Vasey, Paul, 6, 9, 10
Verbal abuse, 151
Verbal bullying, 170
Veterans Benevolent Association (VBA), 34–35
Victory Fund, 80, 82
Victory Institute, 197

Violence against LGBTQ people
in Brazil, 18
and life expectancy, 164
and mental health, 150–152
in Russia, 18
transgender people, 127, 133
See also Hate crimes against LGBTQ people
Visibility of LGBTQ people, 61–88
coming out and, 77
in culture, 195–198
in politics, 79–83
and public opinion on same-sex adoption, 66–69
and public opinion on same-sex relationships, 62–65
in religious groups, 73–74
on television and in movies, 84–88
Voices of Youth Count, 166
Voting rights, of women, 140

Walladah bint al-Mustakfi, 24
Warhol, Andy, 195
Waybourn, William, 80
Weinstein, Netta, 40, 41
"We're here! We're queer!" (slogan), 30, 77
Western Europe, same-sex marriage in, 16
What's Your Pronoun? Beyond He and She (Baron), 135
Whitman Insight Strategies, 189
Wicker, Randy, 37
Willer, Robb, 106–107
Will & Grace (TV show), 86
Williams Institute
on conversion therapy, 157
on demographic data, 178, 181, 184
on religious LGBTQ people, 73
on same-sex parenting, 68
on same-sex parents, 173
Wilson, Lachlan, 88

Women
  bullying experienced by, 170
  equal rights for, 140
  identifying as LGBTQ, 179
  inspection of Olympic athletes, 122
  in poverty, 184
  sexual activity of, 186–187
  voting rights of, 140
  wearing men's clothes, 117
  See also Bisexual women; Feminism; Lesbians; Transgender women
Women who have sex with women (WSW), term, 4–5
"Womyn-born-womyn only" policy, 142
Woodard, Brandon, 80–81
World Athletics, 122
World Health Organization (WHO), 127
Writers, LGBTQ, 195
Wuornos, Aileen, 96
Wu Qing, 22

Xu Xiyun, 21–22
XX chromosomes, 121
XXX chromosomes, 121

XXY chromosomes, 121, 122
XY chromosomes, 121
XYY chromosomes, 121

"Year of the Lesbian Mayor," 82
Young, Lindsay C., 7, 8
Young people
  bisexual, 102, 103
  bullying experienced by, 169–171
  capacity for attraction of, 103
  conversion therapy for, 154–157
  gender transitions for, 129–130
  HIV infection in, 147
  homeless, 166–168
  identifying as LGBTQ, 178, 179–180
  mental health of, 150, 151, 152
  pronouns used by, 136–137
  in rural areas, 182
  substance abuse in, 160
  transgender, 128–131, 166–168
  See also Children
Youth Risk Behavior Survey (YRBS), 170

"Ze/zir/zirs," 137
Zuk, Marlene, 7, 10

About the Authors

Melissa R. Michelson (PhD, Yale University) is dean of arts and sciences and professor of political science at Menlo College. She is a nationally recognized expert on Latinx politics, voter mobilization experiments, and LGBTQ rights, and past president of the LGBT Caucus and of the Latino Caucus of the American Political Science Association. She is the award-winning author of six books, including *Mobilizing Inclusion: Transforming the Electorate through Get-Out-the-Vote Campaigns* (2012) and, most recently, *Transforming Prejudice: Identity, Fear, and Transgender Rights* (2020). Her work also appears in a variety of top-rated academic journals and in popular outlets such as the *Washington Post's* Monkey Cage blog.

Brian F. Harrison (PhD, Northwestern University) is visiting assistant professor at Macalester College and lecturer at the Humphrey School of Public Affairs at the University of Minnesota. His prior affiliations include Northwestern, Yale, NYU, and Wesleyan Universities. Before academia, Brian was a White House appointee for the Department of Homeland Security. He is founder and president of Voters for Equality, an organization fostering political engagement among LGBTQ people in the United States. He has published three books with Oxford University Press, the most recent two in 2020: *A Change Is Gonna Come: How to Have Effective Political Conversations in a Divided America* (2020) and *Transforming Prejudice: Identity, Fear, and Transgender Rights* (2020). An award-winning teacher and author, Brian's interests are in American politics, political communication and political behavior, political psychology, public opinion, and LGBTQ rights.